SHORT GRASS COUNTRY

AMERICAN
FOLKWAYS

EDITED BY ERSKINE CALDWELL

SHORT GRASS COUNTRY

by

STANLEY VESTAL

GREENWOOD PRESS, PUBLISHERS
WESTPORT, CONNECTICUT

To
AUNT ANNE

ACKNOWLEDGMENTS

Parts of this book appeared in Poetry, a Magazine of Verse, *August, 1928;* Folk-Say, a Regional Miscellany, *1929; and* Journal of American Folk-lore, *Vol. 53, No. 207, 1940. All permissions are acknowledged in the text or in footnotes.*

I gratefully acknowledge the aid of Dr. Milton Hopkins, of the University of Oklahoma, in matters botanical.

Part of Chapter 10 first appeared under the title, "The Histrionic West," in Space, *June, 1934; part in* King of the Fur Traders, *Boston, 1940. They are reprinted here by permission of Houghton Mifflin Company, and the editor of* Space.

Contents

SHORT GRASS COUNTRY

1. The High Plains

IT ALL began with the four directions. For a man on the Plains, like a pebble dropped into quiet water, finds himself always at the center of multiplying circles. Nature abhors the straight line, or, at any rate, much prefers the curved. This fact, hidden from men in woodlands and among the hills, is obvious as daylight in open, level country.

On the Plains everything is round. The earth is round like a disk; the sky is round like a dome; the sun and the moon are round; the grass-stems underfoot —in truth, the very body, limbs, and head of the man himself are round. Without landmarks to guide him, he will inevitably travel in a circle. We all know what "going around in circles" implies.

Yet with every step he finds himself still at the center of the visible world, forever prevented from reaching its circumference. He is like a man at sea out of sight of land. The Plains Indian felt this strongly, and his songs repeatedly express that feeling:

> At the center of the earth
> I stand.

So encircled, a man craves orientation above all things. More than that, he requires it for survival.

Without landmarks to guide him he may very well perish, being utterly lost.

This orientation, of course, is provided by the sun. It rises in the east and sets in the west, thereby dividing the south from the north. Thus the Plainsman squares his circle, and finds himself no longer a prisoner, but master of all he surveys.

The Plains Indian was intensely aware of the four points of the compass, which he gratefully symbolized by a cross with equal arms, and the number four became for him a sacred number, a token of the order he perceived in the Universe. To him everything—not merely space—was arranged and divided in fours. Time had four divisions: the year, the moon, the day, the night; the year fell into four seasons; he counted four "divides" or stages of life: childhood, youth, manhood, and old age. He himself had a front, a back, and two sides. To him the number four was the Great Law of God, Man's refuge from the everlasting circle of which he was the inevitable center.

This constant awareness of the four quarters is a possession common to all men who live long on the Plains. Plainsmen resent a winding road. Their farms are laid out in rectangles. They like houses built "square with the world." Even indoors they tend to think in terms of the directions rather than in terms of "left" or "right." Thus you will hear a workman setting up a stove in your house say to his helper, "Move her a little south."

"There are Seven Parts of Everywhere," according to the poet, "East, South, West, North, Up, Down, and Here." Of these, on the Plains, "Here" was always most important. One spot on the mat of grass was like another; it derived importance only from the fact that a *man* stood upon it.

This fact had a profound effect upon the psychology of Plainsmen. The man who is neighbor to a mountain must be reciprocal. He is only half a man in that relationship, the mountain being the other half. But a man on the plain has full possession of his identity. He is conspicuous in the center; he is It—and the rest is only background, setting.

Beneath him is the earth, above him the sky—nothing else; and where there is nothing else, Man is *everything*. Accordingly the Plainsman differs somewhat from the men of the woodlands and the hills.

If these latter had been born in Europe they would, no doubt, have been less well educated, less prosperous, less free. But in other respects they differ but little from their kinsmen across the Atlantic, and therefore many of them, absurdly enough, turn their backs on their own country and look eastward with nostalgic eyes. What happens in Belgrade interests them more than what happens in Amarillo.

Not so on the Plains. There the American came into his own. There he became an independent man, looking in four directions, instead of only one. This may account for his lack of interest, often amounting to indifference, as to European affairs. Left to himself, he would not give a damn what happened in the Balkans. For in that big, open country—so different from the tidy pettiness of Europe—no sane man can long go on pretending to be a European living, like some ungrateful, carping refugee, in an "inferior" country. The bluff is too thin. . . .

On the Plains, as the Indian chief put it, "Grass is the head chief of everything."

From the Saskatchewan River in Canada southward for 1,500 miles, a strip of country averaging some 500 miles in width extends almost to Old Mexico—country once covered with an unbroken mat of buffalo grass, grama, mesquite. These are all short grasses—rarely even six inches high. Of these, the buffalo grass is most abundant; spreading over the ground with runners like a vine, curling back upon the earth, and looking rather like over-size moss.

But this vast area is not a unit. Differences of climate, of soil, of population, and of custom, together with a divergence of the Oregon and Santa Fe trails, divided it. By the Short Grass Country we mean the southern section of the region, the High Plains.

Boundaries of this section may be indicated in different ways.

Geographically, it falls between the 32nd and 40th degrees of latitude, and between the 98th and 105th meridians of longitude.

Topographically, the region is bounded on the east by the woodlands, on the west by the foothills of the Rockies, on the south by the Colorado River in Texas, and on the north by the Republican River of Kansas and Nebraska.

Politically, it includes the western half of Oklahoma and Kansas, Northwest Texas, the plains of eastern New Mexico and Colorado. Its eastern boundary approximates a line drawn through the cities of Wichita,

Kansas, El Reno, Oklahoma, and Fort Worth, Texas. On the west side, the line extends almost as far west as Denver and Pueblo, Colorado, and Las Vegas in New Mexico.

Again approximately, in terms of population, it may be bounded by the Ozark hill-billies to the east, by the Spanish-American sheep-herders to the west, by the cornhuskers in Nebraska on the north, and on the south by the brush-poppers of Southwest Texas.

The Short Grass Country thus includes the much smaller Dust Bowl, which in periods of drought threatens to absorb the whole. It is a country high, dry, and healthy, where the rivers hide under their beds. It is also, as the Englishman said, "a bit draughty."

The Short Grass includes vast stretches of level country, the alluvial apron washed down through geologic ages from the Rockies. But it also includes country of a more varied character: wandering streams, fringed with cottonwood, willow, and elm; broken hills decorated with red cedars; patches of shinnery; shallow lakes, often dry; lonely buttes—the Black Mesa and the Yellow Houses—survivors of erosion; and scattered ranges of under-size mountains, such as the Wichitas in Oklahoma; impressive canyons a thousand feet deep, like the Palo Duro of the Texas Panhandle; barren palisades hemming in the vast levels of the Staked Plains.

The Short Grass is a spacious land of great variety: the land of buffalo hunts and county-seat wars; of roundups, rodeos, and barbecues; of cattle, wheat, and oil; of prairie fires, tornadoes, cloudbursts, northers, and dust storms; of barbed wire, windmills, and branding irons; of boots and saddles, warbonnets and steel helmets—and of the men who wore them.

The Short Grass was the range of Coronado and Buffalo Bill; of Dull Knife, Quanah, and Satank; of "Wild Bill" Hickok, Wyatt Earp, and "Doc" Holliday; of Chris Madsen, Bill Tilghman, and the Texas Rangers; of Billy Dixon and Cynthia Ann Parker; of Charles Goodnight, John Chisum, and Will Rogers.

Over the Short Grass rolled prairie schooners, bull trains, pack mules, "wind-wagons"—and the Pony Express. Across it lie marks of the cattle drives and the ruts of the Santa Fe Trail. It is a land of dugouts, soddies, bunkhouses, and skyscrapers; of ghost towns and boom towns; of Okies and squawmen, *ciboleros* and rustlers and vigilantes; of sidewinders and coyotes and road-runners; of horned toads and prairie dogs, of good women and bad men.

There Tascosa, Dodge City, Abilene throve to the tune of the Sharps buffalo gun and Samuel Colt's patent "equalizer."

The Short Grass has its names of high renown: Adobe Walls, the Battle of the Washita, Beecher Island and Cutthroat Gap, Boot Hill and Hell-on-Wheels. It remembers the mustangers and the *Comancheros*, Cattle Annie and Carry Nation, Baldwin's Charge and chuckwagon "windies," land lotteries and "The Run," Sun Dance and blizzard, redbud and chinaberry, buffalo grass an inch long, and bluestem seven feet tall, *Home on the Range*, and *Bury Me Not on the Lone Prairie*.

The Short Grass has a flavor and an individuality, a history and folklore all its own. And folkways, too—

ways of thinking, feeling and doing, habits and patterns of life not found everywhere or elsewhere.

It is these ways, these people, we have to consider. Who are they? Where did they come from? What did they bring—and find? What are they like—and how did they get that way?

2. Boots and Saddles

The history of the Plains may be expressed in five words:

the arrow,
the branding-iron,
the plow,
the oil derrick,
the adding machine.

ON THE Plains, history was telescoped. Indians now live who hunted with and even manufactured stone arrow-points. White men still breathe who began as buffalo hunters, turned cowboy when the bison vanished, plowed and reaped on farms with the first settlers, freighted goods to the new towns and made fortunes as frontier merchants, drilled oil-wells, dug mines, built factories as industrialists, and ended as financiers sitting behind mahogany desks in skyscrapers. Such men experienced every phase of human civilization in a single life-time. If experience brings wisdom, such men must be very wise.

Indeed, they should be much wiser than old men of long-established, static communities, since these latter have experienced only a single stage of human history. Fifty years on the Plains is worth whole cycles of Cathay. It is for this reason that the old-timers on the Short

Grass are so well worth study, and so well repay understanding.

Oklahoma was the last frontier on the Plains, and in
its western half—its Short Grass region—a man in middle
age may be older than any community in his county,
older than any building, even older than any living
tree. He has seen it all created under his own nose, and
can remember when his home town had no cemetery
—because no one had lived there long enough to die
there. Such a man is likely to take civilization more
casually than others do. At the same time he knows
where its roots lie—in moral qualities.

In long-established communities, it is only in old age
that one realizes—with a shock—that the leaders of the
people are simply one's friends and neighbors, that the
country's "great men" are just the fellows one grew up
with. But the Plainsman always knew that. He saw his
companions create his institutions and traditions as
they went along. And because he knew their weaknesses
from the start, he is all the more impressed by their
strength and their virtues. He is therefore, curiously
enough, more stable in his loyalty to what has been
created by them—and at the same time more willing
to change it; more willing to fight for it—and less able
to revere it! He unconsciously attains a certain maturity
of outlook, a riper wisdom.

This wisdom is not always rightly appreciated by
outsiders, because life on the Plains was so different
from life in the woods and the mountains. In like manner, the man from the Short Grass found men from
other regions hard to understand. To him the men of
old, settled communities sometimes seemed like chil-

dren—their experience of life seemed brief and shallow. They were too easily cast down, too easily disillusioned; some of them appeared to have neither faith, hope, nor charity. Cynical, wary, distrustful, they were forever passing by on the other side. And so he delighted in knocking off their high hats, or making them dance to the tune of a six-gun.

He, on his part, had something of the joyous spirit of old age. If not the heir of all the ages, he was at any rate their contemporary.

He did not expect anything easy, or demand much in the way of comfort—for he seldom encountered it. A man on the Short Grass was expected to attempt somewhat more than he could certainly do; to attempt less was to brand himself, in the words of the Indian, "an old woman."

This way of thought was forced upon old-timers, who had to face their troubles or perish. When Indians attacked, a retreat was generally fatal, whereas a bold stand, or a brisk attack—even in the face of superior numbers—often saved, or won, the day. So too with all the other hardships of the frontier: blizzards, prairie fires, charging buffalo, stampedes.

From this hard experience the men of the Short Grass discovered that when a man is distrustful, he is not—as he imagines—distrustful of others, but only of himself. Such a state of mind was as intolerable as it was dangerous. . . .

One day the small son of an old cowman in the Panhandle of Texas was delighted to receive the gift of a burro. The men were saddling up to ride after cattle, and the boy, eager to try his new mount, went about saddling the diminutive jackass. His father advised him to ride his pony, but the boy had no ears for the timely counsel. He hopped on the burro, and jogged out into the pasture.

Buffalo would seldom attack a man on foot, though often the bulls would charge a horseman. In fact, buffalo bulls have been known to chase a mounted man for ten miles and more, thirsting for his blood. But range cattle are different. Among them a man on horseback is rarely in danger, while a man afoot goes in hazard of his life.

Accordingly, when the boy came along, riding his tiny donkey, the steers came lumbering up to stare at this small person who had so rashly lowered himself to the level of their sharp horns. They crowded close, shouldering each other, staring and blowing, until he found himself entirely surrounded by a milling mob of dangerous horned beasts. His heart was in his mouth. Any minute now, he felt, they would go for him.

Luckily, some of the cowboys happened along, set the steers moving, and the boy escaped. He let no grass grow under his burro's feet, but spurred it to the corral to get his pony. There he met his father, and the old man turned him back. "You forked that burro," he said, sternly. "Now ride him. Get on back to the cattle. Nobody's going to say my son is yellow."

The boy went back, stayed in the saddle all day, helping the men work the cattle. He made his word good. The lesson was severe, but elementary—and typical for that country. Afterward, at college, that boy proved a fighting halfback, and later became a successful cowman on his own account. When he tells the story, it is with pride—pride in his *father's* manhood.

Most men on the Short Grass were valiant, but they had no corner on courage. The women were as brave as the men. They not only endured hardships, they fought conditions with steady valor. Let one pioneer wife speak for her sex:

"Perhaps the most difficult thing I had to do, as I recall now, was to be left alone on the homestead with my small children with only a wagon box to live in protected by what shelter my husband was able to erect at one end, while he went back to Barber county to move back a house for our home.

"Did I ever feel that we must give up and go back? No, not I! My husband was sometimes discouraged, but I was determined to have a home, and where we came from there was neither wood nor water. Here we were on land covered with wood and with two abundant springs of water." *

Hardihood seems to have been in the air of the Plains from the beginning. Of what prehistoric man was like there, we know little. But the early records of Spanish exploration and settlement show clearly that the Comanches and other Indians were plenty able and willing to make trouble for all comers.

These Indians had a cheerful custom of appointing brave young men leaders in their warrior societies, and investing them with trailing sashes of leather, which slipped over the head and one shoulder, and trailed on

* See "Happy to Have Home, Wood and Water," by Mrs. H. V. Sturgeon, in *Echoes of Eighty-Nine*. Kingfisher Times and Free Press, Kingfisher, Oklahoma, 1931. Page 133.

the ground. Each warrior so honored carried a lance with which to pierce the tail of his sash and stake himself to the post of duty, as soon as he encountered enemies. He was under a vow never to retreat until he had killed a foe—unless his comrades pulled up the lance and drove him away with their quirts. This institution persisted for centuries. Indian generals did not die in bed.

Open country means open warfare, for there were no walls, few hide-outs, and attacks were generally too sudden to be prepared for. The best a man could do was to dig a fox hole and stand off his foes. In the great open spaces, men had to be men.

This type of warfare developed fighters of a superior order. All authorities agree that no braver men ever lived than the best of the Plains Indians, such as the Cheyennes and the Sioux. The men who conquered them had to be equally skillful and courageous, for they were commonly outnumbered. One of the bravest fighters, too little known, was Major Frank North, who commanded the Pawnee Scouts in Indian campaigns. He was a warrior in the full sense of the word—a commander who inflicted great damage upon his Indian enemies, yet never lost a man.

There are leaders who say "Forward, march!" There are leaders who say "Come on!" Frank North was a leader who never bothered to say anything.

When he saw an enemy, he charged, and never even looked back to see if his men were following. Always well mounted, he was commonly two hundred yards to half a mile ahead of his scouts. They rode their horses to death trying to keep up with him. His brother, Captain Luther North, was equally courageous.

One of the most regrettable gaps of American history is the lack of a record of the exploits of the scouts, both white and Indian, who worked with the army in subduing the Plains Indians. Few fighting men anywhere can have ridden harder or fought more valiantly than they. One might apply to them in all fairness the praise given by Winston Churchill to the R.A.F.: "Seldom have so many owed so much to so few."

The following account of warfare on the Plains is taken from George Bird Grinnell's *The Fighting Cheyennes,* by permission of Charles Scribner's Sons, who published the book in 1915.

The Death of Mouse's Road

"In 1837, the year before the great fight with the Kiowas and Comanches, the Cheyennes were camped on the South Platte River. A war party of fourteen started south on foot to take horses from the Kiowas and Comanches. Stone Forehead and Pushing Ahead were the two who carried the pipes—the leaders.

"They found the camp of the enemy at the head of what the Cheyennes called Big Sand Creek, which runs into the Red River [of Texas]. That night the Cheyennes went into the enemy camp in couples. Stone Forehead was with a man named Angry. It was very dark. Close behind a lodge which they passed stood a pole with a shield hanging to it. Angry untied the shield from the pole and put it on his back, and they went on, looking for horses. They came to a bunch of fifty or sixty, and went around them and drove them a little way, and each caught a gentle horse, mounted it, and drove off the herd.

"When they reached the place where it had been agreed that they should meet, they found the others of the party already there, excepting only six men. Stone Forehead said: 'We cannot wait here; we must start.' They did so. Stone Forehead and Pushing Ahead went behind, where it is the custom for the leaders to travel, while the others went ahead. They drove their bunches along side by side, but two or three hundred yards apart. When day came they looked carefully at their horses so that they should know them again, and then they bunched the horses into a single herd. The way was so rough that they drove very slowly, and Pushing Ahead, who knew the country, kept saying: 'We are going so slowly that they will surely overtake us.'

"It was a little past the middle of the day when they saw the Kiowas and Comanches coming. There were only a few of them—not over thirty. Then the Cheyennes began to catch the swiftest horses, so that they could get about quickly. Pushing Ahead was a brave man. He said: 'We must not let them take our horses. I do not think there are many of them.' The Cheyennes mounted the fast horses and bunched up the herd, and, sending two young men ahead to ride one on each side so as to hold the horses together, they stopped. One of the Cheyennes got off his horse and fired at a Comanche, and shot his horse through the body. The Comanche rode back, and soon his horse began to stagger, and the Comanche left it and mounted behind one of his fellows. Then the Cheyennes made a charge on the Kiowas and Comanches, and they turned about and went back.

"Of the other six men two, Little Wolf and his partner, Walking Coyote, were alone. They were on the head of the Washita, in level country. They had taken only a few horses. They saw a big party of Kiowas and Comanches coming in two bands. There was a ravine near them, and Little Wolf said: 'These horses are tired out. We cannot drive them much farther; the enemy will soon overtake us. Let us dismount and hide in this ravine.' They ran down the ravine and hid in a little hollow, and lay there. If the Kiowas had looked for them they would have found them, but just then they saw the four other Cheyennes far off, and turned to rush them. Little Wolf and Walking Coyote stayed there till night, and then set off for home on foot.

"When the Kiowas and Comanches charged Mouse's Road and his three companions, the Cheyennes did not run; they rode up on a little hill and got off their horses and began to kill them. They had already left behind the horses they had taken and had only those that they were riding. Now, as the Kiowas and Comanches came up, the Cheyennes were seen to be taking off their leggings so that they could run fast and easily. The enemy charged them, and the Cheyennes fought bravely, though they had but few arrows, for they had been out a long time. In a little while the enemy had killed three of the Cheyennes.

"Early in the fight Mouse's Road's bow was broken in two by a ball, and he threw it away. A Comanche chief, seeing him thus disarmed, charged up to kill him with his lance, but Mouse's Road avoided the blow, caught hold of the Comanche, pulled him from his horse, and killed him with his knife. Mouse's Road was still unwounded. He let the Comanche's horse go, and signed to the Kiowas: 'Come on.'

"There was a man named Lone Wolf, a chief, and a brave man, who had been behind the other Kiowas. He called out: 'I have just come and I wish you all to look at me. I intend to kill that man.' He said to a Mexican captive: 'Do you ride close behind me.' The two charged upon Mouse's Road, and the Mexican rode straight at him, but Mouse's Road, though on foot, did not run away; he ran to meet the Mexican and, springing at him, seized him, pulled him from his horse, and plunged his knife into him several times. While he was doing this Lone Wolf dismounted and rushed up to help the Mexican. Mouse's Road dropped the dead Mexican and rushed at Lone Wolf, who ran at him with his lance held in both hands above his head, so as to deal a blow of great force. As he thrust with the lance Mouse's Road stooped and ran under the lance, caught Lone Wolf by the left shoulder, and struck him a terrible blow with his knife in the hip. Lone Wolf turned to run and Mouse's Road caught him by his hair ornament and with all his force thrust at his back. The knife struck one of the silver hair plates and broke in two, leaving about four inches of the blade on the handle. Lone Wolf screamed for help to his people, but no one came, and Mouse's Road continued to stab and hack and cut him with the stump of the knife until Lone Wolf fell to the ground, pretending to be dead.

"Now came a Comanche chief riding a fine horse, and armed with a lance and bow and arrows. Mouse's Road took up the lance Lone Wolf had dropped, and ran to meet the Comanche. He parried the Comanche's lance thrust and drove his own lance into the Comanche and lifted him high out of the saddle, and the Comanche died.

"Now the Kiowas and Comanches saw something that they never had seen before—a man who seemed swifter than a horse, more active than a panther, as strong as a bear, and one against whom weapons seemed useless. There were more than a hundred of the Kiowas and Comanches, and only one Cheyenne on foot, without arms, but the Kiowas and Comanches began to run away. Others, braver, made signs to Mouse's Road, who had now mounted the Comanche's horse: 'Hold on! Wait, wait. Take that horse that you have. We will give you a saddle. Go on home to your village and tell your people what has happened.'

" 'No,' signed Mouse's Road, 'I will not go home; my brothers have all been killed and if I were to go home I should be crying all the time—mourning for these men. You must kill me.'

"When he said this all the Kiowas started to run, and Mouse's Road charged them. Behind the main body of the enemy were two Kiowas who had just come up. Both had guns, and when they saw Mouse's Road coming they got off their horses and sat down and waited until he was close to them, and then both fired. One of the balls broke his thigh, and he fell from his horse. Yet still he sat up to defend himself with his lance, and the Kiowas and Comanches, though they surrounded him, dared not go near him. One crept up from behind and shot him in the back, and he fell over. Then all the Kiowas and Comanches rushed on him and cut off his head, and when they had done that Mouse's Road raised himself and sat upright.

"The Kiowas and Comanches jumped on their horses in fright, and fled to their village and told the people they had killed a medicine man and he had come to life again, and was coming to attack them. And, the women swiftly packing up a few of their things, the whole camp moved away, leaving many of their lodges standing.

"This is the story told by the Kiowas. The Cheyennes have no account of it, for all the Cheyennes were killed. Lone Wolf lived for a long time, scarred and crippled from the cutting he had received. He died not long ago. The Kiowas and Comanches said that Mouse's Road was the bravest man they ever saw or heard of."

"REMEMBER THE ALAMO"

To the Plains Indian, war was a glorious holiday, a splendid adventure, and a lot of fun. It was his vacation from the hard drudgery of hunting, and his one chance of getting something for nothing—of being paid for what he enjoyed doing. A war party, seeing a stranger on the prairie, immediately lashed their horses into a dead run, whooping and yelling, racing to be first to gain glory, horses, and enemy hair. If, as sometimes happened, they found that the supposed enemy was an ally or friend, nothing could surpass their chagrin and disappointment. The bright face of danger had turned into commonplace.

This spirit was inevitably communicated to the white

men who moved into their country, who hunted, lived, and fought with them. A man who did not enjoy battle did not live long on the Plains in early days. And the pioneer, to give him his due, throve on it. He knew only one bugle call, or maybe two: *Boots and Saddles,* and *Charge!* His motto was: "There they are, boys; give 'em hell!"

When they were attacked, they fought together as a team with admirable *esprit de corps;* as soon as the danger vanished, they were likely to quarrel with each other. The behavior of the heroes at Adobe Walls is typical: while the allied tribes assailed them, the buffalo hunters fought like heroes; a few days later, they fell out, and were ready to shoot each other.

Young, hardy, valiant, and independent as wildcats, they were ready to fight at the drop of the hat. In their hearts they carried memories of how Travis drew the line in the dust of the Alamo with his sword, inviting those who were ready to stay and die with him to cross it, and how the command stepped forward as one man; how Bowie, from his sickbed, commanded his comrades to carry his cot across the line. It was their philosophy that dogs die every day, lions but once.

Those men knew that war played a great part in human affairs, that it had made the nation in the first place, and caused its expansion later to include half a continent. They never supposed that the world could be set right, once for all, wound up like a clock, and let alone; they expected to have to run it, each generation in turn, with blood, sweat, and tears. They knew that war was like childbirth: neither pretty nor pleasant, but glorious all the same.

They were efficient fighters, too. In modern warfare, with vastly improved weapons, it costs around $50,000 to kill a soldier. In those days, a few cents invested in bullets would kill a man, so that a no-account fellow was commonly said not to be "worth the powder and lead it would take to kill him."

Even boys were battlers then.

One night a bandit rode into a farmyard and put up his horse in the barn, intending to compel the farmer to give him supper and lodging for the night. As it happened, the farmer was up in the hayloft putting down hay for his stock when the bandit arrived in the dusk. He heard the noise made by the bandit below, looked down, and recognized him as a wanted man.

As the bandit walked toward the house, the farmer slipped down the ladder. He had no arms, but jammed the handle of the hay-fork between the bandit's shoulder blades, and ordered him to throw up his hands. Taken by surprise, the bandit lost no time in obeying.

The farmer marched him into the house, where his small son quickly picked up the loaded shotgun and covered the bandit. There was no woman in the house at the time, and the father decided to ride to town, bring the sheriff, and collect the reward. It was a ride of some hours.

They made the bandit sit on a chair at one side of the narrow room. The boy sat opposite, pointing the shotgun at the bad man's midriff. Before he left, the farmer gave instructions to the boy: "Son, if he stirs, let him have it with both barrels."

For three hours the pair faced each other in the narrow room.

When the father came back, the sheriff asked the bandit why he had not tried to escape. The bandit laughed shortly. "If it had been a man with that shotgun, I might have risked it. But I knew that boy would surely shoot."

Nowadays the gunmen are in the cities, where they find safety in numbers, and seldom give their enemies a fighting chance. On the Plains the code provided that no one should shoot an unarmed man, or fire without giving him a chance to draw his weapon.

Every man was expected to defend himself, if armed, and where all men went armed a threat invited immediate reprisals.

3. Samuel Colt's "Equalizer"

TWO brothers, Bat Masterson and Ed Masterson, were celebrated for their courage and skill with frontier weapons. In 1874, Bat helped fight off the Indians at Adobe Walls. In 1877, Ed was appointed marshal of Dodge City, then one of the toughest cowtowns in the world The marshal at Dodge was in a tight corner. He had to protect the town from the Texas cowboys on their spree, cowboys who had no love for Yankees; yet he had also to control them without offending them to the point where they would abandon Dodge and take their cattle elsewhere for shipment. Dodge had a galaxy of gun-fighters for marshals that outshone any other: men of steel—Bill Tilghman, Bill Brooks, Wyatt Earp, Charlie Basset, Mysterious Dave Mather, Pat Shugrue, and Jack Allen. Of these the Mastersons were as brave and handy with their guns as any.

One day the Lone Star dance hall was the scene of a quarrel. A man named Moore had won forty dollars from Bob Shaw. Bob, much the worse for liquor, covered Moore. Ed Masterson told the cowboy to hand over his gun. Shaw paid no attention. Then Ed, reluctant to shoot, "whipped" Bob with his pistol. A pistol-whipping was no joke, and when the barrel crashed down across the skull of the victim, he was usually knocked cold, "buffaloed" for fair, and easily dragged off to jail. But Ed was too gentle, and Bob failed to go down.

Instead, he turned, fired, and rendered Ed's right arm helpless. The lead threw the marshal, but he coolly transferred his weapon to his left hand, fired, and hit Bob twice, not to mention two others who happened to get in the way.

Bat and his friends were alarmed at Ed's accident— for which they blamed his carelessness. But their arguments failed to make him realize the danger he faced in being meek and gentle with such butchers. Hardly a year later, Ed tried to tame two other Texans. They killed him. Bat, coming up just then, found his brother dying, and fired two shots. The killers died before they hit the ground. But that had not saved Ed.

Brave, cool, deliberate, he had attempted to argue with armed enemies. Dodge City had to get another peace officer.

So died Ed Masterson and, like him, many a well-meaning but mistaken fellow, too green to know what he was up against: facts, not a theory—a code based not upon law, but upon cruel necessity.

Where all men carry arms, nobody can dominate by words alone. If not prepared to use a gun, why pack it? To carry it and then refuse to draw might well be fatal. To draw it and not fire was certainly quite as dangerous. Therefore, since victory in any argument rested upon gunfire, why waste time in talk at all?

Shoot first and talk afterward. A word and a blow— but the blow first. Action speaks louder than words.

Never pull a gun, unless you aim to use it. The less said, the sooner ended. Do unto others as they would do to you—and do it first. Such were the precepts of the Short Grass.

From this code of silent battle, it followed that boisterous noise was a token of peace and good will. Thus the Plains Indians always entered a friendly camp yelling and whooping, firing all their guns tб empty them in proof of peaceful intentions. Many an employee of the Indian Bureau was scared nearly out of his wits when a horde of painted savages dashed into the agency, yipping and shooting—but with no other purpose than to draw their rations! For it was only in war that the Indian came sneaking. Old-timers were never so wary and uneasy as when *no* Indians could be seen or heard.

Just so it was with the cowboy. When, tired after the long trail-drive, and eager for human society, he came charging down Main Street, ki-yi-ing and shooting up the town, he did so with the best intentions—advertising to all and sundry that he had arrived, with money in his pocket, hell-bent for a good time. And if, before it was all over, he had smashed a few mirrors, he was generally ready to pay for them. But when cowboys were out to kill, they generally rode in silence. It was the custom of the country.

Like the Indian, the white man of the Short Grass was a boisterous friend and a quiet foe; in fact, the quieter he became, the more dangerous he was. The gun-fighter, if he spoke at all, usually uttered the last words of his argument in a whisper.

Strangers with different mores have often come to

sudden grief because they did not understand this. In their own country, they have been accustomed to prevail by bluster and talk and fisticuffs that settle nothing. If they do fight, they are likely to precede their battle by an exchange of loud vituperation.

It is amusing to watch such a man quarreling with a Plainsman of the old school. He thinks he has won at the very moment when the trouble is about to start. For the Plainsman becomes more silent, soft-spoken, and laconic as his dander rises. And then the lightning strikes. On the Short Grass, silence is deadly.

On the other hand, Plainsmen sometimes underestimate the stranger because he is "talky." The two have a different code, a different tradition. It is more fun to see them squabble than to watch a tarantula and a centipede thrown together in a Mason jar.

The Road of Appeasement leads to Death in any country. But on the High Plains that road was plenty short! It led straight to Boot Hill.

Paul I. Wellman gives a graphic account of a shooting affray in his book, *The Trampling Herd;* it is presented here through the courtesy of the author and his publishers, J. B. Lippincott Company:

"Among the hardest individuals who walked the streets of Newton [Kansas] was Mike McCluskie, whose real name was Arthur [or George] Delaney. McCluskie was a night policeman, a fine-looking, squarely built, self-reliant man, chary of speech and bearing a reputation for being tough and ready to shoot.

"Wherever McCluskie went he was followed by a thin-faced, sunk-chested youth named Jim Riley. Nobody knew much about Riley, although it was surmised that he was related to McCluskie. He was only eighteen and appeared to be in the last stages of tuberculosis, with a hacking cough and the hectic red in his cheeks of the fever-ridden. McCluskie, who had never befriended anyone else, had been a good angel to this boy. He "grubstaked" him, furnished him a bed, and always took his part in the quarrels that were forever rising. Riley wore old, patched clothing and had no money. He followed McCluskie around like a dog. They made a strangely assorted pair—the fierce, swaggering gunman and the pale, inoffensive youth.

"Friday, August 11, was a big day in Newton. An election was being held to vote on the subscribing of $200,000 in county bonds for the building through Newton of the Wichita & Southwestern railroad. William Wilson, alias Bill Bailey, a Texas gambler with two or three notches on his gun handle, served as a special policeman at the election and was thoroughly offensive and officious. During the day McCluskie and Bailey met, and Bailey was drunk. There had been bitterness between them over a woman and now Bailey taunted McCluskie over having been arrested a few days previously on a charge of garroting preferred by Captain French, a Texan. The case was heard before Judge Bowman, who dismissed it for lack of evidence. There was no occasion for the gibe by Bailey, but the thought of the woman over whom they were rivals was fierce between them and they quarreled explosively before they separated.

"That evening at 8 o'clock they met again in the Red Front saloon. Bailey, even drunker than before, was very abusive. He demanded that McCluskie set up

the drinks. McCluskie refused. Oaths crackled out, followed by blows. Out of the saloon ran Bailey, and
crouched across the street before the Blue Front saloon.
A moment later McCluskie stepped out of the Red
Front. His six-shooter blazed and the gambler was carried, dying, to a bed in the Santa Fe Hotel, while the
girl from 'Hide Park,' who had been the original cause
of the quarrel, sobbed over him.

"Newton considered the shooting justified, but the
Texas contingent, to which Bailey belonged, thought
differently. To avoid trouble, McCluskie left town for
a few days to allow feeling to die down. He returned
Saturday night, August 19, and in spite of warnings
went to Perry Tuttle's dance hall in 'Hide Park.'

"One of the Texas cowboys who felt most bitterly
over Bailey's death was young Hugh Anderson, who had
just come up the trail with a herd of cattle from his
father's ranch. Young Anderson was dangerous and had
more than one killing behind him. The night McCluskie returned to Newton, Anderson learned of it and
gathering his friends led them straight to Tuttle's place.
It was past midnight, the dancing was over in most
dance halls and the musicians dismissed, but at Perry
Tuttle's the lights still glared brassily.

"Within the building glasses clinked, the hoarse
voices of the gamblers called their bets, and a spavined
piano, a fiddler or two, and perhaps a banjo tinkled out
a tune barely discernible above the shuffling feet of the
steel-limbed dancers on the floor. McCluskie was taking
an active part in all of this, while Riley, with his spasms
of coughing, leaned against the wall near the door. Of
a sudden the door was violently flung open and Hugh

Anderson, with his Texans, stepped grimly in. At one of the gambling tables sat McCluskie, taking a turn at cards. Straight toward him walked Anderson, his revolver in his hand, looking squarely into the widening eyes of the man he had come to kill. What he said sounds melodramatic. But the words were full of deadly realism:

" 'You cowardly dog! I'm going to blow the top of your head off!'

"The young Texan's voice rose in a sudden furious scream and the gun in his hand began to cough ear-splittingly. A bullet ripped through McCluskie's neck and he spun out of his chair to the floor. A second bullet bored through his body.

"The dance hall was in an uproar, the frenzy of fear. Cowboys, gamblers, bartenders, and dance girls, who had filled the floor a moment before, fought to reach the door or find room behind the bar. In the center of this hysteria the little group of Texans stood contemptuously, Anderson at their head, his revolver still smoking in his hand as he looked down at his dying enemy, prostrate on the floor.

"Thus for a moment appeared the scene. Then, without warning and from a quarter entirely unexpected, disaster struck the Texas crew.

"Jim Riley was leaning near the door by which the Texans entered. Before he had a chance to move, his friend and idol, McCluskie, had been shot down before him. For a moment he looked on, as if he had difficulty in comprehending the shocking thing that had occurred. Then the apparently inoffensive youth went berserk. Jim Riley the consumptive, Jim Riley the harm-

less, Jim Riley the butt of jokes, became in an instant
an appalling machine of death. In two strides he reached
the door, slammed it shut, turned the key. Then he
whirled and from somewhere among his nondescript
garments pulled a six-shooter.

"With his back against the locked door and bitter
hate in his face, Riley began to kill. The reports of his
revolver sounded like the reverberations of cannon in
the closed room. Somebody hurled a chair at the lights,
putting the interior in blackness. Still the orange flashes
of flame leaped forth from heated gun muzzles.

"It lasted only a few moments. Quiet came, as appalling in its way as had been the noise of death. Someone managed to find the door, now left unguarded,
and threw it open. A rush of fresh air poured in to
disperse the acrid powder smoke. Men and women who
had been caught cowering in corners rushed to safety.
For long minutes nobody ventured back into the building. Then a bartender had the courage to re-enter and
strike a light.

"Jim Riley was gone; but on the floor lay the victims
of his fury. Nine men were dead or wounded in that
room. Beside McCluskie and almost on top of him lay
Hugh Anderson, gasping and moaning, it seemed at the
edge of eternity. A little to one side sprawled Jim Mar-
tin, Anderson's trail boss, dead. Beyond him lay two
cowboys, Billy Garrett and Henry Kearns, both shot
through the lungs and dying, with Jim Wilkerson, badly
wounded, farther on. In another part of the room Pat
Lee, a railroad worker, was huddled, shot through the
stomach and dying. With him was a track foreman
named Hickey, wounded in the jaw and nose, and an-

other bystander named Bartlett with the blood spilling from an ugly hole in his shoulder.

"Newton was hysterical with panic and indignation. A doctor was summoned and some of the dance hall girls did womanly service in nursing the wounded. Tom Carson, the city marshal, enlisted a posse to arrest the survivors of the Anderson gang, but the Texans gathered in a threatening knot. It appeared for a time that there would be street fighting as an aftermath of' the dance hall battle, but the posse finally dispersed. Even after the withdrawal shootings occurred in different parts of the town. Two white men and a Negro were wounded during the following day, none seriously enough to have their names recorded by the chroniclers of the period.

"That Sunday morning, from 8 o'clock to noon, a coroner's jury sat and arrived at a verdict of murder in the case of McCluskie, naming Hugh Anderson as the guilty person. Shortly after the jury adjourned, each juryman received a brief, grim notice:

" 'Leave Newton at once. If you do not you will be found ornamenting a telegraph pole Monday morning.'

"The messages undoubtedly were from the Texans, who at this time were talking about burning the town and running out all the prostitutes and gamblers. None of the jurors, however, stopped to question the authority behind the warnings. By Monday morning all were gone, three to Wichita on an early train and the other three elsewhere.

"Departure of the coroner's jury removed much of the force of its findings. Hugh Anderson's friends were able to place the wounded Texan on a train where they hid him in a washroom, standing guard at the door all the way to Kansas City. There he received medical treatment and eventually recovered from his wounds sufficiently to travel, but he was permanently crippled and died a few years later.

"And Jim Riley? Nobody ever learned what became of him. For a few lurid seconds he occupied the center of a furious drama, a sudden, incandescent machine of death Then he was gone. He disappeared, where nobody knows, to die in all probability of the mortal illness which had fastened upon him."

But there were occasions when the Plainsman showed courage of an unusual order, without any thought of deadly weapons:

When in 1869 the Cheyenne tribe had agreed to go upon a reservation in what is now Oklahoma, they moved south from the Arkansas River and settled along the North Canadian. As it happened, the new camps should have been along the Cimarron River to be within the boundaries of the land set aside for them, but Congress hastily drew new boundaries to include the camps along the Canadian, rather than enter into any further argument with those valiant warriors.

Somewhat later, John Seger, a young veteran of the Civil War, a carpenter and stone mason by trade, was employed by the Indian Bureau and sent to Darlington, the Cheyenne agency. He arrived one afternoon with his tool chest, prepared to set about building the new school house next morning. Lumber had already been freighted down overland at great expense in wagons from

Wichita, Kansas, a distance of a hundred and fifty miles or so.

No Indians were in camp about the agency, but towards sundown the small group of employees saw a cloud of dust rising in the west, turned to a golden haze by the setting sun. The Indians were coming—wild Indians—Indians fresh from the bloody warpath and the buffalo hunt. The whole staff turned out and stood looking up the valley, saying little. Few of them knew anything about Indians. Some of them were tense and pale, but the young carpenter did not notice this. He had been in some hard fights and was what Plainsmen called "scarefree." He was there to build the school house. Here came the pupils.

A great ruck of Indians horseback and afoot, pack mules and traveaux spread over the grassy bottoms and, like magic, the taper tipis mushroomed along the river. Men began driving their ponies to water, swinging a rope around their heads; women plodded back and forth fetching water, gathering firewood for the evening meal. Bright little cooking-fires sprang up among the tents.

Those Indians nearest the agency soon spied the pile of bright new lumber, and the women began streaming to help themselves to this firewood which the white man had so bountifully provided. Before young Seger, the carpenter, knew what was up, several old squaws were helping themselves and packing off the precious lumber on their backs, while others laid into it smartly with their axes.

This was too much for Seger. He saw his job going up in smoke, and started forward to interfere. The whole agency staff tried to restrain him, "Leave 'em alone. If you start an argument, they will scalp us all."

Seger was not so easily discouraged. "I'll take a chance," he said. "We can't allow them Injuns to burn up that lumber. It's Government property and it cost a-plenty."

Immediately he started forward, marched out, and took his stand on the pile of lumber. He was a small, chunky man. Standing on the lumber brought him about even with the tall Cheyennes, who averaged over six feet in height. Once there he glanced back. The entire staff had fled into the buildings and locked the doors. He was alone, facing that horde of savages.

Indians in those days paid little attention to white men, and laughed at the idea of regarding their wishes in any matter, even the most trivial. Seger did not know a word of their language or understand the language of signs—so he talked to them in English! Apparently they did not hear him or care what he was saying. Therefore, as people will do in speaking to foreginers, he raised his voice, speaking louder and louder until he was fairly shouting at the redskins. The noise he made finally attracted their attention. A crowd of boys and young men gathered round to watch the strange antics of the little white man with the big nose. Steadily the women went on gathering up the lumber.

Finding all his talk useless, Seger laid hold on the planks the women were taking, shaking his head and pointing to some old cottonwood logs which lay nearby, even lifting these and handing them to the women in place of the planks they were taking. By that time his shouting had attracted one of the chiefs, who came forward to investigate what all the yelling was about.

It did not take the chief long to discover from Seger's actions what the white man meant. He spoke to the women, beckoned some warriors forward, and stationed a guard about the lumber to prevent it being carried off.

Satisfied, Seger shook hands with the chief and went indoors to have supper. He found the staff awaiting him, pale-faced and indignant, still terrified for their lives. Only the agent, a dauntless old Quaker, seemed to approve his action.

Next day the chiefs came to the agency to hold council and, to his surprise, they went first of all to the young carpenter and presented their problems to him through their interpreter. Somewhat dumbfounded, Seger led them to the agent and presented their demands. Every day it was the same: whenever a matter had to be discussed with the authorities, the chiefs came first of all to Seger. It was the beginning of a long life of influence among the Indians for him, and eventually led to his being made superintendent in his own right.

One day sometime later, when he had learned their language, he asked the reason for their referring everything to him. The chief explained: "The first time we saw you, you were so determined and talked so loud, we thought you must be a big chief from Washington. . . ."

THE AMERICAN HEROIC AGE

Throughout American history people moved west somewhat faster than the institutions which followed them. Always on the slowly advancing frontier a few bold spirits were in the van well ahead of law and order. As a rule, these pioneers of the mountains and woodlands carried their families with them and promptly set up institutions like those in the settlements behind them.

But when the settlements reached the eastern edge of the Great Plains, law and order halted there while those with families hurried across the prairies to find shelter in the mountains and forests of the Far West. Civilization jumped the Plains, and for almost a century following the first American explorations, the Plainsmen were a law unto themselves. From the date of the Louisiana Purchase by Thomas Jefferson until the Ghost Dance War and the death of Sitting Bull in 1890-91, civilization on the Short Grass was a *natural* growth. Institutions were sketchy or non-existent. The only controls of conduct were the sense of shame and fear of blame in the hearts of individual Plainsmen.

If the tides of population which eventually swept in to submerge the old-time white population and destroy Indian ways of life had been held back for another half-century, the Plains might have developed a culture unique and self-sufficient. As it is, the people on the Short Grass cherish the memory and tradition of an heroic age.

By an heroic age, we mean, of course, some period or system of society in which the individual is captain of his soul, if not altogether master of his fate. Men cast adrift in a vast area, faced with novel and difficult conditions, had to adapt themselves quickly or perish. In the early days, this was largely an individual undertaking, and such groups as were formed continually dissolved. A man on the Short Grass before 1890 was very largely on his own. He had to make his own decisions, use his own judgment, and solve his problems for himself.

Such heroic ages have been comparatively rare in the history of men of European blood, and in every instance have produced a literature and a tradition which men would not willingly let die. The Homeric heroes, the knights errant of the Middle Ages, and the frontier Plainsmen all occupy a place in the memory of man out of all proportion to their numbers and achievements. The Homeric poems, the Arthurian legends, and the heroic stories of the Western Plains possess a vitality, a virility, and an appeal to the imagination of mankind unrivaled by any others, and authors have delighted in working and reworking these materials for the enjoyment and instruction of their readers.

This, of course, is because the chief function of history and fiction is to display human character. Actions speak louder than words, and the man who acts on his own initiative always displays his character more fully than the man whose behavior is controlled by outside forces. No man in a civilized community, living under law and order, can possibly afford as good a subject for an author as the man who acts freely and without interference from others. The Plainsman, quite as much as Achilles or Bayard, was independent, and expressed in his deeds what was in his heart. It is for this reason that stories of the Plains continue to enjoy the favor of such multitudes of readers.

Indeed, the Plainsmen have an advantage over the

Homeric heroes and the knights errant of Romance because they were even more independent. The bulk of stories about Plainsmen is vastly greater than that about the knights and the Greek heroes. Moreover, the Plainsman was no king or aristocrat, but, as a rule, a common man who required as his equipment only a gun, a horse, and a blanket. And he found himself faced at every turn with some crucial decision or some adventure on which might hang his own life and even the future of those who were to follow his trail to the West. Any man could be a hero on the Plains if he had the stuff, and nearly every man was forced to be a hero at some time or other.

If you go through the little towns which dot the Plains today, you find on the newsstands a great array of western story magazines or western books, and often little else. In other parts of the country, these stories and these books may seem to their readers to be sheer fiction or mere fantasy, but to the average man bred on the Short Grass, these stories embody the tradition of the country. They are his historical fiction, the record of his ancestors in a by-no-means distant past. The saddles and guns and horses, the prairie fires, blizzards, and stampedes, the Indians, wild game, and cattle, are things still familiar, things which he himself has seen and heard tell of in the family circle. To him, a rodeo is not an acrobatic show put on by strangers from afar, but a frequent demonstration of practical skills as native to the Plains as they are spectacular and heroic.

As a matter of fact, some of the best rodeos are wholly private and impromptu, put on by amateur riders for their own amusement on the ranch of a Sunday afternoon. And of course, some horses buck every morning, as soon as they are saddled, seven days a week.

The first World War demonstrated that courage is as common as mud, but between wars this fact is lost sight of in old settled communities, where people wonder if they are growing soft and effeminate. Such a notion rarely occurs to the Plainsman because he sees around him the objects and the mementos of heroism and can recall out of his immediate experience or from the accounts of his friends and neighbors examples of valor and fortitude quite ample to maintain his faith in human courage. This tradition on the Short Grass is vitalized by heroic conflicts within living memory. The Short Grass lies squarely between two great memorials—the Alamo in Texas and the Custer Battlefield in Montana, where brave men went looking for trouble and died rather than retreat.

The man who came west expected trouble, commonly carried a chip on his shoulder, and though not deliberately quarrelsome, could seldom brook a rival. No sooner had a man acquired a reputation as a gunman, due to some killing in self-defense, than he was beset and challenged on all sides by ambitious rivals who sought him out with no other purpose than to test their own skill and valor at the risk of their lives. The "bad man" had badness thrust upon him—he had no choice but to fight all comers or leave the country.

The spirit of the frontier is well expressed by the old story about the pioneer in Tennessee who learned that the Texans were fighting for their independence against the Mexican dictator. The Tennessean took his long rifle and set out for the West with blood in his eye.

One of his friends asked him where he was bound. Sternly the traveler answered, "I'm goin' to Texas to fight for my rights."

This willingness to fight is a regional tradition.

When Congress passed the Peace Time Conscription Bill, there were already so many enlisted in the National Guard and in the regular armed forces of the Nation that the first draft was almost a dead letter on the Short Grass. The quota had already been filled up long before the bill was passed. Texas had more volunteers for the Army than any state in the Union, and it has been claimed that there are more Texans in the Royal Canadian Air Force than there are subjects of King George.

A good part of the Short Grass was inhabited by people who came west after the Civil War before they had had their fill of fighting. What they had been unable to do in battle, they managed to do in feuds and private wars. The Civil War was fought hand to hand or with single-shot rifles at close range. This tradition persisted long after the Spanish War. If my memory serves me right, there was at least one fight on the school ground in our town every day, and frequently half a dozen.

Nowadays, whether because warfare in our time consists in hurling high explosives at an unseen enemy, or because of the multitude of school-marms in the educational system, or for whatever reason, there seems to be much less fighting between the boys and young men than formerly, but the old fighting spirit is not dead—only kept under. On the Short Grass, the boy who does not look forward to an opportunity to go to war for some good cause would be regarded as definitely odd.

People would think there was something wrong with his glands.

One day at a rodeo, a bucker fell on his rider, pinning the cowboy to the earth. His friends ran out to save him, calling, "Take it easy. We'll help you up."

"Hell," the bronc-buster replied, indignantly, "help the *horse* up. I'm still in the saddle."

To understand any man or any region, it is not enough to see what the man is: one must also arrive at an understanding of how the man thinks about himself. On the High Plains, where almost every boy regards the cowboy with an admiration amounting to reverence, the notion persists into later life, and the tradition colors his thinking down through the years. He may never wear boots or mount a horse or know one end of a gun from the other; still the influence is felt, and to some extent, modifies his conduct and shapes his ideas to the end. In regions where the cowboy was never known, this fades away rapidly in adult life; but in cow country it persists, because everyone understands it and is friendly towards it, since it is the tradition of the region.

4. The Age of Rawhide

SPARSE population and the sheer necessity for getting things done developed a talent for improvisation in even the most stodgy and conventional settler. There were no barriers to his thought short of the horizon and he quickly developed a willingness to try anything once. He was always ready to hear or to tell some new thing, but especially ready to try one. In this the Plainsman was in strong contrast to his neighbors, the Arkansawyers in the Ozarks to the east, and the Spanish-Americans in the Rockies to the west. Compared with these mountaineers he seems as progressive as a rocket.

Every able man became a Jack-of-all-trades, like the fellow described in Mark Twain's *Roughing It*, who was "hotelkeeper, postmaster, blacksmith, mayor, constable, city marshal, and principal citizen." The Plainsman was compelled to make the attempt to fulfill John Milton's requirements for an educated man: "fitted to perform . . . all the offices, both public and private, of peace and war."

This kept him as busy as an ambidextrous centipede, and many were the inventions and devices he employed. Thus Charles Goodnight invented the grub-wagon or chuckwagon—at first called the "cupboard" wagon— hung all around with victuals (salted, smoked, or dried), heaped with sacks of flour and beans, with the high box at the back divided into partitions to contain the smaller cooking utensils, molasses, shortening, and seasoning, and the compartment just in front to hold the dutch ovens, pothooks, and pans. In such a wagon, besides the sacks and barrels, would be the carcass of a steer and the cook's bedroll. Underneath was slung the canvas " 'possum-belly" full of firewood. Without the chuckwagon the life of a cowboy would have been a cheerless existence indeed, and though he used the term "the Wagon" to include the bed wagons containing the bedrolls of the men, his first thought was of the chuckwagon. If necessary, he was always ready to "wait for the wagon."

Buffalo Bill developed this idea into the traveling kitchen used in the Wild West Show, which was faithfully studied by military men when the show visited Germany, and is supposed to have been the original of the rolling kitchens used in the first World War.*

BAREHANDED

Buffalo hunters learned to take refuge from a blizzard in the disemboweled carcass of a freshly killed bull or pony, and sometimes found themselves frozen in when the blizzard had passed. Men caught by a prairie fire when hauling water, cut their teams loose and saved themselves by submerging in the water barrel until the flames had passed. Sooners—that is, men who staked claims "too soon" (in advance of the opening of Indian

* See *Diary of Annie Oakley*, quoted on pages 293-94 of *The Making of Buffalo Bill* by Richard J. Walsh. Indianapolis, 1928.

lands to white settlement)—deceived the officers by throwing a bucket or two of water over their horses and rubbing their hides into a lather with soap. When the grass gave out, cattlemen went round with blow torches and burned the spines from prickly pear to provide feed for their cattle.

To keep off chiggers, people filled their boots or the cuffs of their trousers with sulphur flowers.

Army men introduced camels for ships of the desert in the West—though this innovation never caught on.

There is a story of an English gentleman who, having been reduced by the blizzard of '86 from a cattleman to a hog-farmer, was at a loss to know how to dress the pork for market. Having been told that he must scrape the bristles off, and having no knife, he used a set of fine razors, of which he had seven, one for each day of the week. One surmises that he let his beard grow after that experiment.

With this talent for innovation on the plains, went a certain impatience, a desire for quick results. Thus when a horse died in the trail, no one stopped to bury him. They simply drove around, letting the buzzards, coyotes, and tumblebugs remove the offal.

When oil came in and smoking was forbidden about the rigs to prevent fires, oil men who were confirmed smokers formed the habit of having a "dry" smoke, gradually chewing an unlighted cigar to bits. One nervous man in an office, who found that he puffed his cigars too fast to enjoy them, formed the habit of lighting two at once which he puffed alternately.

In the old days the prairie was dotted with the bleached and crumbling bones of millions of buffalo, antelope, wild horses, and other game. Travelers often marked their course by piling up a few skulls into a landmark, or, like Brigham Young, writing the direction and record of the day's march on the broad forehead of the cranium. The early trails were easily followed if one could read the meaning of these markers.

But in the hard times following the first settlement of the country, the settlers turned bone pickers and went about gathering up the bones by the wagonload. They hauled them to the railroad, where, awaiting shipment, they were stacked into great heaps extending for hundreds of yards along the tracks. Even today one may occasionally pick up a hoary, flaked buffalo horn down by the railroad in little frontier towns. On the High Plains the bones were apt to be very dry. Selling by the pound as they did, they brought little enough. Sometimes the men who loaded the cars took pity on the bone pickers and drenched the load with water, thus greatly increasing its weight.

Many of these bones were used for fertilizer in the East, but they say some were shipped abroad and made into bone china.

This traffic in bones from the Plains is by no means ended. In hard winters when hosts of wild horses freeze to death, one may see stacks of bones in little way-stations heaped higher, sometimes, than the station-house roof.

On both the Santa Fe and Oregon trails ingenious pioneers set out for the mountains in light wagons rigged with sails, hoping to cruise like so many ships across the boundless sea of grass. One old-timer told how he saw one of these wind-wagons on the Oregon trail. The men had a set of harness made to fit their own bodies so that they could draw the wagon whenever the wind failed.

Such resourcefulness has always been an American trait. A new country inevitably prompted experiments and inventions, and new folkways grew from new conditions. Since the High Plains presented conditions more widely different from Europe than anything in the woodlands and hills of eastern states, resourcefulness was more in demand there than elsewhere. The climate also was temperate and highly variable—a climate supposed to favor the use of intelligence. In fact, the pioneer not only applied his resourcefulness to practical necessities; he actually delighted in inventions as absurd as they were logical.

There was the man who proposed, on learning that rattlesnakes were nocturnal in their habits, that all snakes should be painted with luminous paint—so that the wayfarer could see them in his path, and step to safety! It would be a sorry cowboy who could not think up as good a one as that any day between chuck and bedding down.

Prairie dogs were a curse to some ranchers. They were disposed of by backing a motor car up to the hole, and filling it with carbon monoxide from the exhaust.

One day John R. (Jack) Abernathy, cowboy and U. S. Marshal, took after a big "loafer" (*lobo*) wolf. When he reached the animal, he found one of his dogs slashed and dying by the loafer's teeth. Jack jumped from the saddle to rescue the dying dog. The wolf leaped for his throat. Somehow, in fending it off, Jack's hand got into the wolf's throat, his fingers closed on its lower jaw behind the sharp canine teeth. Both went down, and in the rough-and-tumble Jack was surprised and delighted to find that he could hold the wolf so without being bitten.

From that day he hunted wolves bare-handed with striking success, shaming all the heroes who told of battles with the savage beasts. Though the animals sometimes scratched his shirt to ribbons before he could master them, he caught many—brown, white, gray, and black—which had been the terror of the cattle all over that part of Oklahoma. Jack carried some baling wire, with which he wired the jaws of his captive together, then carried the harmless creature home alive across his saddle.

One day at Frederick, Oklahoma, he gave an exhibition of his skill in a cage, and his fame spread throughout the country. When he met a wolf, he simply "gave it his hand."

When Teddy Roosevelt came west for a wolf hunt, Abernathy went along on invitation from the President, and caught a wolf for the President—after which the three of them were photographed together, while Jack held the helpless wolf by the jaw single-handed. Some of the animals he caught weighed as much as 125 pounds. His feats were also recorded by motion-picture cameras. But the dignity of his office prevented him from giving exhibitions for pay. Photographs and detailed accounts of Jack's hunts appear in an interesting book called *In Camp with Theodore Roosevelt, or the Life of John R. (Jack) Abernathy,* published by The

Times-Journal Publishing Company of Oklahoma City in 1933.

Pioneers on the Short Grass had to do a good many things bare-handed, but they were not afraid to try. In the early days—down until the end of the free range—the Plainsman placed his chief reliance upon rawhide. After the Age of Rawhide came the Age of Baling Wire. One or the other was used for every conceivable odd job, repair job, or substitution on the Plains. Turn a man loose there with a piece of rawhide, or a coil of baling wire, and he could rig up anything from a set of harness to a patch on his pants.

The windmill was one of those institutions which underwent transformation on the Short Grass. The massive towers of Holland with their vast soaring wings gave place to a lean structure of steel with a buzzing wheel that faced every which way and caught the power of all the winds that blew. It was bolted together, or—if the bolts wore out—wired together. Its clanking made the music to which ten thousand homesteaders dreamed of rich wheat and fat cattle. Whatever else failed on the Short Grass, wind *never* failed.

Today you may sometimes see several windmills standing close about a water-tank in a pasture. If you rashly ask why there are two or three, the poker-faced native will answer, "Well, you see, there is too much wind for one mill to handle!"

In recent years a windmill with a propeller blade has been widely used to generate electric power.

Barbed wire was another invention—or perhaps discovery—which found wide use on the Plains. When the cattlemen found that the blue blizzards had driven their cattle miles and miles away, they built drift fences running along the edge of their holdings to catch their neighbors' cattle drifting in, and their own when drifting out. These fences, being made of smooth wire, would not hold the steers, who blundered through, yanking the staples from the posts. Some say that a rancher noticed one of these staples clinched about the wire of his wrecked fence, and got the idea that staples clinched on at regular intervals along the wire might discourage cattle from breaking through. However that may be, barbed wire soon crisscrossed the prairies. The invention was patented by J. F. Glidden, November, 1874.

The new fencing had a profound effect upon our history. It not only helped to bring an end to the free range, thus changing all the habits of man in that region; it also helped destroy the herds in the great blizzard of 1886, which wiped out the investment of a thousand cattlemen. It protected the nester's little farm from passing cattle, turned wandering Indians back, blotted out the old trails. In World War I it had no small part in stopping the Kaiser.

It also helped put an end to the nefarious raiding of cattle-thieves, and sent the sheepman back to his adobe abode in New Mexico.

The Indian, though a conventional person, had his share of this pioneer resourcefulness. For he also was, often enough, a newcomer to the Plains, having moved to the Short Grass only a generation or two ahead of the white pioneer. He quickly learned to use the inventions of the white intruder, and made not a few improvements on these for his own needs—some of which were later adopted by his teachers. Thus, the Plains Indian, being a vain person, delighting in personal adornment, avidly bought the small mirrors offered him by the trader. But the redskin warrior soon found new uses for the looking-glass.

He noted that the mirror would reflect the sun, and that the flash was visible a long way off. It occurred to him that he had found a wonderfully convenient way of communicating with his fellows.

The most authentic account of this use of mirrors is to be found in Captain W. P. ("White Hat") Clark's classic of the Plains, *The Indian Sign Language;* Philadelphia, 1885. Clark says:

"There is not a very extensive code with a mirror. Its principal use is to attract attention, give warning, etc., and the number of flashes are often determined on, just prior to its use, by special decision of the participants. Its particular value is the power to communicate intelligence over great distances in an instant of time, provided always that the sun shines.

"Though there is no special code, yet the mirror is used to impart information in regard to the pursuits of life which are nearest and dearest to an Indian heart, namely, love, war, feasting, and hunting.

"A young man, armed with a looking-glass, will seat himself on some little eminence near the camp, where he can see the tipi of his sweetheart; she appears at the door of the lodge, the flash of light from the mirror falls upon her, and then moves to the right or left. Even if this arrangement has not been preconcerted she divines the meaning, and is suddenly seized with a desire to go after wood or water in the direction which the flash indicated, and a meeting is the result.

"To call people to a feast some previous arrangement has to be made. Sometimes it is understood that the invitation will be issued in this way, and of course the flashes are looked for, and they are not particular as to the number. An old Indian illustrated its use by saying, 'Suppose eight or ten of us were seated here smoking and became hungry. Knowing someone in camp who had plenty to eat, one of our number would go to the man's lodge and hint that something be cooked. His suggestion meeting with success, he would excuse himself for a moment, step outside the tipi, and signal us to come; and on the strength of this information we would, one after another, happen around to the lodge, and of course be invited to eat when everything was ready.'

"In hunting, suppose the scout sent on in advance discovered four bands or herds of buffalo, and then many scattered over the country, four distinct flashes would be made, and then a fluttering motion given to the mirror.

"Information in regard to any other game would be communicated in a similar manner, and its location to right or left of the advance scout be made known by turning the flash to the right or left. By preconcerted arrangement the kind of game would be determined by the number of flashes.

"For war purposes. Suppose the scouts sent on ahead discover a large number of the enemy close at hand, a continuous, quick, vibratory, tremulous motion is given the mirror; no distinct flashes. The party in rear scat-

ter and secrete themselves. Should there be distinct
flashes, the party in rear hurry forward, moving to right
or left as the flashes may indicate.

"The system to be used is talked over, thoroughly
understood, and agreed upon by the party before the
scout or scouts are sent on in advance. . . ."

Such devices were employed to get the best of white
men, long after the Indians were placed upon reservations.

When the Texas cattlemen pastured their steers upon
the grass in the Cheyenne and Arapaho Reservation in
Oklahoma, during Cleveland's administration, the Indians were dissatisfied with their cut of the income.
They felt, too, so they say, that since the white men
had killed their buffalo, they had a right to shoot a
few of the white men's steers. Accordingly, every morning every cowboy found himself trailed at a discreet distance by two Indian riders armed with looking-glasses.
Wherever he went, they followed—always the same distance behind, following him like wolves, but apparently
doing nothing more. If he halted, they halted; if he
rode, they followed.

Every day the boss would find a steer, killed silently
with arrows, and neatly butchered—or, rather, he found
the spot where the steer had been butchered, since an
Indian butcher leaves no offal. Not once did a cowboy
come upon an Indian butchering. For always the riders
who trailed him signaled his approach to the Indians
who were killing steers. To stop the business was impossible, unless the cowman hired a personal guardian
for every steer. For the Indians far outnumbered the
cowboys, and under regulations, had the right to go

anywhere they chose on their own reservation. It was a feast every day for the Cheyennes, and a headache every day for the boss. And it was all done with mirrors.

There are people who think Indians are not inventive or ingenious—and have no sense of humor! The Texans, as they say, "learned a heap different."

This use of mirrors for signaling was soon brought to the attention of officers of the Army in the Indian wars, and they adopted the idea, developing it to make the heliograph—widely used in the Boer War by the British. Is it too great a stretch of fact to see in the flashing lights or "blinkers" used as signals in our Navy the ingenuity of the Plains Indian?

At any rate, the redskin showed how much store he set by his looking-glass by the decoration he lavished upon its wooden frame, which was all carven and painted and studded with brass tacks, and often a foot in length. An unusually fine specimen may be seen in the Museum of the Panhandle-Plains Historical Society, a Museum entirely devoted to the Short Grass Country, at Canyon, Texas, adjacent to the Palo Duro State Park. No lover of the High Plains should fail to visit it.

The Indian found ammunition hard to get, and after metallic cartridges came into use, learned to re-load cartridge shells. This practice was also adopted by white men.

Moreover the Plains Indians appear to have invented the smoke screen for use in war. They say this was at first an accident, which developed when they tried to drive their enemies out of position by firing the long grass in the bottoms where they had taken refuge. The burning grass threw up a heavy smoke curtain, and the

Indians found they could charge safely up behind this, until they had their foes at short range.

The smoke screen was used by the allied Kiowa, Comanche, Cheyenne, and Arapaho in the fight with Kit Carson's command at Adobe Walls, 1864. It is now an established technique in warfare, on land and sea and in the air. Possibly Europeans invented it before the Indian discovered it; in any case, the Indian may claim to have made the discovery independently.

The Indian scout also used the flint and steel in early days for signaling—a use which, I believe, was not an invention of the white men. When bent on stealing horses or scalps, Indians would creep near the hostile camp, and send a scout forward to reconnoiter. The scout, using pre-arranged signals, would face his own party, draw his blanket over his crouching figure, and by striking sparks from his flint, convey silently information as to the number of horses, enemies, or lodges of the camp.

Smoke signals also seem to have been an Indian invention. Popular belief would have it that the redskin made these by spreading a blanket over the fire, and releasing puffs of smoke, but though I have talked with old warriors of nearly every Plains tribe, I have yet to find one who had ever seen any such method employed. They say that separate fires were used, each of which, quickly burning out the small quantity of green stuff thrown upon it, ceased to smoke, while another was made to smoke a minute after. Two parallel columns of smoke meant good luck. Sometimes a returning war party merely set fire to the prairie on nearing home, as an indication of a successful raid.

Again, after they got horses, Indians would signal from a distance by riding in circles on a hillside. The larger the circle, the bigger the herd or band of enemies they had discovered. A common alarm signal was made by tossing a double-handful of dust high in air, where the wind made a banner of it. This was in imitation of the dust pawed up by a bellicose buffalo bull, and meant immediate fight: "Enemy close by!" or "Charge!"

Little has been published from first-hand sources on this matter of smoke signals. I am happy to quote the following passage from the unpublished memoirs of the well-known Oklahoma pioneer, Mr. Chal Byers, offered here through the kindness of my colleagues, Dr. Cortez A. M. Ewing and Dr. Ralph H. Records, of the University of Oklahoma.

"For some reason or other, I stayed all night at an Indian camp on the Caney River. That in itself was not an unusual thing for me to do, for I was living about as much with the Indians as with people of my own race. Early on the morning after, Alvin Ward came riding into the awakening camp and announced that General Custer and all of his soldiers had been killed. The general was well known to the Oklahoma Indians and they had followed his actions with considerable interest.

"The Indians in the camp were visibly excited, but I noticed that none showed any skepticism concerning the announcement. But not caring to swallow so important an announcement without more information than Ward had given, I asked him how he knew that it had happened. 'Smoke, smoke,' he answered. But that seemed more like an evasion than an answer to me. I went on home that morning and told my father what I had heard. He wouldn't believe it. Eventually we learned that the report was true. The question always stayed with me as to how Ward knew that Custer had been killed on the morning after the great battle in the Little Big Horn country.

"Of course, we had no telephones in those days, and it was over forty miles to the nearest telegraph office. And from the Montana battlefield, it must have been much farther than that to a telegraph ticker. Our most widely read newspaper was the *St. Louis Globe-Democrat*, and we didn't get it until it was over a week old. But the Indians knew that Custer was killed before, probably, the type was set on the paper announcing the startling event. . . .

"The news must have been relayed to Oklahoma by means of signal fires and smoke. As a matter of fact, several groups of Pawnees were on the road to join Custer, even as Custer and his force were annihilated. Captain North, one of Custer's best officers, had come to Oklahoma to get thirty-four Pawnees to act as scouts during the northern campaigns. The Pawnees were notorious as scouts. They were very elusive fellows, who lived by their wits. Captain North was not able to recruit so many Pawnees as Custer wanted, so he left word for others to follow him as he went to join Custer.

"A few days after North departed, a hunting party of Pawnees returned to their lodges and heard of North's mission. Straightway they started up the trail after him. We saw them as they passed, walking and each leading a pack horse. A few days later, another group passed on the way to Custer. Thereafter, there were three or four of these Pawnee parties that passed, at intervals of a few days each, up the trail toward the Missouri River forts. It was only a day or two after the last party departed before Ward made the announcement that I have described.

"Moreover, in a day or so after the battle of the Little Big Horn took place, the last party of Pawnees came back down the trail, headed for home. My father, knowing their original intentions, asked them why they had returned without joining Custer. They answered: 'No use. Custer dead!' Up along the trail, the isolated Pawnee bands had secured the information concerning Custer's defeat, had received it long before the papers were out, even before the country-at-large knew of it.

"One may think what one may concerning my explanation of the grape-vine telegraph. Without contradicting evidence, I'm inclined to believe that it was true in regard to the Custer episode. Of course, with Negroes in African jungles, the news may be carried across the continent in a short time through the use of huge drums. Noise is easily detected. A stranger within the hearing range of the drum might note its existence, even though he might be unable to decipher its strange code. Smoke would, to the uninitiated, be a very common thing. In fact, it would scarcely be noticed. But the keen eyes of an Indian would be able to read the fire or smoke message from great distances.

"Again, there was no possibility of Indian runners having carried the news from the Montana plains. The time was too short for that great distance. Even with relay devices, modern high-powered automobiles would not be able to negotiate the distance in so short a period as that which was represented in Alvin Ward's news flash. . . ."

Recently, in a newsreel, we have seen how the U. S. Army ferries light cars across streams by making a "boat" of a waterproof tarpaulin drawn up around the vehicle on all sides to keep out the water. This is a device also evidently borrowed from the redskins. Just so Plains Indians ferried all their belongings across rivers, floating them in the hide covers of their tipis.

There is no end to the ingenuity of Plainsmen; even bandits displayed it.

An honest man can get along with a few friends, but a bad man must have friends everywhere. Whether he is generous by nature or not, he has to play the part of Robin Hood or perish. Only one bandit in the west was actually the "Lone Rider" of legend. This was a desperado who operated in Colorado, known as Black Jack. Having no friends, he improvised them, setting up dummy gunmen in the bushes around the spot where he intended to hold up the stage. These dummies, with dummy guns, helped him by keeping the travelers "covered" while he relieved them of their valuables. Black Jack worked fast, and the robbery was over before the fraud could be discovered.

Free land sometimes left the landholder wondering, like the dog that caught the skunk, what to do with it. Some lived upon wild game for a while, or on the neighbors. Others found methods of cashing in on whatever the land produced. In the '90's some enterprising ranchers killed and dressed prairie dogs which they shipped east to market as "prairie squirrels." They were so much in demand for a while, that buyers were sent west to contract for shipments. This unforeseen development led to trouble.

Such misunderstandings were very minor difficulties as compared with the broad social disturbances brought about by the sudden influx of men from all quarters of the country, bringing different mores, diverse ideals, and often enough prejudices and passions inflamed by years of conflict, not to mention the stress of prolonged hard times.

Much of the trouble on the Plains was a hangover from the Civil War. The Southerners who came to the Short Grass, some of them members of guerilla bands like Quantrell's Raiders, were still ready to fight the Yanks at the drop of the hat. They felt that they had been "outnumbered," not defeated. They believed in their lost cause and resented the loss of their slaves and their political rights. In a troubled world they felt that courage and shooting were the only protection for the values they held dear. It is a curious fact that they expressed their hatred of industrial civilization by the use of the Colt's revolver, one of the first machines to be manufactured with interchangeable parts.

Medical science was one of the last blessings to find its way to the Short Grass. Calomel, laxatives, cholagogue, soda, and alcohol were for a long time almost the only remedies available. Even snake-bite was treated by applying soda and alcohol until the patient recovered—or died.

REMEDY WORSE THAN THE DISEASE

George Bent, half-breed son of Colonel William Bent, builder of Bent's Old Fort on the Arkansas River in Colorado, used to tell the story of how an Indian medicine man saved his father's life. Colonel Bent was afflicted with a bad case of what was then known as "putrid sore throat." His throat was so inflamed that the decayed flesh was about to choke the Colonel to death. At all costs, a channel must be kept open.

All over the Plains there are patches of sandburs. This grass produces small burs of about the diameter of a small pea. Each one is armed with a number of barbed hooks, all pointing one way. The medicine man gathered a dozen of these, pierced each one with an awl, and strung them on a slender thong with a loop in the end, taking care that the barbs all pointed in the same direction, opposite the loop in the thong. He then notched a twig, put the notch into the loop, and so pushed the thong gently down the sick man's throat. It went down smoothly, since the barbs all pointed up.

Then, while others held the Colonel's head, the medicine man pulled the thong out. The barbs bedded in the rotten flesh and brought it all out, leaving the throat lacerated but open. The treatment was severe, but the cure was certain. Colonel Bent lived many years after and showed no loss of his unusual vigor.

To some it may seem strange that Bent, himself a practical doctor, who served all the people within a week's ride of his fort, would look to a medicine man for treatment. But no old-timer would have thought so. On the Plains, the Indians were the most numerous inhabitants, who had been living in tune with conditions there for many generations, and had discovered how to cope with emergencies which arose there. In fact, the Short Grass was effectively Indian country until 1890. What the redskin had faced, the white man who followed had to face also; no one can understand either those problems or their solutions who ignores the ideas and devices of the red brother.

Sometimes the red brother himself was the problem that inspired ingenuity.

BALDWIN'S CHARGE

The Army, too, has its examples of ingenuity on the Plains. In 1874, when General Nelson A. Miles was trying to round up the hostiles of the Short Grass, detachments were sent after the Cheyennes under Gray Beard. These Indians had several captives, including the Germaine sisters, of pathetic memory. On November 6, a troop of the Eighth Cavalry ran afoul of a hundred warriors, and had to send for reinforcements. Two companies of the Tenth Cavalry were sent under Major Price, who failed to accomplish anything.

Lieutenant Frank D. Baldwin, a dashing officer, known familiarly as "Lucky" Baldwin, and the only man of his day who received the Congressional Medal twice, was assigned to the Fifth Infantry. He had with him a detachment of cavalry, and a number of wagons, besides the infantry. He went after the hostiles with his

usual drive and dash, and came up with them on the
north branch of McClellan Creek. His scouts reported
a large camp just over the hill.

Price was nearby, but Baldwin could not wait for
him. Outnumbered as he was, he knew he had to make
the most of what he had. The infantry could not keep
up with the cavalry in a charge, and without a charge
he could not hope to handle the Indians; surprise was
vital. Yet his force was too small to be divided.

Baldwin thought fast, and gave his orders. The soldiers ripped the wagon sheets from the bows of the
wagons, and the infantry climbed in. Baldwin formed
the wagons in a single rank, with cavalry on each flank.
"Charge!"

The bugle sounded, the teamsters lashed the mules
into a dead run, and the cavalry rode hell-for-leather
alongside. Over the ridge they went, bouncing like blitz-
buggies, and rolled down the slope upon the camp of
the astonished Indians, while the infantrymen cut loose
with everything they had from the wagons.

For half a minute the Indians stood with their
mouths open. Then they took to their heels, leaving
their lodges and everything else behind, riding and
running to escape. Two of the Germaine girls, pitiful
waifs, were left behind, unharmed. Baldwin had won
against odds. His was our first approach to mechanized
warfare on the Short Grass. . . .

Maybe it was the bareness of the country that caused
men to rely upon themselves. Nowhere was it barer or
flatter than on the Llano Estacado, the Staked Plains

or Palisaded Plains. These vast levels got their name, some say, from the fact that they were shored up at the edges by steep palisades; others claim that the name arose from the fact that travelers had to set stakes to mark the trail—though one wonders where they got the stakes and how many wagon loads of stakes it took to mark a trail across that country.

Llano Estacado

For hundreds of miles there was not a tree worth mentioning. The Comanches, with typical Indian wit, dubbed the band which ranged on the Staked Plains the Back-Shade Folks—since they could only sit in the shade of their own backs! When a cowboy slicked up to go to a dance, he judged of his appearance by watching his shadow as he rode, there being no pools in which to admire his manly beauty. It is said that a certain gambler, driven out upon that plain, got the idea for a patent corkscrew by contemplating his own shadow.

When the sun was hot, riders used to get off and sit in the shade of their horses, while the animals rested. Dogs learned to run in the shadow of a horse when the sun threw it to one side or the other. And there is a story that the Staked Plains got their name from the attempt of a man, lost and crazy with the heat—a man who tried to stake the darkness down at night, so that he would have some shade to sit in next day. In doing this, he smashed his thumb with the hammer, and put it in his mouth to relieve the pain. The thumb swelled so

that he couldn't get it out, and he choked to death before sun-up. But the stakes are still there—*if* you can
find them.

Just ride two hundred miles straight west, and turn
north.

Buffalo—grama—mesquite—the true Short Grass—
grows best on level land or on the long slopes of rolling
prairies. But in stony ground or sandy soil, near sloughs
and sink-holes, in river bottoms and in timber along the
creeks many other species—some rare, some common—
some worthless, some useful—are found. For the whole
region is as hospitable to grasses as it is hostile to trees
and shrubs.

Many of these are plants which offer good grazing,
and protect the soil from erosion. For, as the short
grasses are to be found far to the east of the Short Grass
Plains, so the taller grasses make themselves at home in
the West. In Kansas alone there are sixty different
groups—almost two hundred species. Oklahoma and
Texas are similarly blest, and the value of these plants
is shown by the popular English names applied to them.

Your Plainsman will know Bottlebrush Grass, June
Grass, Western Wheat Grass, Red Ray, Ever-grass,
Needlegrass. Nodding Wild Rye, Feathergrass, Prangle
and Crabgrass; White Grass, False Buffalo Grass, Slough-
grass or Bull Grass six feet tall, Windmill Grass, Naked
Beardgrass, Hairy Mesquite, Black Grama, Side-oats
Grama, Texas Grama, Marsh Foxtail, Beard Grass,
Poverty Grass, and Woolly Triple-awned Grass, grow-
ing in dry thickets.

He will recognize Feather Bunchgrass, Sweetgrass, Red-Top, Creeping Bent Grass, Spider Bent Grass, Fly-Away Grass, Foolhay, and Nimble Will; Big Sand Grass, Pancake Grass, Hairgrass, Dropseed, Satin-grass, Rush Grass, Saltgrass, Red Oats, and Alkali Grass.

With these, others are seen: Lacegrass, Blow-out Grass, Speargrass, Strong-scented Lovegrass, Candy Grass or Skunk Grass; Pink Grass, Spikegrass, Wild Chess, Cockgrass, Manna-grass, Frisky or Evergreen Grass, Pigeon Grass, Green Bottle Grass, Jungle Rice, Billion Dollar Grass, and the annoying Sandbur.

The list includes Fingergrass, Panic-grass, Knot-grass, Devil's Grass, Spreading Witchgrass, Ticklegrass, Tumbleweed, Range-grass, Grapevine Grass, Deer Tongue Grass, Switchgrass, Blue-joint and all the other big and little Bluestem grasses.

Added to these native stocks are the imported and cultivated plants which play so great a part on the Plains: Johnson Grass, Feterita, Kafircorn, Bermuda, Broom corn, Sorghum, Cane, Milo Maize, and Sudan Grass.

Add to these the vines, shrubs, weeds, and trees native to the region, and you can understand the blank amazement of a Plainsman who hears some dude complain that the Short Grass country "lacks variety."

SKY GARDEN

The ancients never became aware of the beauty of the Alps. To them, those mountains were just so many big stones in the road to Gaul. Some people are just as stupid nowadays. To them the Plains are only so much distance to be traversed. They complain that the Plains are flat and bare. Naturally—that is the beauty of them. The scarcity of landmarks, the scale and sweep of the High Plains are what make their sublimity. But they are never monotonous, never twice the same.

Anybody can admire a mountain or a tree—but the subtle undulations and gracious contours of the Short Grass require a sensitive eye for their appreciation.

For, as a matter of fact, the level ground is never exactly horizontal, nor the horizon precisely a circle. It is their approximation to these fundamental ideas that make the Plains so spiritually stimulating. The ideal is always unattained. But whoever may fail to enjoy the beauty of these dimensions may at any rate appreciate the skies. Nowhere is there a greater glory of the heavens, nowhere do the stars shine brighter, or the rising columns of warm air pile up cloud towers to heights so incredible. The Plains are one great Sky Garden.

The buffalo grass clothes the earth as with a sheer garment, and every contour, plane, and curve of the land appears fresh from the hand of those oldest of sculptors, the Wind and the Rain. A man is in despair because his hands are too small to caress those carven hillsides, tilted planes, arcs, hollows, and gracious undulations. The High Plains are not easily painted, only a sculptor could hope to render them adequately—but there is no stone large enough to carve them on.

The songs of the Short Grass are full of this. Too often we forget the obvious fact that many pioneers went to the West and lived and died there because they loved its beauty:

And often at night when the heavens are bright
By the light of the glittering stars,
I have stood there amazed, and asked as I gazed
If their glory exceeds that of ours.

In such a land, a lair is better than a nest. People all over the Plains make a practice of sleeping out-of-doors. In summer it is cooler; usually, before morning, a blanket is needed.

One old cowman so loved his nights under the stars that he continued to sleep in his bedroll to the end of his days—though he was rich in oil. On his regular visits to his son's home, he appalled his fastidious daughter-in-law by refusing to occupy a bed in her luxurious city house. All during his stay, the old-timer slept in his blankets on the well-kept lawn.

The man who sleeps in a bedroll learns to undress in a certain routine which often differs from that of other people. In going to bed he takes off his boots first, then his pants, his shirt, and his hat. In getting up, he reverses this order, gradually emerging from the shelter of his tarp. This custom, which always marks the seasoned cowman, is followed unconsciously by others who have picked up the regional folkway.

Other old habits have maintained themselves, in spite of the changes in living which followed the motorization of our material culture.

In the old days when an Indian returned to camp, he led his horse to the door of his tipi and unsaddled there. His wife led her pack-horses to the same spot and

stacked the traveaux close by the tent. Just so, the pioneer settler drove his wagon up to the house for safety
or convenience before he unhitched his team.

Today this folkway persists all over the Short Grass.
Wherever you go, you will find cars parked on the lawn
or on the parking rather than left in the drive. It
is one of those customs unconsciously followed from
old times. A man leaves his car where it is safest and
most convenient.

THE RED RIVER VALLEY

Sometimes it was death that inspired resourcefulness,
sometimes the threat of death.

In the old days when Indians buried their dead fully
equipped for the Happy Hunting Grounds, the body
was sometimes deposited in a vehicle in some small
canyon or grove of trees. When the land was settled,
a settler found one of these dead Indians lashed up in
blankets, seated in a new buggy. He buried the corpse
and surprised his family with the magnificence of his
new rig.

Once in Oklahoma two outlaws, brothers, handcuffed
together were being taken from one jail to another for
safety. Their enemies attacked the guards. In the fracas
that night, while the officers and the opponents were
shooting it out, the outlaws leaped from the buggy in
which they were riding. One of them was shot dead.
The other freed himself by cutting off the hand of his
companion with his pocket-knife.

Even the Army showed originality on the Short Grass,
if the following tale be true. It happened, they say, at

one of the western posts. One of the soldiers had been badly beaten up and thrown out of a honky-tonk in the nearby town. The next day he and his comrades returned to seek vengeance, but found their enemies gone, whereupon that night, while the officers were all at a dance, it is claimed that the men took out a battery of three-inch guns and prepared to bombard the town from a neighboring hilltop. Fortunately one of the officers learned of the project in time to interfere. If this be legend, it is at any rate in line with old-time conditions on the Short Grass.

During the drouths in the early '30's, three men went out to shoot wild fowl on the Red River. The river at the time was low, a mere trickle through a mile-wide bed of sand. A flock of geese flew over, high out of range, and alighted on a sandbar a quarter of a mile away. Two of the men remained in the blind while the third volunteered to circle round and flush the birds back toward his comrades. The wind was high and blew up such a dust screen on the river bed that he was able to approach the geese behind this curtain unseen.

This true story might seem incredible to one unfamiliar with the Plains, where, when the wind gets up, it raises the dust first of all in the river bed. One may trace the course of the stream miles away by the clouds of tawny sand which mark its wanderings.

After all, on the High Plains, the great fact is the *weather*.

5. The Age of Baling Wire

> After dishing out almost everything on the list Friday—record temperatures, dust, high winds, clouds, showers, lightning, and brilliant rainbows—Oklahoma's weather Saturday was settling down to a prosaic "fair and warmer."—*The Oklahoma Times.*

DWELLERS on the High Plains had to be resourceful. Their first problem was shelter, making the most of materials at hand. The climate—or rather the weather—offered a man-size challenge to their ingenuity.

The climate was generally dry, but brought terrific downpours and beating hail which searched out every crack and crevice of a building. Strong winds demanded a staunch structure. At times these winds were bitterly cold, again hot and parching, warping every log or plank exposed to the sun. Yet most of the year the wind was pleasant, and the only relief from summer heat. Snow was sometimes heavy, and roofs had to be steep enough to shed it, strong enough to carry it, yet at the same time flat enough not to be suntraps. And the extreme variability of the weather presented an ever-changing problem in heating and cooling arrangements.

These exactions forced men to devise all-weather shelters, staunch, proof against hail, rain, snow, wind, heat, drouth, and cold. A major problem in the Southern Plains was ventilation.

All these tests had to be met with materials at hand. Stone, timber, lumber were, in most places, unobtainable. There was only the earth, the grass, some slender trees and scanty brush—and the skins of wild animals. To complicate matters still further, the business of Plainsmen in the early period made constant travel necessary during a great part of the year. Even a vacation there meant, as a rule, a trip. Always far horizons beckoned.

Long before cattle and cowboys reached the Short Grass, the Indians had worked out shelters which—for outdoor, active men—met the challenge of the climate adequately.

Of course the Indian was hardy and, except in blizzards and cold rains, seldom felt any need for shelter from sun and wind. He wore no hat on the hottest day, and his clothing of buckskin was proof against most weather.

When warm rains fell, he simply stripped to the gee-string, stowed his clothes in a dry place, and let the rain run off his own waterproof skin! If the ground was muddy, or the snow had melted to slush, he removed his moccasins and went barefoot—with no fear of pneumonia. When the traders introduced brightly colored umbrellas, you might see a warrior carry his under his arm through the heat waves rising from the blistering prairie only to raise the gaudy decoration over his head after he had found a seat in the shade of the agency office! Even in weather twenty degrees below zero, old-time Indians made long journeys afoot naked above the waist, protected only by a buffalo robe. The Plains Indian could take it. At the same time he liked his comforts.

In the summer he was content to sleep and eat in a mere windbreak made by sticking a few willow shoots upright in a circle and tying a piece of tent cloth or a buffalo hide around these on the windward side. Even where tipis were available, young men seldom slept inside in summer. They lay in their blankets on the grass under the stars, where any prowling enemy would be sure to stumble over them. Any healthy young man found hanging around his mother's tent in daylight was likely to get a lecture from his grandfather; his place was on the prairie with his ponies.

The tipi belonged to the woman, and the Indian woman on the Plains was a careful, busy housewife who could make a snug home wherever grass grew. A well-bred Cheyenne woman was the equal of any Dutch *vrouw* at making her family comfortable. I have lived in the homes of both, and I know.

It was Indian women of this sort who contrived the tipi—by all odds the best tent ever invented. Twenty or more long, straight, taper poles—pine or cedar—peeled and seasoned, were artfully stacked in a cone against a tripod and then tautly covered with a semi-circle of canvas or tanned buffalo hides neatly sewn together. This covering was pinned up the front with wooden skewers the size of a lead pencil, and was pegged to the ground all round. In a permanent camp all the poles were set two or three feet deep in the earth, so defying all but the most violent winds.

The tipi was not a perfect cone, but tilted slightly

back, so that the smoke-hole was on the front above the pins and the entrance. This made the tent a thing of beauty, showing a different silhouette from every angle. On either side the smoke-hole was a wing or flap or "ear," managed by an outside pole. By shifting these poles, the "ears" could be raised or lowered or moved about to create a draft for the fire inside and so carry off the smoke. These "ears" rather resembled the lapels of a coat with the collar turned up. They made the tipi an airy, well-ventilated home. It was, in effect, a conical chimney.

Since the bottom of the covering was usually two or three inches above ground all around, plenty of air came in below to carry the smoke up and away; there was a continual draught blowing in all around the bottom of the tent.

To keep that draught from striking the backs of her family as they sat facing the central fire, the Indian housewife lashed a sheet of canvas to the poles over each pallet four or five feet up. This canopy or lining hung down inside the poles and was tucked under the edge of the bed behind. Thus the air coming in under the bottom of the outer covering was automatically deflected upward by this lining, and never struck the people about the fire.

Since the poles sloped inward, the lining formed a canopy over the bed, and so turned any rain that might fall through the smoke-hole, or beat through the outer covering. Thus the windbreak was built *inside* the tipi proper—making the whole as snug as it was well-ventilated. Because of its sloping walls, which reflected the heat of the fire downward, a fire no bigger than a dinner plate kept a tipi warm as toast.

I remember how, one bitter night when we had guests, a sudden norther blew out our north windows and made the whole house icy cold. I was unwilling to have the party broken up, and invited my guests to move out into the tipi which I kept pitched in my back garden—as a kind of outdoor "den." They were all very dubious, but put on their coats and followed. In a few minutes I had a fire going, and soon had them all backed up against the sides of the tent, their faces glowing. For three hours we continued our party while the wind howled and sleet covered the tent as with ground glass.

In like manner Reservation Indians usually moved out of their Government-built houses into tipis for the winter—in order to live comfortably. Indians have been much criticized for thus going "back to the blanket," but no one who has lived in a tipi in winter can doubt that they were right in doing so. The white man's frontier shack was a mighty poor makeshift compared with a good tipi.

It shed wind and water, it was snug and warm and airy. Two women could pitch a big tipi in fifteen minutes—if necessary, one could do it—and it could be transported at the rate of fifty miles a day, horseback.

In hot weather, the outer covering could be raised a foot or two to let the breeze through, and a few leafy cottonwood boughs leaned against the tent on the sunny side broke the force of the strongest sun. In warm weather, too, cooking was done outside in a windbreak or "kitchen," thus leaving the tipi fireless and cool.

But in a permanent camp the Indians added a brush "arbor" or "bower" to their establishment, under which the whole family found refuge from the sun. This was about twenty feet square, and consisted of a flat roof of leafy willow brush supported on stout posts seven or eight feet high, planted in the ground at intervals of about six feet. The sides were open to let the breeze sweep through, but, when high winds blew, the careful housewife stretched a wagon sheet across the windward side.

When traveling, a tent-fly over a ridge-pole served a similar purpose. Thus the Indian made himself comfortable. In early days a traveler could distinguish an Indian cabin from afar by the brush arbor alongside—even though the owners had departed with their tipi.

Not a few white men adopted the Indian arbor as a notable addition to the regional culture. Today it assumes the form of the screened porch—or outdoor living room, open on three sides—found everywhere on the Short Grass.

The white men, however, have not learned the lesson of the tipi. In the beginning, their scorn of everything Indian made them too contemptuous to see its merits. More recent builders have been unaware of what it has to teach us. As a result, there is as yet hardly any building on the Short Grass which solves the problem of shelter for this region so successfully. Here our architects have failed.

Of course, the tipi failed too in one respect—it could not exclude dust. But neither do our houses. For our builders have not only failed where the Indian succeeded—they have not even succeeded where the Indian failed. Dust remains the housewife's curse, and allergy is fast becoming a regional disease.

In the absence of any local solution, people simply give up and buy their house-plans by mail order, as their fathers bought stoves and saddles—house-plans devised by architects of the woods and mountains—who have no conception of the weather on the Plains. New England, Virginia, Mexico, and Italy provide our builders with models—could anything be more absurd?

Some attempts have been made, chiefly in Kansas and Texas, to build something suited to the region—and these are often as beautiful and convenient as houses anywhere. But in the main, architects are either esthetic in their approach, or devise mere streamlined versions of the Texas ranchhouse. The architects have sidestepped the basic problem of devising a house suited to the climate of the Short Grass.

Some think air-conditioning is the answer—and it may be, for indoor workers. But it is too expensive for most people. Moreover, most of the people on the High Plains spend their waking hours out-of-doors. Such people might find an air-conditioned house simply an expensive means to a bad cold.

When the first white settlers came to the Short Grass, the buffalo were almost extinct. There were no more hides for tipis. Those homesteaders lacked the campers' tradition. They came west land-hungry, with visions of farmhouses like those of the states they had left behind.

As for tents, they knew only the wall-tent, and being practical men, had no intention of living in that most uncomfortable of dwellings—unventilated, unlighted, unheated, freezing in winter, suffocating in summer, hard to pitch, easily blown down, and rarely proof against the beating rains of the Short Grass. That tent was abandoned there even by the Army, which improvised a one-pole tipi (the Sibley tent). A covered wagon was better—except in bitter cold.

In fact many a pioneer first established his family in a covered wagon-bed set flat on the prairie. There they lived until something more permanent could be provided.

The settler, as a rule, had three choices. He could make a dugout, build a sodhouse, or freight in expensive lumber by wagon from the nearest railroad town —often a hundred miles or more away. Even men who filed on claims with no intention of living on them, were required by law to erect a house of some kind before they could prove up and obtain title to the land.

The dugout was usually cut back into a hillside—a rectangular hole four or five feet deep, open at the front—and covered by a ridge-pole from front to back supporting planks, logs or a pole-and-brush roof of sod and earth. The roof extended a foot or more beyond the hole on either side. The low walls—of wood or sod— were erected near the eaves, thus leaving an inside ledge or shelf about shoulder high on either side. Windows were sometimes made in these walls above the level of the ground outside. A door—with leather hinges—was set up at the entrance in a wooden wall. If no slope offered, so that the dugout had to be made in level ground, the door sloped like an old-fashioned cellar-door. At the back a fireplace might be dug out, with a flue leading up. Or a stove-pipe was run up through the roof. Sometimes these dugouts were quite small.

Again they might be roomy, with space for two double-decker bunks on each side. If the roof were tight, such a shelter might be very snug in winter, cool in summer, and dry always. But if carelessly built, centipedes, snakes, scorpions, and tarantulas found entrance, rain dripped in, and of course ventilation was always a problem.

Nowadays the dugout is rare, inhabited by underprivileged people, or used as a stable. Few remain, since a dugout requires constant attention to be kept habitable.

But in early days a good housewife could make a dugout into a real home, with curtains at the windows, gay quilts on the bed, a shining cook-stove, and a row of plates on the mantel over the fire. The hard red clay walls were smooth as plaster, and rugs or sacking carpeted the earthen floor.

The dugout may have been suggested by the spring-house or root-cellar of older settlements. It had two big advantages—it was cool, and it generally survived tornadoes.

"Papa made a dugout for me and I lived in it until I proved up the claim. He split rails and put over the top, and covered it with dirt. I had the chills and one day was lying on the bed, when I looked up and saw a big snake crawling just over me on a rail. I got up and tried to get it but it got away from me." *

After people had left their dugouts for houses above ground, they reserved them for use as cyclone-cellars or " 'fraid-holes."

* See "Remembers First Burial, First Train" by Mrs. M. L. Jones, in *Echoes of Eighty-Nine*, page 39.

Recently a modification of the dugout has come into considerable use—cellar rooms, for offices, for games, or even for bedrooms. The coolest, snuggest place on the Plains is still underground. Some cellar rooms are cooler by ten degrees than the house above.

The sodhouse was above ground—made of slabs of deep prairie sod, laid up like brick, roofed in the same way as the dugout, and often plastered inside and out with mud or with the fragrant white gypsum of the region. Rarely, small windows were glazed with thin sheets of transparent—or translucent—crystallized gypsum from the Glass Mountains in Oklahoma.

In spite of, or rather because of, the limitations of the builders—inexperience, native materials, the stern requirements of necessity—such houses were often quite pleasing to the eye, often more pleasing than some more pretentious structures since erected where they stood. They were functional as few houses have been since.

The sodhouse might be a roomy structure as pioneer houses went. On my uncle's ranch in the Cheyenne and Arapahoe country there was a sodhouse containing four spacious rooms. When I saw it he was living in a frame house and used the soddy as a stable. I have seen twenty horses and mules stalled in it.

Owing to the gradual settling of the sod walls, such houses were never of more than one story. They fell to pieces quickly. If not well built and well kept up, a sodhouse was a sorry shelter. In such a soddy, the saying went, it "rained outside for one day, and inside for two days afterward."

Today our builders are realizing the usefulness of this type of construction. One of the handsomest tourist camps in the Southwest is built of brick made of mud, oil, and straw—a thoroughly modern, air-conditioned establishment. The walls are painted white and appear quite smart.

The first houses, even those put up with studding and clapboard, after the usual manner, seldom had any plaster. The house was "ceiled" with canvas or cheesecloth, on which the wallpaper was pasted. On a calm day, such a house seemed like any other. But when the wind was up, as usual, the stranger was likely to be startled at the way the walls billowed and fluctuated. One tenderfoot, frightened, ran out of the building, supposing he was in an earthquake. Needless to say, such homes were frigid in a blizzard.

"The house was so loosely built that every high wind blew pictures from the walls. I remember an afternoon when I had invited the senior class to dinner and couldn't keep the oven fire lighted in my gasoline stove. But we were never afraid the house would blow over, no matter how hard it shook, because the wind blew right *through* it.

"It was in that house that I passed eighteen of the happiest years of my life. I soon thought it a pretty place. Honeysuckle and trumpet vine covered the porch, a big sweet-briar rose grew by the steps, the mulberry trees attracted thousands of song birds, not only the mocking birds, but meadow larks, orioles, brown thrushes, blackbirds, scissortails, song sparrows and many others, and a mother quail leading her brood of downy chicks was no uncommon sight in our yard. Even in late summer, when the hot winds had burned everything a uniform brown, there was one oasis, the home on the bank of the creek." *

The pioneer often preferred to build a shack of planks, sometimes covered with tar-paper. This, raised a few inches off the ground, seldom painted, rarely plastered, without porch or fireplace, was a bleak, cheerless, cramped dwelling. Occasionally today you see one standing deserted and forlorn in the midst of a quarter-section of buffalo grass, with nothing between it and the North Pole but a barbed wire fence.

Most people on the Short Grass live now in frame houses, more rarely in homes of bricks and stone—houses which might stand anywhere in the Mississippi Valley, except that modern plumbing, gas, and electricity are rather more common here than in the older communities. In open country new ideas travel fast.

To make these "outlandish" houses comfortable in summer, people resort to various methods more or less experimental and makeshift: hollow tile walls, insulation in walls and ceilings of frame houses, fans and ventilators in the attic, air filters or coolers—boxes of Spanish moss or hay kept damp by dripping water—over bedroom windows, adjustable metal shutters or some device for air-conditioning the whole house.

What is needed is a house which can be thrown wide open to the night winds—which are nearly always cool—a house which can be shut tight against dust-storms, northers, hail, and hard rain—a house with outlets from the ceilings and attic to release warm air quickly as soon as the sun sets—a house with some kind of heating

* See "Brief History of Kingfisher College" by Mrs. F. L. Drake, in *Echoes of Eighty-Nine*, page 79.

system that can be quickly turned up or down to keep pace with the sudden variations of temperature—a house with double walls and roof, perhaps, so that air may pass freely, *automatically*, between them and so keep the heat from inner walls.

The most comfortable houses seem to be those which have a big fan or blower in the attic with a grill beneath it opening on a central hall or (better) a shaft into which open vents from the surrounding rooms. The fan, electrically controlled, swiftly sucks up the warm air and drives it out through attic louvres in the gable-ends, producing a lively breeze in any room where the windows are open.

A refinement at the windows is a box filter which cleans and cools and moistens the air, excluding dust. Such a house, if well built and insulated, is much more comfortable than one entirely air-conditioned, and much less costly. But such buildings are few and far between.

The Short Grass is in the same latitude as North Africa.

Of course, housing is equally deplorable all over the United States, lagging far behind population. Considering what people pay—and what they get—it is a wonder anybody builds at all. The motto of the industry seems to be: millions for materials and labor, but not one cent for imagination or common sense. Someday we may change all this and get a house designed for living. So far, the vaunted resourcefulness of the Westerner has failed him in this matter. We are not as quick even as the pioneers before us. The Indian has left us in the dust.

The problem of clothing for the Plains was more easily solved, and it *was* solved. In that region of sudden extremes, it is said, a man is prepared for the day only if he wears rubber boots, a slicker, and an overcoat, and carries an umbrella and a palm-leaf fan. At one time of day he may need a coat to turn wind or rain, and at another may wish to ventilate his skin for coolness.

The Indian solved the problem with buffalo-robe or blanket, which he could use as a hood, overcoat, bed or saddlepad, or carry folded, belted about his thighs. When it was cold he snuggled in it; when he was too warm, he dropped it from his bare body. And, gracefully draped about his tall frame, it served admirably as a formal cloak on occasions demanding a show of dignity.

The cowboy adopted a costume equally well suited to the climate. His felt hat turned wind and water and sun alike. The handkerchief about his neck protected it from sunburn, and could be lifted to cover his mouth and nostrils in thick dust. His shirt, always worn with the long sleeves buttoned at the wrist, kept off sun and wind, and in this his vest helped. The vest, like the Indian's blanket, could be loosened for coolness. It also had pockets for matches and tobacco and cigarette papers. His close-fitting pants or blue denim levis made the saddle comfortable, while leather chaps, if he wore them, protected his legs from brush, contact with corral posts, lunging animals or rope-burns, besides adding a weight to his legs which helped keep him in the saddle of a bucking bronc. The high-heeled boots prevented his feet from slipping through the stirrups and also put the brakes on a roped steer or horse when he was afoot. The coat and slicker tied on his saddle were ready for cold or wet, and his gloves prevented too much wear and tear on his busy hands. Add the rope coiled on his saddle and the gun in his holster, and you have a man ready for anything.

The homesteader dressed much like the cowboy, except that he had no use for chaps or boots. Overalls took the place of levis, and he might omit the handkerchief around the neck, and the vest—carrying his Bull Durham and papers in the pocket of a hickory shirt.

Sometimes he preferred a straw hat, though in general a straw hat was a badge of social inferiority on the Short Grass. It marked a man as a stranger, or a "sissy"—an indoor person, or one ignorantly unprepared for that climate. In early days, men who turned up in straw hats often had them knocked off, fed to a horse, or tossed into the fire. It was all good clean fun, helping a man become acclimated. If the boys liked the way the stranger took his initiation, they might chip in afterwards and buy him a proper Stetson.

So, until recently, no he-man felt comfortable in a straw hat. Only Indians wore their shirts outside their pants. Knickers, riding breeches, golf stockings, slacks, and sandals were laughed at on the streets. I well remember the first time I saw a male in a bathing-suit, and the scorn it provoked. We soon peeled it off the wearer to see if he had a man's fixin's, then threw him into the river as God made him. Only women wore bathing-suits in those days.

But it was seldom that anyone objected to "regular" fancy clothes on the High Plains. In fact, many of the leading heroic figures of our history were out-and-out dandies, who spared no pains with razor, brush, and soap, no cost in buying frock-coats, fine boots, or "flower-bed" vests. Following the example of the gorgeously arrayed Indian, they dressed their heroic part to perfection—as fighting-cocks have done in all ages. Trader and trapper, buffalo-hunter and soldier, gambler and cattleman—all dressed up (on occasion) fit to kill. No star in Hollywood gets himself up with more care than did Wild Bill Hickok, Charles Bent, General Custer, or Buffalo Bill.

The love of fine clothes, fine weapons, fine saddlery is one of the strongest traditions of the High Plains. Only the nesters, in their poverty, were unable to keep the pace. Long hair and buckskins were not in their tradition.

But public opinion expected the fine costume to be *manly*—and appropriate to the region, the climate, and the outdoor life.

Nearly all male animals go gorgeously arrayed, particularly those with any fight in them. So it was on the Plains. Of course, sartorial glory diminished somewhat with the passing of the gun-fighter, though one sees some handsome outfits at a good rodeo. Yet even today, I have heard a Westerner in New York say he wanted to get back home where he could see some well-dressed people.

But nowadays, with women underfoot everywhere, men are beginning to dress—or undress—informally like them.

Since World War I, riding breeches have been tolerated in the West, because our soldiers glorified them in battle. And the tourists of these days rush through the Plains at such a rate that folks have no time to educate them. The Short Grass, thank heaven, is not a tourist country.

Without seeming *laudator temporis acti,* may one still marvel at some of the costumes one sees? Sitting Bull wore his shirt-tails outside his pants, because he had no pants into which to tuck them. But what shall be said of people who have, and nevertheless do not? Wild Bill and General Custer would stare. And what a target those shirt-tails would make!

Fashions in felt hats have varied with the years. A century ago the Plainsman generally wore a low-crowned headgear of felt or "wool," water-proofed with paint. With the Civil War, the high-crowned campaign hat reached the West.

When the Texas cattlemen started their trail drives in 1865 and '66, some of them were still in Confederate uniforms, and the white hat soon became the standard for cattlemen everywhere. The black hat of the Union soldier, issued to Indians after the War, was long preferred by them—partly because it was the color worn by the victors, partly because black was the traditional color of victory among Plains Indians.

According to Indian notions, war was like fire. When the fire was put out and peace returned, only charcoal and ashes remained. Therefore, victorious warriors painted themselves with charcoal before returning home. When the agents and the missionaries discouraged facepaint, Indians could still wear black—in black hats. Usually they preferred to wear them as they came from the bandbox—uncrushed.

In some parts of the Plains, sheep-herders wore black hats—and this made cattlemen in those parts refuse anything but white or gray felt.

The Mexican sombrero was tall and broad-brimmed, and it is claimed that the modern ten-gallon hat was developed to outdo the Mexican headgear.

At first the mark of a cowman, the ten-gallon hat became the headgear of the oil-man when oil came in. Nowadays it is often worn by dudes, or artists.

Some peace officers prefer the big hat. It makes them taller. Moreover, if someone takes a pot shot, there is a lot of hat to shoot at above the top of the skull.

Taste in food on the Short Grass has always inclined to meals that will stick to the ribs. Beef was the basis of the usual cuisine, whether Indian, Mexican, or Anglo-American.

The Indian's cookery aimed primarily at retaining the juices of the meat. He therefore either boiled it to rags in a kettle, or ate it so rare that the flesh might be said to be warmed rather than cooked. When butchering, the Plains redskin never cut the meat across the grain, with the result that even his dried meat and pemmican was flavorous and tasty.

The Mexican cut his steak very thin, and cooked it until it was almost charred. The Anglo-American swung between these two extremes, generally preferring his steaks well done, or medium. His taste is well illustrated by the yarn about the cowman in New York who found his portion too rare and sent it back, saying, "I've seen Texas steers that were hurt worse than that, and lived."

Nowhere is there better beef, or more people who

understand how to prepare it for the table. Some will have it that men make the best cooks everywhere. However that may be, on the Short Grass men certainly make the best when it comes to a barbecue. Put one of those experts at an outdoor pit with proper fuel and the right sort of beef, and he will turn out something, dressed with his own sauce, that will live in your memory forever. I have seen such a man do his work in a cloudburst, and still produce a dish that makes my mouth water to think of it now.

The cook of a cowcamp was an arbitrary person, lord of his limited domain. His way of announcing that dinner was served was to yell at the top of his voice, "Come and get it, or I'll throw it in the creek." After a hard day working the cattle, few cowboys dallied when that signal sounded. The cook might not be a master chef, but the nearest kitchen was too far away to encourage any argument from his patrons. They came a-runnin'.

From the beginning, the staple of the Short Grass has been beef and potatoes, black-eyed peas, beans, and biscuits. In early days, dried apples supplied most of the fruit ration—and many yarns have been told of how greenhorns filled a kettle with these, put in the water, and were disconcerted to see the kettle boil over, spreading the swelling apples over the prairie for miles around—so that the cattle bogged down and had to be dragged to safety with ropes!

This reliance upon beef has not changed. When a Plainsman thinks of food, he visualizes a steak a yard long, fried potatoes, and black coffee. In his more luxurious moments he fancies fried chicken, flap-jacks, ham and eggs, corn on the cob.

In early days, wild game added much variety to the diet on the Short Grass, but since the sale of wild game was prohibited and the country was settled up, game has been rather a luxury, not to say a rarity, on the table.

Milk, in the old days, was almost unknown—as no self-respecting cowboy would stoop to milk a cow. Even now, on some farms, milking is the work of women. Usually, chili con carne, tamales, or some other common Mexican dish can be bought at the short-order counter. For tourists, these are tempered to meet a timid palate; but the old-timer likes his Mexican food well peppered, "so hot that you have to wait for a norther to cool you off before you can swallow it."

People with Southern traditions, ignoring vitamins, still relish hot bread, molasses, ham hock or salt pork to cook with vegetables, turnip greens boiled to rags, grits and rice, pork chops, friend chicken, and fried potatoes. But the Plainsman, as a rule, prefers fresh vegetables, beef, pie, and is much less partial to grease. Malnutrition is no part of his heritage.

When all else failed, the Plainsman relied upon whatever was available, throwing it into an iron pot kept boiling on the fire—a pot which was constantly replenished with whatever came to hand. Such a hodge-podge or pot pourri or hunter's stew is known on the Short Grass as Son-of-a-Gun Stew. Sometimes it deserves—and receives—a stronger name.

Nowadays, of course, with people from all over the world congregating on the Plains, cookery in the home

is much like that everywhere in the States—a mixture
of dishes of every sort, adapted to the taste of individual families. There are as many good cooks on the
Short Grass as anywhere else in America, and the same
abundant rations. But, since the region is not a tourist
country, good eating places open to the public are few
and far between.

The Fred Harvey railroad restaurants first set the
pace in good eating there. With the development of
motor travel, these first-rate houses have been supple-
mented by restaurants in towns along the main tourist
motor-routes to the Rockies. In these, one finds beef
and fried chicken, turkey, and—in the mountain states
—trout, well cooked and considerably cheaper than elsewhere in the country.

In almost every hamlet there is to be found one good
boarding house, where plenty of wholesome "home
cooking" can be obtained. But first-rate restaurants
are rare. The Short Grass is rather larger than France,
and dotted with small towns and cities, yet on consult-
ing the 1941 edition of Duncan Hines's *Adventures in
Good Eating,* one finds only forty-one towns listed where
the traveler can be sure of finding good food well prepared.

That is rather less than one town in ten. Such public
restaurants are given as: in Colorado, nine; in Kansas,
thirteen; in New Mexico, seven; in Texas, ten; and in
western Oklahoma (one of the most densely populated
parts of the region), only two. So much for what the
gourmets think of our cooking. Every one of these restaurants listed are to be found on one or other of the
main roads frequented by tourists.

No doubt there are others which are as good, judged by the best palates of the region, but which might not appeal to travelers from outside. Still, this is hardly a state of affairs of which Short Grass folks can be proud.

For, except in the best places, one cannot look for really good soups, hors d'œuvres, pastries (except pie), or salads. The soup is likely to come out of a can and to be served without coming to a boil; relishes are also out of bottles and cans—I once stayed at a small hotel where an entire "line" of sauces and seasonings was grandly arrayed in a permanent column down the middle of the long table; pastries are inferior; and the so-called salad is generally a dreadful concoction of canned fruit, soggy cheese, whipped cream, languid lettuce, and slices of tomato. Whatever else you lack in these sad establishments, you never miss sliced tomatoes.

Few of those cooks ever heard of lemon and olive oil dressing, or vinegar and oil. Sauces come from a bottle and are made of who knows what. For frying, butter—or even lard—is seldom used. Instead, they offer some dismal vegetable oil, which will not melt at body heat, and so remains a cold lump in the stomach for hours after. And sometimes the food is soaked in grease, half raw, and served on cold plates—even in the dead of winter.

One cannot help wondering where these cooks themselves eat; surely no sane man would prepare such dreadful provender for his own use.

But the worst atrocity is the coffee—which everybody drinks. Not even the British could brew worse coffee than is commonly served in the cheaper restaurants on the Short Grass. And this is the more amazing, in that so many of the people are from regions where good coffee is available everywhere.

One need not subscribe to the Brazilian faith, that coffee, to be good, must be "hot as hell, strong as death, black as night, and sweet as love." One need not even insist that it be prepared as in New Orleans—though this would be heresy all along the Gulf. Still, there can be no excuse for the coffee served in some of the restaurants on the Short Grass. It is muddy, tasteless, boiled, stale—as uninviting as hogwash. All you can say for it is that it is hot.

In the old days, you had to ride a hundred miles to find good water: now, if you eat in restaurants, they say, "you have to drive a hundred miles to find good food."

Chambers of Commerce on the Plains are continually demanding that the natives "give up their boots and spurs, quit playing Indian and cowboy, and call attention to the industrial marvels and natural resources of the country." There is no likelihood that this advice will be followed. But, if our businessmen really want to bring tourists to the Short Grass, there is one sure way to do it: bring *all* the restaurants up to standard. Some people travel for scenery, some for climate, some for historical sites, some for fresh human contacts, some just to be moving. Now, the Plains are short on monuments, scenery, population, pleasant summer climate; few tourists who can see the Rockies looming in the west will linger long on the lone prairie. Only one thing will stop them—good food. They all want good food—and plenty of it.

Shakespeare understood the minds of travelers perfectly, and repeatedly makes his characters, on arriving in a town, inquire first of all about the *food*. Thus, in one of the old plays, we find the typical traveler's idea in a nutshell:

> *After dinner we will view the city.*

Chambers of Commerce should read Shakespeare, and put their faith in *good cooks, well paid.*

If they can do that, the reputation of the High Plains for resourcefulness will be vindicated, and the tourists will come—and stay. It could be done. Plainsmen generally do what they think worth doing—and do it well. There are any number of instances to show that.

Take, for example, making flap-jacks. A really good cook can squat in the fireplace, throw the flap-jack up the chimney to the stars, and catch it when it comes down, t'other side up. . . .

But the best example of the independent ingenuity of people from this region follows: An Oklahoma lady, very fond of gardening, was compelled to go and live in New York City. Her apartment was not far from Central Park. She bore her exile from her beloved garden as long as she could; then she bought some potted plants at the florist's, set them out in a secluded corner of Central Park, and tending them daily was happy again. By latest reports her garden is still thriving, for she is still in the big city.

6. Jack and Jill

A CHEYENNE BLANKET

THE Cheyennes, like other Indians, do not speak to each other when they are away from the camp. If a man goes away from the village, and sits or stands by himself on the top of a hill, it is a sign that he wants to be alone; perhaps to meditate; perhaps to pray. No one speaks to him or goes near him.

"Now there was once a Pawnee boy, who went off on the warpath to the Cheyenne camp. In some way he had obtained a Cheyenne blanket. This Pawnee came close to the Cheyenne camp, and hid himself there to wait. About the middle of the afternoon, he left his hiding place, and walked to the top of the hill overlooking the village. He had his Cheyenne blanket wrapped about him and over his head, with only a little hole for his eyes. He stood there for an hour or two, looking over the Cheyenne camp.

"They were coming in from buffalo hunting, and some were leading in the pack horses loaded down with meat. A man came along, riding a horse packed with meat, and leading another pack horse, and a black spotted horse that was his running horse. These running horses are ridden only on the chase or on war parties, and are well cared for. After being used they are taken down to the river and are washed and cleaned with care. When the boy saw this spotted horse, he thought to himself that this was the horse that he would take. When the man who was leading it reached his lodge, he dismounted and handed the ropes to his women, and went inside.

"Then the Pawnee made up his mind what he would do. He started down the hill into the village, and walked straight to this lodge where the women were unloading the meat. He walked up to them, reached out his hand, and took the ropes of the spotted horse and one of the others. As he did so the women fell back. Probably they thought that this was some one of the relations of the owner, who was going to take the running horse down to the river to wash it. The Pawnee could not talk Cheyenne, but as he turned away he mumbled something—m-m-m-m—as if speaking in a low voice, and then walked down toward the river. As soon as he had gone down over the bank and was out of sight, he jumped on the spotted horse and rode into the brush, and pretty soon was away with two horses, stolen out of the Cheyenne camp in broad daylight.*

Ways and Means

The pioneers, accustomed to moving on wagon wheels the flimsy shacks built to prove title to a prairie claim, adapted the practice to their county-seat wars.

* This is one of the stories in George Bird Grinnell's Pawnee Hero Stories and Folk-Tales; it is reprinted by courtesy of the publishers, Charles Scribner's Sons.

While one town slept, their sly rivals would go into town in the darkness, lift the courthouse onto the running gears of a wagon, and decamp, taking building, records, and all to their own community.

Governor Haskell, the first Governor of the State of Oklahoma, in a somewhat similar manner moved the State Capitol from Guthrie to Oklahoma City, they say. He simply loaded the Seal of the State, and all essential records into a car, and drove away with them. Since that day, the capital has been Oklahoma City. But we cannot go into the tricks of the legal profession here; that would require more volumes than this series of books affords.

We shall be better entertained, if we consider the ingenuities of the cowboy and the frontiersman, since they are more representative of the region.

In Dodge City there was once an altercation in one of the saloons, and a certain man who does not wish to be named was arrested and thrown into the jail—a dry hole in the ground, like a well—to await trial next day. He was in an anxious frame of mind: his enemies knew he was there, and might at any moment come and shoot him down from above.

He heard the beat of hooves above, and expected his death without delay. But a lariat dropped down, striking his shoulders, and he heard a low voice call, "Hang on!" He grabbed the rope, the horseman quirted his animal, and the prisoner was dragged to safety.

Few men have contributed so many fresh ideas and folkways to the High Plains than Charles Goodnight, "Father of the Texas Panhandle." He was constantly on the alert to improve the cattle, the land—even the people—of the region.

Charles Goodnight got together a considerable herd of buffalo which he developed over a long period of years. At one time some attempt was made to break a team of buffalo to harness. The animals were fairly docile, but with typical buffalo bull-headedness they liked to keep on going once they got started. The problem was to turn them at the corner of the section. Perhaps it would be incorrect to say that they took the bit in their teeth, but nobody was able to turn the team by any ordinary method.

An old-timer, who was a cowboy on the Goodnight ranch at the time, tells how the problem was solved. A windlass with a crank was rigged up at the front of the wagon by the driver's seat and a rope was stretched from the animals' heads to the windlass. On approaching a corner the driver frantically wound up the windlass on the side toward which he wished to go, thus pulling the buffaloes' heads around in that direction and eventually making the turn. By this ingenious method the team could be directed with some hope of arriving at the intended destination. . . .

Jack and Jill, who went up the hill to find water, were surely bred on the Short Grass—where streams are full near their sources and almost dry up before they reach their mouths.

Another odd custom concerns the use made of cottonwood. General G. A. Custer relates the following anecdote in his book, *My Life on the Plains,* published in 1875:

"During the winter campaign of 1868-'69 against the

hostile tribes south of the Arkansas, it not infrequently happened that my command while in pursuit of Indians exhausted its supply of forage, and the horses and mules were subsisted upon the young bark of the cottonwood tree. In routing the Indians from their winter villages, we invariably discovered them located upon that point of the stream promising the greatest supply of cotton-wood bark, while the stream in the vicinity of the vil-lage was completely shorn of its supply of timber, and the village itself was strewn with the white branches of the cottonwood entirely stripped of their bark. It was somewhat amusing to observe an Indian pony feeding on cottonwood bark. The limb being usually cut into pieces about four feet in length and thrown upon the ground, the pony, accustomed to this kind of "long for-age," would place one forefoot on the limb in the same manner as a dog secures a bone, and gnaw the bark from it. Although not affording anything like the amount of nutriment which either hay or grain does, yet our horses invariably preferred the bark to either, probably on account of its freshness."

But, if the uses of cottonwood seem strange, what shall be said of the mesquite tree? It is generally so thin and so slight of foliage that only a snake could contrive to lie in its shade. A more hopelessly useless tree—to look at it—could scarcely be imagined. It is rarely thicker than your wrist. Yet it provides the Plainsman with firewood, believe it or not.

For on the High Plains men mine wood. Above ground, the mesquite tree is puny, scrawny, worthless. But it has immense roots awaiting excavation.

The yucca is another deceptive plant.

The yucca, or soapweed, sometimes called Spanish bayonet, is one of the hardiest and most useful plants on the Plains. The central stock, the tall spike carrying many creamy white blossoms, sometimes referred to as Madonna candle or the candle of the Lord, is surrounded by an abattis of sharply pointed stiff leaves. These are so stiff and sharp that one must be careful not to blunder into them. There is always a chance that one of the points may puncture a vein in the leg and fill one's shoe with blood. The yucca is a plant useful as well as beautiful. From its fibers ropes are made, from its roots soap. The ripened pods were ground to flour by the Indians, and innumerable eyes have been gladdened by the beauty of its blossoms.

EROSION MAKES A PROFIT

When the soil began to blow away during the great drouth, various schemes were tried to hold the soil where it belonged—most of them without much success. One farmer, finding himself hedged in north and south by lands whose owners took no measures to conserve the soil, was in despair. The wind sweeping across the section on either side scoured his land with the dust and sand from the adjoining farms.

The prevailing winds blew north and south. Accordingly he decided to plow his land with a lister, running the furrows east and west. The listing plow threw up a big ridge with a trough on either side, a formation which tended to break the force of the wind sweeping across and so conserve the soil. This device worked well enough, and to his surprise, added to the richness of his soil rather than depleted it. When the wind blew from the south the soil from his neighbor's farm on that side filled the furrows on his land. When it blew from the north, his land was enriched by the soil from his neighbor in that direction. Before long the furrows were an inch or two deep in loose soil and sand.

Still it did not rain. The farmer began to wonder how he could hold the soil with which his careless neighbors had enriched him. He hooked up his plow again and "busted back" down the middle of the ridges, throwing these to either side into the troughs, thus anchoring the soil which had blown in. In that way one farmer acquired the rich topsoil of the two adjacent farms and found his land an oasis in the middle of the desert. The rains finally came, and with them some potato growers from Idaho who planted potatoes on his land and so produced an excellent crop.

The Indian Police Obeys Orders

"To a white man, rules and orders are abstractions, or ideals, the enforcement of which is on a 50% level, but the Indian policeman entertained no such irrational ideas; to him orders meant what they said, and rules were rules. Graft and leniency were contrary to his notion of the police function. New agents, not understanding all this, were often embarrassed. I recall one such incident. Information came one evening that some ten miles out, a certain white man with an Indian wife was on a drunk and threatening to kill his family. He was said to be a bad man when running amuck. The new agent called in a policeman and ordered him to arrest this man. Thinking it necessary to be emphatic, he said, 'Bring him dead or alive; do not come back without him.'

"Before the lone policeman arrived at the scene, an Indian had killed the desperado in self-defense and the family had laid out the corpse. The policeman astonished everyone by announcing that he would take the body to the agent. Neither remonstrance nor threats availed; the policeman would take the body or fight to the death. 'Agent's order,' he asserted. So he borrowed a wagon and started on the long, slow journey alone. About four o'clock in the morning, while it was still dark, he drew up in front of the agent's house, unhitched the team, gave them some hay, then thumped on the agent's door. When the agent looked out the Indian, pointing over his shoulder, said, 'Him there in wagon,' turned on his heel and went to the barracks, with the feeling of a hard job well done." *

ONE WAY OR ANOTHER

Cowboys as a rule are not marrying men, but when they fall in love the matter is serious. In one of the immense counties of Texas, one of the boys fell in love with a nester's daughter. She was willing, but insisted on a proper wedding. There was no Sky Pilot within a day's ride. The boys, therefore, got together, organized, and elected one of their number Justice of the Peace. In the cowcamp there was no book but the brand book, but the J.P. was undaunted. Using the brand book as a

* Reprinted by courtesy of the author, Dr. Clark Wissler, from his book, *Indian Cavalcade*. Sheridan House, N. Y., 1938. Pp. 119-120.

Bible, he improvised a ceremony to the satisfaction of all concerned. The cowboy "put his brand" on his bride, and the two were "hitched to run in double harness."

STRAW MAN

Out in the Panhandle there was a farmer whose hired man was too fond of the bottle. The old man liked a nip himself on occasion, and kept a jug in his house concealed from the watchful eyes of his wife, who was a strict dry. Every time she found the jug, she threw it out of the house, and the farmhand would find it, go on a bust, and be worthless for forty-eight hours. Finally the old man buried the jug in a post-hole in tall grass on the hillside, at a spot he could see from the house. But the farmhand soon learned from the old man's movements where the jug was hidden, crept through the tall grass, and drank all the liquor through a wheat straw.

PRAYER ON THE PRAIRIE

It was in 1878 when some three hundred Northern Cheyenne Indians, led by Little Wolf, Dull Knife, and Wild Hog, defied the Government and fled from Darlington, Oklahoma, back to their home country in the North. On their way they fought several times with the troops and killed a number of civilians. This was afterward known as the Dull Knife Raid.

Charles F. Colcord, one of the foremost builders of Oklahoma, began life as a buffalo hunter and ended as an industrialist and a financier. He was President of the State Historical Society at the time he made the address

quoted (in part) here following; the address is incorporated in the twelfth volume, 1934, of the *Chronicles
of Oklahoma*. At the time of the Dull Knife Raid he
was a range boss of the Jug Cattle Company.

"The morning of the Indian raid, Reuben Bristow
and Fred Clark left our ranch headquarters on Red
Fork Creek, driving a team of mules, with a wagon, en
route to the Cimarron Salt Plain, for a load of rock salt,
for use elsewhere on the range. They had evidently just
reached the high divide between the Cimarron and Salt
Fork watersheds near Jug Mott, when they met the
band of Northern Cheyenne warriors, by which they
were quickly surrounded. From the tracks and marks
around where we found them, we could tell that the
Indians had come up all around the wagon and had
shot Reuben Bristow in the head from behind. The
mules the boys were driving were very much afraid of
a gun and the marks in the ground where they had
been standing showed that they had been very restless.
The tracks of the Indian ponies indicated that the Indians were all around the wagon and one could see
plainly where, at the crack of the gun, the mules had
plunged forward and jerked the wheels off the ground.
Then the Indians had chased the wagon, filling the bodies of both boys full of arrows. The panic-stricken mules
ran down the slope from the high divide into the valley
of a small branch or ravine, where they were brought to
a sudden stop by a thicket of willows which were of sufficient size and elasticity to lift its wheels from the
ground when the mules could drag it no farther. The
Indians had cut the traces and taken the mules, leaving

the bodies of the two youths in the wagon-bed, where they had fallen.

"I pulled four arrows out of Bristow's heart, shot in from the right side under the arm, and drew three or four out of Fred's body. . . .

"A site for a grave for the burial of the remains of our slain friends and companions was selected, back up the slope, near the divide where they had met their tragic fate. The September weather was intensely hot and dry, there having been no rains for several weeks. It surely was a hard job to dig that gravel with shovel and spade in that dry joint clay.

"Always, two of us would dig while the third member of our party would remain on watch at the highest point on the nearby divide. When one of the two diggers would get tired, he would mount guard on the high point, while the one thus relieved would go down and take his turn at helping to excavate the grave.

"Finally, when the grave was large enough to hold the two bodies, our next effort was to extricate the wagon which was resting on those bent willow saplings. Some of the largest of these had to be cut. . . . Then, with riatas tied from saddlehorns to wagon-tongue, it was pulled up the slope, out of the ravine, and into position at the grave. The transfer of these remains from the wagon into the grave—swollen as they were by decomposition to twice their natural size—was a gruesome task as well as a sad duty.

"When we had finished covering the bodies in the grave someone said that a prayer should be offered. All three of us were uneducated cowboys who had had no chance to attend church services or Sunday school, so none of us knew what to say or do under the circumstances. Both of the other two declined to do what all of us thought should be done, so both said to me, 'Charley, you will have to say something.'

"Now we all believed, as all men who are reared out in the open must and always will believe, that there is a God, who rules and overrules in the affairs of men. We had watched the sun, moon, and stars in their courses; we had night-herded by the North Star, for years, using it as a time-piece; every spear of grass in the prairie verdure, every flower that spangled its face, every wind that swept the plain and every note sung by the birds bore witness to the existence of a great, unseen, Divine Power. So, knowing in my own soul the existence of such a Supreme Being, I took off my hat and raised my face to the skies as I said, 'God, take care of these poor boys.'

"Such was the prayer that I offered."

7. The Spider's Web

IN A great, open, "unoccupied" country there are few
dark corners where superstitions and primitive ideas
can breed or linger. In mountainous regions or islands,
peninsulas or remote valleys we are likely to find ves-
tiges, at least, of the oldest beliefs and institutions
known to man in those regions. But the High Plains
were swept clean every year by winds from all four
quarters. They are open to all new ideas, which speed
over them as rapidly and unimpeded as cloud shadows
on a windy day.

It is true that Europeans crossed these Plains more
than sixty years before the first settlements were made
in Virginia and New England. Coronado led his expedition through them in 1541, and for some two centuries the French and Spanish struggled intermittently
for possession of the land. But these made no permanent settlements there and left few tokens of their
passage. The Anglo-Americans who moved into the
Plains in the nineteenth century found what seemed
to them a new and unspoiled country. Moreover, these
newcomers, the American pioneers, were, for the most
part, white Protestants, originally from the north of Europe, with a firm belief in education and enlighten-
ment.

Here they met conditions very different from those in the woodlands and hills from which they had come. Today the Indian finds that with the extermination of the game animals he can hardly carry on his ancient rituals, because the feathers and skins used in those rituals are no longer obtainable. The white pioneer discovered a similar difficulty in carrying on the rituals of his superstitions. On the Plains it is not always easy to knock on wood, since the nearest fence post may be twenty miles away. Not even the old weather signs held good on the Plains, and many of the superstitions taken seriously in other parts of North America perished or were kept up only as a sort of nostalgic revival of ancestral customs.

A man could hardly be superstitious about beginning something on Friday when he had been so long away from home that he had lost count of the days of the week. Phases of the moon meant something quite different on the frontier, where moonlight meant only the probability of a Comanche raid. There were no black cats to cross the trail, few dogs to howl, no wishing wells, no haunted houses. The old superstitions, like all other importations to that country, faced a hard test— a test which many of them could not pass.

And so we find that folks on the Short Grass kill frogs, crickets, and spiders without compunction. They walk under ladders, start on a trip on Friday, sit nonchalantly on tables, climb through windows when necessary without fear, and count the cars in a funeral procession without loss of sleep. They step on cracks (they had to, on those old boardwalks in frontier towns), willingly eat the last piece of bread on the plate, sweep out pins, drop dishrags, cut their hair or their nails without thought of how the moon may like it. They marry in any month of the year and, in short, are careless of or unaware of the fears which haunt their contemporaries in other parts of the world. The contempt of the Plainsman for old superstitions was clearly shown by his habit of smashing to pieces the mirrors in the saloons he shot up.

New superstitions were slow to develop, but as time went on new conditions provided the materials and there was also some carrying over of superstitions of other peoples, the Spanish and, particularly, the American Indian. These were not always taken too seriously, and some have been reinforced recently by the development of local pride and civic enterprise. But gypsies do not flourish on the Short Grass, fortune-telling is generally banned by law, people sleep too well to pay much attention to dreams, and few have time to worry about numerology, astrology, or palmistry. The wonders of science among the well-informed people have put witchcraft in the shade. Even the Plains Indians are a literate people, having been compelled to attend Government schools for two generations. Negroes and European peasants have never been numerous on the Plains.

The richest source of current superstitions on the Short Grass is the lore of the Indian, who only a few years ago could be found living in tipis and grass houses, wearing blankets and observing ancient rituals. Some of these are still observed—for example, the Sun Dance of the Cheyenne and Arapaho tribes—though on a much reduced scale. Though only about 15,000 in number at the turn of the century, these Indians of the High

Plains loom large in the consciousness of Plainsmen everywhere. Texans, Kansans, New Mexicans, and the people of the Colorado Plains had suffered their depredations and respected them as fighting men, and in Oklahoma they are now fellow-citizens recognized as having a contribution to make to the culture of the region. Their folklore and beliefs still play some part on the Short Grass, where there is no social barrier between whites and Indians as such.

Hunting for a living was hard work. Since the game played out, Indian men have been given a bad name for laziness, because they had nothing to do and so had to lie around camp most of the time. But in the old days, Indian men were always working—that is to say, hunting. And, being human as the rest of us, they often wished they could take a day off. All hunters therefore envied the spider, who was so smart he never had to leave his lodge to hunt—the acme of Indian felicity.

But the wise old men revered the creature for reasons more profound. They had observed that the spider spun his web out of himself, and for them the spider became the symbol of the Creator, the First Cause, and his web a symbol of the World.

In old Indian pictographs you will find the world commonly represented by a spider web—diamond-shaped, or in the form of a square—with four main strands running at right angles from the center to the corners, thus forming a cross with equal arms to indicate the four directions. Around this web, otters or other aquatic animals are shown swimming to suggest the waters that surround the land. The cross arms (projecting beyond the web), each with an otter trailing, form a pattern all too familiar in our day—the Swastika.

For all that, the Indian pictograph is not the same as the Nazi swastika. It has a very important difference, as an old chief was careful to point out to me. Said he, "The sun rises in the east, passes round by the south, and sets in the west, passing under the earth by way of the north. In like manner, all good things, all helpful,

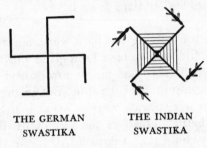

THE GERMAN   THE INDIAN
SWASTIKA   SWASTIKA

beneficent things, move *sunwise*, like the hands of a white man's clock. Thus, Indians go into their tents and walk sunwise around the fire to their places; they pass the pipe sunwise: everything that is good follows the path of the greatest power of all, the Sun. So it is here: the otters swim around the spider's web in a *sunwise* direction. So you can see the Indian swastika is good; it is helpful.

"But Hitler's swastika is not like ours. His swastika turns the other way: it moves against the sun, against all good things. It is therefore evil, and it cannot win. For nothing can defeat the Sun, and the path of the Sun is the sure path to success in life."

Among the Arapaho, the spider—and its divine counterpart—was known as Ne-aw'tha, and when white men appeared wearing clothing woven of threads, as the spider's web was woven, that name was applied to the white man also. Some conceited white men have contended that the name was given them because of their "superior" intelligence. This seems too good to be true. Old-time Indians were like the rest of the human race: when they met someone who thought differently from themselves, they regarded him as *less* intelligent, not more. Even today, you could safely offer a big reward for the capture of an Indian who thinks the white man in any real way superior.

At any rate, Ne-aw'tha was the hero of a thousand tales, in which he appeared as a smarty, a trickster, or a fool—a person who relied upon sharp practice, wit, cunning, or intelligence—and often relied upon them to his own undoing. Thus the Arapaho Neawtha corresponds to Unktomi of the Sioux, Old Man of the Blackfeet, and Coyote of other tribes. No book on the Short Grass would be complete without a story about Neawtha. He was a lovable fool—sometimes triumphant, sometimes just a wise guy sticking his neck out.

The story which follows here was first printed in *Folk-Say, a Regional Miscellany,* edited by B. A. Batkin for the Oklahoma Folk-lore Society and published by the University of Oklahoma Press, 1929:

NEAWTHA'S WARPATH

"Everybody in the Arapaho Indian camp was wide awake and busy—everybody but Neawtha. He was still lying in bed, wondering what his mother would cook for his breakfast.

"While he lay there half-asleep, he heard someone talking about him. It was the man who lived next door —in the next tent, and the man was scolding. 'What a lazy fellow that Neawtha is! Still lying in bed when all the other boys are outside hunting or playing games or racing their ponies! I don't see what his mother means by letting him act so. Now, my son Hawkan is wide awake. He is going to war right away. But that lazy Neawtha—he will never amount to anything.'

"When Neawtha heard that, he sat up, stretched, yawned, and rubbed his eyes. Then he ate the breakfast his mother had prepared for him. After that he got up and put on his moccasins. 'I guess I shall have to show these folks how great I am.' he said to his mother. Then Neawtha went out of the tent.

"The tents of the Arapaho Indians stood in a big circle on the prairie, and Neawtha could see a number of young men and boys marching around the camp, singing war songs. All the people stood and watched them, and the boys were very proud. For all the men and women were cheering them because they were going to war. Pretty soon the boys and young men returned to their tents, got their things together, and prepared to start.

"While they were packing up their food and extra moccasins, Neawtha came up and said, "Well, boys, I guess I will go along with you. It is time I showed you how great I am."

"Then all the young men and boys laughed at him. The leader said, 'No, Neawtha, you are lazy. We do not want you. You cannot go to war. You stay with your mother where you belong.'

"Neawtha smiled. 'All right,' he said. 'You go on ahead. I will come along later on. When you need me, I shall be on hand.' And he went back to bed.

"While he was lying there that evening, he heard the man next door scolding again. 'That lazy Neawtha! He will never amount to anything. He has been lying in bed all day while my son Hawkan and the other boys are marching to war. But they will come riding home on the ponies of the enemy. Then Neawtha will wish he had walked away to war with the rest.'

"When Neawtha heard that, he sat up, stretched, yawned, rubbed his eyes. Then he ate the supper his mother had prepared for him. After that he put on his moccasins and got up. 'Mother,' he said, 'I guess it is time for me to show these folks what a great man I am.'

" 'You have guessed right,' said his mother. She was a little tired of his laziness. He took his buffalo robe off the bed, picked up a stick and started out.

" 'Why don't you take your bow and arrows?' asked his mother.

" 'Pshaw, Mother,' said Neawtha, 'the enemy will have plenty of those.' And he went on out and got on his pony. Then he rode away on the trail the young men had followed. In a short time he overtook them. But he did not let them see him. He rode around, ahead of them, tied his pony to the trunk of a tree in the creek bottom, and walked back on the trail they were following.

"When they came along, tired and dusty after their long walk, they found Neawtha, all clean and fresh, sitting beside a nice fire, with some meat cooking on a peeled stick. 'Well,' said the leader, 'here is that lazy

Neawtha. He must have come here in a dream. He is
too lazy to walk so far.'

"'Yes,' said Neawtha, 'I told you I would be on hand
when you needed me. Sit down and rest and eat some
of my meat.'

"In the morning they all got up early and started off,
but Neawtha lay in bed. He was too lazy to get up early.
So the others went off without him. 'He will never
amount to anything,' said the leader. But when evening
came, Neawtha caught his pony, rode ahead, and had
dinner ready for them when they arrived. And every
day it was the same, and the young men began to look
for Neawtha whenever it was time to eat or sleep. He
was always on hand at those times. 'Eating and sleeping
are the only things he thinks about,' said the leader,
Hawkan. 'He will never amount to anything.'

"Finally they reached the enemy's country and found
the trail of a village on the move. They followed it to
the edge of the prairie, and there they lost it. The grass
and the ground were so dry that they could not find
which way the tracks were going. When Neawtha saw
that trail, he got off his pony and turned it loose.
"Aren't you going to ride your pony into the fight?"
said the leader.

" 'Oh, pshaw,' said Neawtha, 'the enemy will have
plenty of ponies.'

"They were all standing helplessly around, wondering what to do. One of the young men said, 'If I could
find a piece of boggy ground, soft mud, then I could
find tracks in it and tell which way to go to find the
enemy.'

"Another young man said, 'If I could find a little

bush pushed down by the drags of the enemy, I could tell which way the enemy was going.'

"Another young man said, 'If I could find some stones that had been kicked aside by the hooves of the ponies, I could tell which way the enemy was going.'

"So they all began looking for mud, bushes, and stones, on the prairie. And while they were looking, Neawtha took a nap. He knew there was nothing of that kind on the dry, grassy prairie.

"When they were all tired out, they came back, and the leader said, 'Look at that worthless Neawtha. He will never amount to anything. He is so lazy he won't even move out of the path of those ants. See! They are crawling right across his body.' And so they were.

" 'Well,' said the leader, 'what shall we do? We cannot find out which way the enemy went from here.'

" 'Oh, is that what you want to know?' asked Neawtha. 'That is easy. Wait until I ask this ant here— Hold on, Brother ant,' said Neawtha again, 'tell me which way the enemy went. Please, Brother ant, wait a moment and tell me which way the enemy went. Please, Brother ant, wait a moment and tell me which way the enemy went. . . .' And Neawtha began to follow the ants through the grass.

"All the young men were laughing at Neawtha for running after the ant and asking it to tell him. 'He will never amount to anything,' said Hawkan. 'He is not only lazy, but silly too.'

"But just then Neawtha called the others to him, and said, 'The ants say that the enemy went to the west. Look! There on that big ant hill is the track of one of the enemy's drags.' And so it was. The men did not laugh at Neawtha then.

"That night they crept up close to the camp of the enemy and hid in the bushes along the creek. Across the creek they could see the white pointed tents of the enemy—and the ponies tied beside the doors. They waited for the people in the tents to go to sleep, and while they waited they whispered together. Each one was telling what he intended to do that night. Neawtha went to sleep.

" 'I shall capture the horses of the enemy,' said one of the young men. 'That will be the best thing for me to do. I want a lot of fine horses.'

" 'Horses are good, but I shall try to carry away some fine bundle of clothes from some tent. I love good clothes. That is what I want to capture,' said another young man.

" 'Clothes are all right," said another young man, 'but what I want is to touch the enemy. That is the bravest thing of all, to be so near the enemy that you can feel him with your body.'

"Hawkan saw Neawtha sleeping, and poked him in the ribs. 'Wake up, lazy bones,' said Hawkan. 'Tell us what you are going to capture there. What are you going to do in the enemy camp?'

"Neawtha sat up, stretched, yawned, and rubbed his eyes. 'Why, I guess I shall try to capture some of that meat I can see hanging to dry on the racks outside the tents. Now that you have waked me up, I feel hungry.'

"The other men laughed at Neawtha. They thought he would never amount to anything. 'You will have to wake up,' they said. 'When the enemy begin the fight, then we shall have to run and be very active.'

" 'Pshaw,' said Neawtha, 'I thought that surely when we got to camp we could rest awhile.'

"When everything was still, the young men went into the camp of the enemy. One began to gather up the horses. Another began to slip into the tents, looking for fine clothing. And Hawkan, the leader, was waiting to get a chance to touch the enemy after the others were through with their work. But Neawtha went up to the racks where the meat was hung out to dry, and began to eat a nice piece of buffalo meat. Pretty soon the dogs began to bark at the other end of the camp, where his friends were busy. But Neawtha threw pieces of meat to the dogs at his end of the camp, and they were too busy eating to bark at him.

"Neawtha stood near a very large tent, the headquarters of a Warrior Society; and when the dogs began to bark, he went to the door of this big tent and leaned back against it beside the door. The big tent was full of warriors—all the warriors in the camp—and they came running out of the tent as soon as they heard the dogs barking. One after another they came running out, and hurried off to the far end of the camp where the noise was. And as each ran out, Neawtha touched him lightly with his hand. By the time the last one was outside, Neawtha stopped eating his meat, went into the tent, and gathered up all the bundles of fine clothing. Then he went out, still eating his meat the best he could—for both hands were full—and saddled all the horses picketed outside. After that he packed all the bundles on the saddles, cut the lariats, and rode away.

"Pretty soon he heard somebody running. 'Pshaw,' said Neawtha, 'I almost forgot those fellows back there. I suppose they will want to ride some of my ponies home.' So he stopped and called to his friends to come and ride with him.

"They came running, out of breath, with the enemy running after them. They were in too much of a hurry to laugh just then. They jumped on the ponies and galloped away. They were glad to have Neawtha help them.

" 'What a lot of horses you have here!' said one of the young men.

" 'What a lot of bundles you have captured!' said another.

" 'You must have all the bundles and horses in the camp,' said Hawkan. 'There were more than twenty warriors in the camp.'

" 'Yes,' said Neawtha. 'Twenty-four. I touched them all.' And they saw he had twenty-four horses and twenty-four bundles. And he had a piece of meat besides. They said nothing.

"But Neawtha took a lariat and tied himself to his saddle. 'I feel sleepy,' he said. 'Wake me up if you need me, my friends.' And when they got to camp, they took Neawtha off his horse and put him to bed. He did not wake up. He always said there was no use staying awake worrying, unless there was something important to do."

8. Home on the Range

ALL men who ride much alone are likely to occupy their thoughts by singing, making up stories, or rephrasing ideas common to their kind. This was true of the Indian, who was forever singing riding songs, war songs, or hunting songs as he rode across the prairie. But it was even more true of the cowboy—if only because the cowboy was so much more alone.

In fact, the cowboy was very often creative, as his wealth of songs, stories, and vocabuary abundantly proves. Out alone all day on the grass, riding fences, riding herd, or trailing cattle, he was seldom too busy to think up a joke, a telling phrase, a story, or to put new words to an old tune. Most of the cowboy songs so popular today on radio programs were in fact new versions of old traditional songs, revamped to suit life on the praries. Scholars have traced these borrowings.

In the bunkhouse, too, or in his lonely line-camp, the cowboy had ample time and little reading matter. Sometimes a man of education, familiar with good literature, he passed the time concocting parodies or producing original work. When, later, he met up with his fellows at the chuck-wagon or the bunkhouse, he knew that he would be expected to contribute *something* to the entertainment of his comrades—if nothing more than a practical joke. They all took delight in a vivid comparison, an apt caricature, or a witty tale. Sentiment also was welcome at times to men so far from women and children.

It is noteworthy, however, that the sentiment of the early days was not what it has been since. In the old days, the homesick cowboy lamented his loneliness, or begged that he might *not* be buried "on the lone prairie." Now that the old free range is gone, cowboy songs—seldom composed by cowboys—express a nostalgia for the good old days on the frontier, and we hear about the last round-up, south of the border, empty saddles in the old corral.

On the whole, the cowboy's impromptu literature was witty, salty, pungent, expressive of the truth. Will Rogers, ignoring the old saying that brevity is the soul of wit, has declared that truth is the soul of wit, which is perhaps more accurate. Will Rogers carried on the old tradition. We loved him because he put his finger on the fact. He called us many a hard name, but he smiled when he said it.

The folk-songs found on the Short Grass are legion, and include many that were composed elsewhere. It would be impossible to name all those familiar to the Plainsmen, whether sentimental, heroic, patriotic, historic, or those merely sung for fun to express high spirits. In Texas, of course, old Southern melodies and ballads, along with *Dixie,* persist; while in Kansas, *John Brown's Body* and many another Civil War song is known to everybody. All over the Plains, Custer's war-song—or war-tune, at any rate—*Garry Owen* is remembered, and the even better-known tune to which he marched away to his death, *The Girl I Left Behind Me.* The Rough Riders have not let the region forget *There'll Be a Hot Time in the Old Town Tonight,* so familiar after the Spanish War. And everybody knows the songs of the first World War. Though not a song, the Rebel Yell should not be omitted from any record of vocal folklore; it needs to be heard to be appreciated.

Among Indian songs remembered by white men, the death song of the Kiowa Chief Satank (Setangya) is most poetic, with its refrain (freely translated): "O Sun, Thou endurest forever; but we warriors must die." Naturally, few songs in native languages have been able to escape into English versions. Few white men can sing Indian music.

John Avery Lomax has collected the cowboy songs of the Old West, and anybody interested will certainly know his books—particularly *Cowboy Songs and Other Frontier Ballads,* 1938—where all are rounded up. Here I can only suggest some of the more familiar folk-songs, most of which have by now found their way onto phonograph records. They are sung by everybody, and by folks who never heard a phonograph record of a cowboy song.

Home on the Range is a masterpiece of romantic song—so romantic that hardly any two lines have any logical or intellectual sequence. But it expresses what men feel about the Plains perhaps better than any other. God forbid that we should enter into the fierce controversies as to the state in which it was composed! Read the State *Guides* of the Plains, and make up your own mind on this question.

Texas, Kansas, Oklahoma all claim it; and New Mex-

ico sings it as her State Song. Probably an "author"
could be found in Colorado—or Montana! It is probably
the best known and most often sung of all indigenous
ballads. If that one does not rouse an appropriate emo-
tion in your heart, you have no business on the High
Plains!

*Bury Me Not on the Lone Prairie, Git Along Little
Dogies, The Red River Valley, Little Joe the Wrangler,
The Cowboy's Lament, The Cowboy's Dream, Prisoner
for Life, The Days of Forty-nine, Jack o' Diamonds,
'Longside the Santa Fe Trail, Billy Venero, The Texas
Cowboy, Jesse James, The Old Chisholm Trail, The
Roving Cowboy, Dying Cowboy, Lonely Cowboy, Bury
Me Out on the Prairie, Billy the Kid, Ridin' Down
That Old Texas Trail, The Little Old Sod Shanty on
the Claim, The Dreary Black Hills, California Joe, By
the Silvery Rio Grande, The Strawberry Roan, Mus-
tang Gray, Sandy Land, Good Old Turnip Greens,
Suckin' Cider Through a Straw, Take Me Back to Okla-
homa, Frank Baker, Kansas Land, Cattle Annie, Lay
Down Dogies, Cowboy's Evening Song, Hell Among the
Yearlings, If Your Saddle Is Good and Tight, Following
the Cow Trail, Cowman's Prayer, Rounded Up in
Glory, Cowboy's Love Song, The Gambler, Utah Car-
roll, Sam Bass, The Two Soldiers,* all these are well
known, and date back far enough to be called genuine
folk-songs, though some were composed by men still
living. With these should be included *Here's to the
Texas Ranger, Last Great Roundup, When the Work's
All Done This Fall, The Texas Rangers, Zebra Dun,
The Trail to Mexico, The Sioux Indians,* and *Down
on the Rio Grande.* In presenting these lists, I grate-

fully acknowledge the assistance of Mr. Samuel E. Asbury, of College Station, Texas, who has kindly given me the benefit of his wide knowledge of regional folksongs.

Of course everybody knows *Frankie and Johnnie,* and some version of *The Bastard King of England* to be sung only before appropriate company. *Turkey in the Straw, Oh Susannah,* and the immortal Adbul's burlesque ballad have come in from other parts.

The type of frontier ballad is now so well established, and its conventions so well understood, that occasionally something new wins a position among old favorites, even though written by persons who never saw a cowboy. For the most part, the "cowboy" songs plugged on radio and screen sink into the obscurity they deserve.

The songs of the Short Grass, though frequently sentimental and sad, are not so uniformly melancholy as those of the woods and mountains on their eastern borders. The cowboy was a cheerful fellow, as a rule, and seldom nourished a grudge or a grievance. Some of his songs express his awareness of his own rough character and shortcomings, but very few—if any—are tainted with moralistic musings or convincing signs of repentance. He was too hopeful for that.

Someone should work out the inter-relation of cowboy ballads and breakdown songs; it would be worth the trouble.

Rarely, one may hear songs popular among the trappers and scouts on the Plains around Bent's Fort on the Arkansas a hundred years ago: *Money Musk, The Mellow Horn, The Days When We Went Gipsying, The Minstrel's Returned from the War,* and other melodies

antiquated even then. And, of course, a large repertory
of hymns. I was once startled, in a remote Indian camp,
to hear the strains of an organ issuing from a Cheyenne
tipi. It was one of those worked by foot-power, and the
owner—a young woman—played on it very well.

Johnny Get Your Gun and *When Johnny Comes
Marching Home Again* have enjoyed a revival recently.
Ragtime Cowboy Joe is a favorite, and recent events
have produced a ballad entitled *The Dust Bowl Blues*.
Of course, blues and spirituals are known and loved,
but they are importations: few Negroes are to be found
west of the 98th meridian. Even before the prohibition
of slavery beyond that line, Negroes were rare in the region. The Short Grass has always been white man's
country.

Many of the settlers have brought with them various
"cures" for ailments, but few of these are magical. Most
are of the practical sort: poultices, suffusions, and herbs.
One local poultice, apparently native to the region, is
made of the pulp of prickly pear. It is one of the best,
and much less harsh than the old frontier gunpowder-
and-white-of-egg poultice.

There are, of course, persistent legends which will
not die, in spite of historians, as for example, that Rain-
in-the-Face ate Tom Custer's heart after the Battle of
the Little Big Horn. There is the mystery as to why
the ridge-pole of Hanrahan's saloon at Adobe Walls
cracked like a rifle-shot the night before the Indians
attacked, and so kept most of the men awake trying to
repair it—though the story goes that they could never

find any crack in the log at all. At any rate, the noise waked them, and the need for repair kept them awake and saved their lives.

But the Plains are happily free from Maiden Leaps, which have become such a tiresome feature of American landscapes. Indian women must have committed suicide at an appalling rate, to furnish such a lot of leaping rocks for tourists. The Plains Indian maiden was no good at leaping, apparently—or maybe rocks were too hard to find—she generally hanged herself, when despondent—*if* she could find a tree!

There are many tales about horned animals, however. The famous collection of horns at the Buckhorn Saloon in San Antonio is known to thousands who never saw it.

Oddly, the Plains are alive with stories about caves. For some reason, the Plainsman appears to be particularly interested in caves—maybe because he often lived in dugouts. There are a dozen versions of the story of the warrior who wakened in a cave where he had taken shelter, sensed that someone was in the cave, felt about, and found an enemy, or a panther, or a bear. Of course, the dangerous bedfellow lay between him and the entrance every time! But, as Josh Billings would have said, "Half the lies they tell ain't true."

In western Oklahoma is the country known as the Gyp (gypsum) Hills, which might well be called the Land of Hollow Hills. These hills are not lofty, but many of them contain caverns more or less large, so that they echo to the hooves of a horse passing over them. The largest is the Alabaster Cavern, containing more than fifty "rooms."

Where the soft stone has faulted, one may sometimes find entrance to these caves, and here and there about the region are caverns of considerable extent, some with water in them, others high and dry. They are of local repute only, for the most part, but the natives have had their adventures in exploring them.

In the dry caves skunks, and even wildcats, are sometimes encountered. The favorite story is of a man named Bill who followed, as he supposed, a coyote into the cavern. At first he could stand almost upright, then he had to get down on his hands and knees, and finally wormed his way along on his belly, as the cave contracted. Near the end he found himself face to face with an angry cat. They say Bill came out of the cave backward so fast that when the two of them emerged, the wildcat was wearing Bill's shirt.

In these hills crevasses are found. Recently the body of an officer was found in one of these where it had been left by his murderers.

Sometimes great sinks or pools are found in the middle of the prairie, quite hidden from the eye of anyone even a few yards away. There are the usual tales of blind fish in these caverns. What truth there may be in such yarns who can say? But bats abound in the dry caves.

There was once a farmer's daughter beloved by a cowboy. Her father forbade her to have any truck with the knight of the saddle, and kept the shotgun loaded and ready. But the youngsters found a way to keep in touch, even though they could not meet. Every day the young man plucked one of the bats from the walls of the cave where they hung sleeping, and carried it up the canyon to a hollow tree, where he left the creature in a pasteboard shoe-box. The young lady managed to visit the tree, and would tie her message to the leg of the furry creature, leaving the lid of the box off. Since bats always return, if possible, to the cave they inhabit after the night's hunting, the cowboy had only to visit the cave next morning to receive his sweetheart's message. In this way he learned when the old man was going to town, and the lovers would take advantage of his absence, and meet in secret.

There is a story to the effect that smugglers of narcotics used a similar method in getting the "snow" across the Mexican border, sending hundreds of bats back and forth. If the range of bats is wide enough, this method might be useful in communicating across international borders in war-time. Probably the bat would not fly so fast or so far as a carrier pigeon, but he would have the advantage of traveling by night, and of being hard to catch or shoot. Any parachutist could deliver a bushel of bats, each of which could carry a message back to its home in the cave.

In the old days, when malaria was the scourge of the Plains, canny travelers always made camp, when possible, near a bat-cave, knowing that the animals would clean out the fever-bearing mosquitoes in the neighborhood. On the prairies, few people have any fear of bats, or regard them as allies of the Evil One.

Neither is there any fear of the bullbat, or nighthawk, such as haunts those who hear his cousin, the whippoorwill, in the woodlands. He is rather regarded as a friend —strange though he may be, with his nocturnal habits, his "rubber" beak, and his whiskers.

The bullbat is a most erratic flyer, wheeling and plunging, banking and turning like an airplane, in his continual dogfight with the insects on which he feeds. The white spots which mark his wings complete the resemblance.

On quiet evenings, just after sunset, the darting bird dives at one's head roaring like a bomber. Then a boy can have fun playing games with the creature; tossing sticks high into the air to watch the bird feint at them and dart quickly up again on narrow, angular wings, to wait for the next missile.

MAKING IT RAIN

In dry country, rain-makers are bound to flourish.

The great Sun Dance of the Plains Indians, often lasting a week, an annual festival more spectacular than any Indian ceremony on the continent, was basically a rain-making rite. Besides, many of the sacred bundles of individual Indians served that purpose. The bundle of Sitting Bull, the famous Sioux, could be used to make either rain or wind, as desired. Sitting Bull used it to make rain after the long drouth of 1890, and before that, on the warpath, to drive his enemies away by making a strong wind, or—by making it rain—to put out grass fires set to drive him from cover. Many stories are told by Indians of such use against powerful enemies. After the Indians took to farming, such bundles came in very handy on the arid plains.

But the white men on the Short Grass soon acquired the Indians' faith in rain-makers. Or, at any rate, became so desperate for water that they were willing to try any method, however fantastic. Being hunters, the Indians put their faith in animal helpers; the white men, being machine-minded, generally put their faith in machines. One works as well as the other, probably.

The most generally used method in early days was to fire cannon into the clouds, or set off dynamite on hilltops, in the hope that the explosions would cause a downpour. Believers in this method pointed out that very often, after great battles, heavy downpours followed.

The white men, however, were canny. They only paid when the rain-maker delivered. In the nineties an Australian came to the Plains and attempted to make it rain by means of chemicals, releasing hydrogen, which it was thought would unite with free oxygen and so cause rain.

At Goodland, Kansas, two rain-makers actually incorporated, and sold shares in their company. Later, it is said, the Mexican government employed them—with what result is not of record.

Rain-makers who failed often met with strong opposition; no less did those find themselves unpopular who had caused too much rain. In 1912 the Cheyenne medicine man was so successful at the annual Sun Dance in the Canadian bottoms that the whole camp was flooded before the ceremony was half over, and the Indians had to pull out to higher ground. The old fellow was greatly distressed, called a mass meeting, and assured the assembled tribesmen that he had not intended any such disaster. Said he: "I did not know my power was so great!"

Some years ago I was on the French Riviera writing

my biography of Sitting Bull, and had with me the old chief's medicine bundle, which was guaranteed to make it rain. His nephew had given me the bundle, and had taught me the ritual to be used. I was told how to make rain, and also how to make the wind come up. To do this, the owner wore wristlets of buffalo hide, chewed a bit of calamus root, made a sacrifice of his blood—or of some scarlet cloth—and sang the appropriate song. On two occasions I had used the bundle as instructed, with satisfactory results.

It was the height of the season at Juan-les-Pins, and the little town was swarming with tourists. At our hotel, meals were usually served at tables in the garden between the sea and the mountains. It rained so rarely that the landlord had turned his indoor dining-room into a dormitory, in order to accommodate the thronging guests.

One day, as I sat writing at my table in the garden under the gaudy umbrella, I happened to glance up and saw mine host and his wife wringing their hands, and anxiously staring at the Maritime Alps. I asked what the matter was. They pointed to a thunderhead rapidly advancing towards the sea and the town. It was almost the hour for lunch, and if rain fell during that time, their guests would be soaked, or get nothing to eat. The two were in despair.

Hoping to cheer them up a little, I suggested that I could drive the thunder-cloud back into the mountains by means of Sitting Bull's medicine bundle. They both seemed to think that I was jesting at a very bad time. I therefore withdrew my proposition, saying, "Of course, it is nothing to me. Have it as you wish."

At that the man hesitated, glanced at his wife, and replied, "It can do no harm to try."

My bluff was called. I hurried to my room, brought back the bundle, and opened it, spreading the paraphernalia upon the table. As I did so, a crucifix fell out. I had forgotten that it was in the bundle. It was one given to Sitting Bull by the missionary, Father De Smet, and I had stowed it in his bundle, though it did not belong there.

Seeing the crucifix, the pair were plainly shocked, evidently thinking that I intended working black magic. I quickly put the crucifix aside, assuring them that it was no part of the apparatus. They relaxed then, but I saw that they were now in the mood for a miracle.

As I went through with the ritual, the whole staff gathered, forming a line facing the cloud, with their backs to the sea. I sang the song in Sioux, and prepared to wrap up everything again. I said, "Right away, the wind will blow."

Immediately, a sudden gust swept in from the sea, striking them all in the back and fairly lifting the umbrella from the table. Jean, the waiter, jumped two feet in the air with alarm, and indeed everybody but myself seemed thoroughly astonished at the instant fulfillment of my prophecy. Amazed, they stood looking up at the thunder-cloud, which presently began to break up and drift away from the town. Believe it or not, this happened. My family can bear witness to the truth. Whatever the cause, the storm was averted.

Thereafter Jean's demeanor towards me was one of awful respect. He could scarcely bring himself to approach my table near enough to serve me, and put dishes before me at the full length of his arm. He evidently thought me in league with the Devil.

The Sioux certainly have faith in that bundle. During the last fearful dry year on the Plains, when the dust storms were sweeping away the very earth from beneath their feet, Sitting Bull's nephew wrote me from Dakota, begging me to return the bundle, so that they could break the drouth.

They have it now, and the old men assure me that, if Hitler's luftwaffe comes over, they will blow it out of the sky.

TWISTERS AND TORNADOES

Plains Indians believed that whirlwinds were evil spirits. I have seen an old squaw pursue one of these little twisters across the prairie, after it had wrecked her tent, screaming and throwing stones at it. When thunderstorms approached, old-time Indian women would rush toward them and try to frighten them away by waving their blankets. While this was going on, the younger women, who had gone to school, were busy hammering down the tent-pegs. No one who has seen one of those Plains thunderstorms could fail to understand why people should regard it as malevolent.

When tornadoes appeared, everybody ran to the " 'fraid-hole" or "cyclone-cellar," a deep dugout behind the house. There they cowered in the darkness, like so many people in a bomb shelter, waiting for the storm to pass. One day a family hurried to their 'fraid-hole as the dark, funnel-shaped cloud swept toward them. The mother was the last to go down. Just as she reached for the door of the cellar to close it, she turned to look at the house. The wind swept her skirts over her head for an instant. She pulled them down again. The house was gone.

All sorts of stories are told of the freaks perpetrated by such storms—which would blow a piano away and leave a floor lamp standing undisturbed. The difference in pressure between an enclosed room and the outer air as the storm went by often caused the building to explode. Trees also seemed to be softened up in this manner so that straws were driven into them like nails inches deep.

Nothing can stand against such terrific forces. Chickens were stripped of their feathers. Survivors laughed to see these poor creatures sneaking about and hiding behind anything they could find, as if ashamed of their nakedness. Farm tools and even automobiles were blown away.

One afternoon a tired homesteader came to the little shack which he occupied one day each month in the course of proving up on his claim. Worn out, he flung himself down on the bed and promptly went to sleep. Some time later he was vaguely conscious of the rattling of the windows in the flimsy shack, but did not fully waken. Then he heard a sudden *"Zow, Zow,"* and found himself muffled in a quilt lying on the ground at the edge of the floor of the building.

Everything but the floor had vanished. He fought his way clear of the bedding, stood up, and watched the storm tear off across the prairie. He was unhurt, but now that it was over, found himself much shaken. His knees trembled so that he could hardly stand. His barn was also gone. Following the wind came the downpour.

He hurried to the corral to catch one of his horses and ride to the nearest neighbor's for shelter, eight miles away, but his horses' hides were full of splinters from the vanished barn and the animals would not be caught. He had to leg it all the way to find a dry bed and get supper.

Certain towns on the plains have been repeatedly destroyed by tornadoes, while others have never been touched. Snyder, Oklahoma, is one of these ill-fated towns, having twice suffered destruction by tornadoes. People say that the Indians warned the settlers against building the town in that spot; if this is true, one wonders how the Indians knew it would prove dangerous.

For the proverb goes: "Only a fool or a stranger forecasts weather on the Plains." But then, of course, the Plains Indian was neither.

POPULAR LEGENDS

A persistent legend told about an old Indian warrior who had gone blind, is that he put out his eyes rather than see the white man's civilization supplanting the ways of his people.

Some of the legends of the Short Grass have to do with historic events: all over the Plains, at cards, aces and eights are known as the "dead man's hand," because this was the hand held by Wild Bill Hickok when he was shot down by Jack McCall at Deadwood. The man drawing this hand expects an untimely end.

There is also a legend of Sand Creek, the Indian massacre in Colorado, November, 1864, when the Colorado

volunteers under Colonel Chivington practically exterminated a band of Cheyennes and Arapahos, who had
come in to Fort Lyon to make peace. The white men
destroyed men, women, and children impartially, with
circumstances of appalling barbarity. I have recast the
legend into ballad form and have provided the anonymous avenger with a name:

SAND CREEK

Between the dawn and the daylight
While the snow lay on the ground,
The Cheyennes camped on Sand Creek—
Their sleep was sweet and sound.

They had come in to smoke the pipe,
The peace was to begin;
They came and camped near the Army post
To turn their captives in.

Between the dawn and the daylight
They heard the bugles scream,
The roar of rifle and howitzer,
The hoofbeats up the stream. . . .

A hundred women and children
The soldiers scalped that day,
But the cruellest killer of them all
Was the Volunteer, Joe Gray.

For when the fight was over
Four prisoners were found—
Three Indian women and a girl
With the dead upon the ground.

"Stand back," Joe ordered his comrades,
"Stand back and watch," he said.
"Today we take no prisoners—
All good Indians are dead!

"Stand back," he ordered his comrades,
"Stand back and watch the fun."
The screaming women turned to fly—
He dropped them one by one.

The little girl ran to him,
With outstretched arms she pled;
He shot her down with a bitter smile,
"Nits make lice," he said.

She lay there on her painted face
In buckskins all arrayed;
He turned her over, hand in hair,
He drew his shiny blade . . .

"You might ha' held your bloody hand
Till you saw her skin was white;
You might ha' spared that pretty face
To be some man's delight."

"Shut up!" he said to his comrades,
"I've killed enough today—
This is my little sister
That the Indians stole away!"

He folded her cold white hands across,
He kissed her pale cold cheek;
He saw the Indians pulling out
Far up the sandy creek.

He jumped into his saddle,
He galloped on their track,
Unarmed, alone, on his horse he charged . . .
They dragged him from its back.

9. *Thunderbird and Water Monster*

The Thunderbird

IN THE sign language of the Plains Indians, a man indicates "water" by holding his cupped hand to his lips, as though drinking from it. This sign is also used to indicate the idea of "anxiety," or as an adjective, "anxious." On the Short Grass, before the days of windmills, people were often worried about finding water.

Naturally enough, then, many striking legends and myths have to do with water. Of the mythological creatures of which Plains Indians tell, none is so well known as the Thunderbird. It is familiar to everybody, and now forms the insignia of the 45th Division, U. S. Army.

This fearsome creature nests on some high, rocky hill or peak somewhere to the west, from whence the storms come. All winter it stays there. Its return to the Plains is heralded by bellowing thunder, and this first thunder in the spring was celebrated by the Indians with appropriate rituals all over the Short Grass.

Many Indians claim to have seen one or more thunderbirds. Both the Cheyennes and Arapahos describe the Thunderbird (*Ba-a*) as a huge bird like an eagle, dark blue, or showing the color of cut lead like a thundercloud, with red zigzag markings running from its heart to the tail and wing-tips. In its talons the bird carries arrows with which to strike its enemies, and therefore the Indians believe that the eagle on our coins is a Thunderbird. The creature makes lightning by snapping its beak or winking its eyes; the thunder is the sound made by the beating of its enormous wings; and the downpour which follows is explained by saying that the bird dumps the lake carried on its back.

No one who has seen such a deluge fall will be surprised at this notion. Sometimes four or five inches of rain fall within a few minutes; afterward, as the cowboy said, "the water stands three feet deep on the hillside." Within the week, as I write this, the Short Grass has had two such downpours: the weather bureau reports that the first dropped 4.6 inches of rain, the other 5.6. Last night, since midnight, 3 inches of rain fell here. This makes a total for the first week of June of 8.87. Not so bad for what strangers like to call "the Dust Bowl!"

But there are "evidences" other than thunder and rain to show that thunderbirds exist. In Dakota, large round boulders found on the prairie are said to be its "eggs." And the Comanche tell of a spot on the upper Red River where the grass remains permanently burned off over a space having the shape of a huge bird with outspread wings. They say the Thunderbird once alighted there.

Once, they say, a hunter wounded a large bird, and brought it down, but was afraid to go close enough to kill it. He went back to camp for help. When his party approached the ravine where the bird had fallen, they heard thunder and were blinded by terrific flashes of lightning coming from the ravine. Still they kept on, until one of them was struck dead. Then they all high-tailed it back to camp. Such stories are legion.

Numbers of my old friends among the tribesmen have seen one or more Thunderbirds. Gray Whirlwind of the Hunkpapa Sioux once saw four together, perched on a high bluff. Chief Hump, of the same tribe, actually captured a strange bird with zigzag markings, which he believed to be a Thunderbird. A man so favored, or any man who dreamed of the Thunder, was thereafter in a class by himself. He was believed to have a strong heart. Strong hearts are no rarity on the Short Grass.

The Thunderbird has even been celebrated in some anonymous verses, burlesquing the belief of the medicine men, entitled "Medicine Hat."

> *I caught the great, original*
> *And only mythological*
> *Fulmineous Thunderbird!*
> *Since then, when I put on my hat*
> *And sing a certain song,*
> *The clouds assemble at my call*
> *(At stanza four the rain will fall)*
> *From the place where they belong.*

THE TURTLE

The turtle is another creature which plays a large part in Plains mythology—perhaps because· he too is connected with water. He it was who dived into the

wilderness of waters in the beginning, and brought up
the mud from which the earth was made. No doubt
this story was prompted by the fact that the turtle himself is a symbol of the world. His shell is flat like the
earth, domed like the sky; between this earth and sky
is his flesh—symbol of all living things; he has four
legs to mark the four directions, and is entirely surrounded by water. He is also noted for his trickiness.
Watch him: There he lies on the log, asleep. But try
to catch him, and in a second he is safe in the water
below.

WATER MONSTERS

Everywhere on the Short Grass, and indeed the whole
Plains region, you will hear stories of mysterious creatures called Water Monsters. These are generally rep-
tilian in form, but have horns like a buffalo. They live
in lonely pools, sinkholes, or rivers. As a rule, they are
friendly to all men who honor them with appropriate
gifts, such as feathers, paint, and white shells. According
to the stories, they have often saved defeated warriors
from pursuing enemies by ferrying them across dangerous floods, for which service the proper fare was an
eagle feather tied to each of the monster's horns. One
prominent Arapaho family were under the protection
of a water monster, and had his triangular visage, horns,
feathers, and all, regularly painted upon their tipi doors.

There is a widespread story about one of these creatures:

Two hunters were out on the Staked Plains, and
became hungry. As they walked along, they happened
to find four eggs in a damp spot. Neither of them had

ever seen any eggs like these. But they were famished, and one of the young men proposed to eat them.

His comrade objected. Said he, "These eggs are different. We do not know what creature laid them. They may be mysterious (sacred). I do not think we should touch them."

"Well," said the other, "I'm hungry. My belly is cut in two. I am going to eat them." So he took them, broke them, and sucked the contents, raw. The two of them went on, and made camp as the sun set.

In the night the one who had eaten the strange food waked his comrade, and said, "Brother, I feel funny. Something has happened to me. Feel my legs."

The friend felt of his comrade's legs. They were all scaly, and stuck together. The young men were frightened.

They did not know what to do. But as the night wore on, the sick one kept complaining. "Brother, feel my body."

And when they laid hands on his body, they found it was now scaly too. Much alarmed, they waited for daylight.

As soon as it was light, the sick one said, "Brother, something has happened to me. I am terribly thirsty, but I cannot walk. Carry me to the nearest water. I can smell it; there must be a lake over the hill."

His friend was afraid to pick him up, for the sick one had changed fearfully. He no longer had a human head; his head had changed its shape. It looked like the head of a lizard or a horned toad. Two horns were beginning to sprout there, and his tongue was forked.

But he could not refuse his friend's request; moreover, he was afraid to. So he picked up the strange creature, and lugged it over the ridge. Sure enough, there was a pool. He carried the thing down to the bank, and put him down.

The other scrambled into the water, and seemed to feel great relief. But he did not turn back into a man. After a while, he said, "Brother, I am not going home. This is my home now. I am become a water monster. Tell my people to come here and bring me presents when they are in trouble. I can help them."

Then he submerged and sank from sight.

Long after, whenever his people were in trouble, they used to visit this pool and throw in their offerings. Then the monster would rise up and speak to them. By that time, he had long horns, and was covered with scales.

Water monsters are said to inhabit—or to have inhabited—St. Jacob's Well in Clark County, Kansas, and the pond at Dripping Springs, near Clinton, Oklahoma, as well as certain pools in the Staked Plains. Some say there was one in Dead Horse Lake, in Kansas, near the Colorado line. Dripping Springs is now a swimming pool. Nobody so far has reported seeing any such creature there. But I believe few Indians go there for a swim.

None of these pools is large, but even in the dryest seasons, St. Jacob's Well never goes dry. Nobody has ever found bottom in that rockbound pool.

RATTLESNAKES AND HORNED TOADS

Rattlesnakes have always been front and center in the folklore of the Plains. In the early days they abounded there, and in some communities rattlesnake drives are still held annually to rid the neighborhood of these reptiles. On the Santa Fe Trail the progress of a wagon train was punctuated by continual popping of guns as men killed rattlers. On the march across the Plains during the Mexican war, officers, in order to conserve ammunition, had to issue orders forbidding the men to shoot snakes. Now and then one sees enormous snake skins hung up in curio shops, or nailed to a barn door. Tales are told of snakes twelve feet long, thick as a man's leg, having a hundred rattles. You may take those or leave them. Probably in the wild days on the Plains snakes lived longer and therefore grew longer than they do today.

But do not count your rattles unless they are attached to a live, or recently killed, reptile. For it is possible to piece together rattles from several snakes and so make a monster rattle—for the admiration of the unsuspecting dude.

People believed that a snake grew a new rattle every year, so that you could tell its age by counting the rattles on its tail. Some claimed that a snake must drink water after biting someone and that a wounded snake would commit suicide by biting itself. It was claimed that old snakes swallowed the young, and that a snake cannot strike beyond its length, or when it is not coiled. Snake rattles tied to the hatband are believed to prevent headaches.

It was believed that rattlers lived in amity with prairie dogs and burrowing owls, sharing their nests underground. This is hardly scientific. The burrowing owl, comical as he is, was hardly fool enough to make friends with a rattler, and certainly no prairie dog ever willingly shared its hole with such a dangerous companion. Rattlers were, of course, found in prairie-dog towns. They went there to gorge themselves on the young of their unwilling hosts.

Prairie dogs, like jackrabbits and eagles, are said never to require water. Certainly their towns were often miles from water on the high prairie at places where the water table was far underground. Yet prairie dogs in captivity drink water readily enough, and rattlers living in dogtowns certainly required water and never stayed long far from it.

The snake was not, as is commonly believed, a lover of hot sunshine. If kept under a hot sun for several hours, he would die. His habits are nocturnal and he generally contrived to find some shelter from the heat at midday. Dangerous as he is to those who meddle with him, the rattler is not a troublemaker. He is not eager to fight; he needs his venom for his hunting and is loath to spend it on some animal, like man, too big to swallow. Popular opinion gives the rattler little credit for his good motives. He has only one virtue. Once a lady teacher in an Indian school was informed that the chief had given her a name. Flattered, she asked what it was. "*Rattlesnake*," he replied. "I have watched you and you always warn before you strike."

One superstition about the rattler is still widespread, namely, that he will not cross a hair rope coiled around the bedroll. This fond belief, now disproved by photo-graphic evidence, has enabled hundreds of men to sleep soundly in rattlesnake country.

The rattlesnake has had his effect upon the folkways of the Short Grass. He, more than anyone else, made the High Plains a hard liquor country. Every pioneer kept a jug of spirits handy, believing it a sure cure for snakebite.

The horned toad enjoys a happier reputation. He is a little creature for which everybody feels some measure of affection. Of course, he is a lizard, not a toad; but he is not slick and slithery like other reptiles. Instead of scales, he is covered with small horns, like a miniature prehistoric monster. Harmless and easily caught, he is warm in the hand, and his little heart beats at such a rate that his captor is bound to feel sympathetic. No decent man could deliberately kill a horned toad.

Sometimes when captured, though unharmed, the horned toad sheds a few drops of blood. It is said these are "shot" from his eyes, though for what purpose no-body seems to know. He is often made a pet of, and will arch his little back when you scratch it. He is welcome in a garden, and stays on the home range, living year after year in the same narrow neighborhood, a real homebody. Though no chameleon, his color varies somewhat with the character of the country where he is found. He is droll in action, with his puny legs, tiny tail, and fiercely horned head. His body, mottled in chestnut and buckskin colors, is round and flat, so that he looks like a small animated pancake. Probably no small creature on the Plains is so well liked.

If kept shut up in a box, he will live for incredible periods, weeks, perhaps months, without food or water. Stories are told of horned toads found deep in the earth, enclosed in hard rock, apparently centuries old. Some believe he feeds on air and is immortal. On one occasion a live horned toad was put into the tin box enclosed in the cornerstone of a public building, with the sure expectation that he would be alive, awaiting the demolition of the structure by generations yet unborn.

The Black Widow has no friends on the Plains. It is a small black spider with a brilliant red spot shaped like an hour-glass on its body. Its bite is venomous and, some claim, fatal. Folk-Lore interprets the hour-glass marking as meaning that the victim has only one hour to live. Certainly it makes the headlines oftener than its competitor in evil, the rattlesnake.

Legends about horses are many, as is natural in such a horseman's country. Of these Professor J. Frank Dobie and the Texas Folklore Society have collected many in *Mustangs and Cow Horses,* published in 1940. Some are to be found in Phil Stong's *Horses and Americans,* New York, 1939.

One of the most persistent, though false, legends on the Short Grass is to the effect that Indians first got horses by stealing from, or picking up animals lost by, Coronado and other early Spanish Explorers. Modern research has disposed of this legend. The Indians got their horses later, in trade, or sometimes perhaps by theft. Spanish records are explicit and give careful accounting of government property lost on their expedi-

tions. Very few horses were lost, and these not in regions where they were afterward numerous.

Redskins generally held the horse to be a sacred animal and would starve before they would kill one for
food. A dead horse they would eat, but they would
never kill one for that purpose. During the depression,
at one of the agencies, Indians were in such dire straits
that the agent himself killed and butchered a number
of wild horses. He hung the carcasses in the commissary
and called in the Indians: "There it is, if you want it."

The Indians wasted no time and saved themselves
from famine. But until the agent killed the animals,
they would not stir.

Flowers and Feathers

Sandhill cranes, seen occasionally on sandy river beds,
or flying with trailing legs along the bottoms, are a
characteristically hardy breed. The Indians say they will
attack children playing on the sandbars; that Indian
mothers have to warn their little folks to be on the
lookout, or they will have their eyes pecked out. This
fact gives the crane a literary interest, recalling its wars
with the pygmies in Homer—

That small infantry, warred on by cranes.

On the Plains there are no whistling skinks, no belch-
ing baboons, no pygmy anteaters, or blood-lapping bats.
No four-eyed fish swim in the waters, and the grison
is never seen there.

But Short Grass creatures have charms all their own,
and the vegetation is varied and beautiful. The silver

sage and the sandbur, the burdock and the rose mallow, the bush morning glory and the ball cactus with its deep pink flowers; the silken yellow blooms of prickly pear, the wild rose, the buffalo bush with its silver leaves and tasty berries, the roundleaf salt-bush and the rabbit-bush with its greenish flowers, the smelly creosote bush, and the greasewood, loving shale and alkali, rival in their beauty the false scarlet mallows carpeting the ground with their reddish-orange flowers; the evening primroses covering the hills and plains with their sul-phurous yellow glow. In the Panhandle in early sum-mer you may see large clumps two and three feet high of the prairie bearded-tongue with great spikes of soft lilac or orchid-colored flowers.

Then, too, blossoms the yellow bladder pod, cover-ing the ground like a carpet; the dwarf aster, the only spring flowering aster in the Southwest, standing six or eight inches over acres of ground; the spiderwort, with its blue flowers like lilies; or the beautiful dwarf shrub called catsclaw, with its pink pea-like flowers covering sandstone outcroppings. There are sunflowers and dwarf sumac, coreopsis and the gaillardia, verbena and dwarf white daisies found interspersed among the others. This white daisy is a miniature Vassar daisy on a short stem.

Loco weed is common. It causes mental disturbances in animals foolish enough to eat it, and takes its name from the Spanish word *loco*—crazy.

Among trees the cottonwood is king, raising its white branches high into the air above the scrub elms, western juniper, hackberry, and persimmon trees. Dogwood blooms along the streams and redbud flourishes every-where.

The most individual tree of the region is perhaps the mesquite tree. This has very little foliage and bears a leaf reminding one of a honey locust or sensitive plant. The tree is rather scrawny and awkward-looking, growing scattered on the prairie and casting very little shade. At a distance a grove of these trees looks like an abandoned peach orchard.

In Colorado there is a brome grass called rattlesnake grass, so-called because it rustles when trodden on. There too grows the bee-plant with its purple flowers in clusters, the butter weed, the sneeze weed, the yellow evening star. Cane cactus grows four feet high, flaunting its red and yellow flowers in June.

Wild silver sage (*Artemisia*) is abundant in many parts of the Short Grass. The tribesmen hold it sacred, and use it in their ceremonies, spreading it down to sit on, when engaged in prayer or singing. Wreaths of sage are worn in the Sun Dance, and if a man has broken any taboo, or touched any holy thing, he purifies himself by rubbing himself all over with this plant. Some Indians believe that sage is the food of ghosts—and the fact that white men used it as seasoning in their dishes was to them startling. People sometimes chew it, for the taste.

Willow is clean and therefore used in making the mats or head-rests of marriage beds, when young folks set up a tipi of their own. In the old days, Indians peeled willow sticks with their teeth. Scalps were commonly carried home in triumph attached to willow wands. At night, when old warriors bring out their trophies at dances, one may sometimes see scalps doing a mad jig from the top of willow wands, vibrant with the vertigo of the dancers.

Dancing Birds

Evidently, Indian dancing on the Plains is in imitation of the prairie cocks; no other creature dances with such ecstatic, quivering rigidity. On the Short Grass, people sometimes organize parties and go out into the blackjacks at the right season to watch the chickens dance. It is a notable spectacle, if you can get to see it. The blackjacks (scrub oaks) extend in wide belts across some portions of the Plains. On old maps, these belts were known as the Cross Timbers. They made travel by wagon difficult; some say that, but for the Cross Timbers, the Santa Fe Trail would have run from the Indian Territory across Oklahoma, instead of swinging through Kansas as it does.

The prairie squirrel, or spermophile, is like a chipmunk: active, sleek, striped, curious, and quick. His round little burrow is easily recognized, being hardly larger than his body—or a broomstick. In the spring his prolonged vibrating whistle trails off into silence on fine mornings, a peculiarly sweet and appealing sound. It is easy to drown him out of his burrow, and if taken young, he makes a charming pet, always ready and eager to see his master, and agile in captivity as when wild. Though no climber, he will try, if his cage offers any hold to his small feet. If not quite as perky as a chipmunk, he has a sweeter disposition.

The badger is found everywhere on the Plains, and his holes and "diggings" make riding dangerous. Horses are also shy of him, and will sometimes buck when they see or smell him. He is a sturdy beast, with massive shoulders and long claws, bench-legged as a bulldog, with the power of somehow submerging his head and bones in the mass of tough muscle when attacked. His long hair, loose hide, stout body, and sharp teeth make him a tough customer for the average dog or wolf. And once he gets his head and shoulders into his hole, it is a man-size job to pull him out.

But Striped Face is not a savage creature, and once tamed, makes a most amusing pet. I once owned a badger which followed me everywhere, and showed an affection and devotion as real and touching as any dog could have displayed. When put into his pen, he would dig out and be at my heels before I could get out of the yard. If I attempted to shut him up even while I brought water to him, he would dig out and be at my side before the bucket could fill from the hydrant. There was never any choice; one *had* to take him along, and short-legged as he was, he nearly always kept up. Dogs learned to give him a wide berth. But one day, when he was trot-waddling along down the street, hot on my trail, some idiot shot him.

The prairie dog also makes a pet, if caught when a pup. But there is no nonsense about him. He likes his master because he likes company—and a good meal. He is the Sancho Panza of the Plains. Here is how he strikes me:

PRAIRIE DOG

Here's a right-thinker, prosperous and proud,
Provincial, curious, insolently sure;
A town-dweller, and pleased with his home town;
Saucy when safe, but when a keener wit

Than his approaches, he will jerk his tail
(Defiant shred of dignity) and plunge
To his ancestral, labyrinthine dark.

But the prairie dog is a true Plainsman. Settler and nester though he is, he will pull up stakes and hit the trail any time, ready to stake a claim and start a new town elsewhere.

When the prairie dogs had swept their home range bare of grass, or even before, they would migrate in vast hordes, like lemmings, swimming rivers, scaling bluffs, crossing open plains, covering the earth in swarms thick as Mormon crickets. The Sioux say the dogs even rode buffalo to their new home.

They explain that, in the old days, buffalo went to water two or three times a day, traveling single-file along narrow paths leading to water. The Plains, wherever buffalo ranged, were cut by innumerable such paths, varying from eight to ten inches in width. Where the ground sloped steeply, the rain washed out these paths into deep trenches, so that often, where they led down to the river, they were as deep as the buffalo was tall. Such deep-cut paths can still be seen in places where cattle have made them, or where the soil has been hard enough to keep them in their original form. It was possible for the prairie dogs to lie in wait for the bison at the edge of one of these deep cuts, where they could drop upon the huge animal's back and hang on by clutching his wool with their claws.

This may seem a tale of incredible tallness. But Charles Goodnight once made a pet of a prairie dog which behaved in a manner to lend color to the story.

Goodnight was swimming a herd of cattle across the Platte, and found himself alongside of a migration of prairie dogs crossing the stream. He lifted one of the dogs from the water, placed it on the back of his horse behind the saddle; it rode there until he reached the bank. Afterward it traveled in the chuck-wagon, clear to the Pecos. "At night . . . the cowboys . . . turned it out to graze, and 'had a hell of a time playing with it.' " *

Goodnight has something to say about the migrations of the dogs, and their spread to the southeast during his long life on the Plains.

There is a small owl, a ground bird, which nests in prairie-dog holes, and is usually seen hanging about dog towns, dreaming in the sun. One seldom sees two of these birds together, and never perched in trees.

This little bird is surely the most comical of all owls, both in appearance and behavior. He is long on legs and short on feathers, and bobs apologetically at you. He seems almost too small to swallow a mouse, and utters a curious cry—a cry imitated by certain Indian dreamers called Contraries, whose sacred duty it is to do everything backwards.

Contraries are men who have dreamed of Thunder, and this tremendous distinction and evidence of divine protection makes it obligatory upon them to humiliate themselves publicly in this way. These men painted themselves white all over, wore weeds in their hair in-

* For this matter of prairie dogs riding, see *Charles Goodnight, Cowman & Plainsman* by J. Evetts Haley, Boston, 1936, page 426; also *Red Hunters and the Animal People* by Charles A. Eastman ("Ohiyesa"), N. Y., 1904.

stead of feathers, and were under obligation to do the exact opposite of whatever they were told to do. They were the butts of the ignorant, but honored by wiser men. In battle, if ordered to retreat, they charged, and their daily actions were ridiculous. No more appropriate war-cry for them could be imagined than the cry of the burrowing owl! But not even the Contraries could act so absurdly as this little bobbing bird.

Once, while on my way to visit the Sioux on a research expedition, I made camp in a schoolyard on the prairie not far from Bear Butte. Very early in the morning I awoke to find four of these quaint birds perched on the ground about my head in a semi-circle, all regarding me gravely. This was astonishing to me. But when I stirred, an even more astonishing thing happened: they all flew up and perched on the schoolhouse roof.

I had never seen one of them alight on anything but the ground before, and their conduct in grouping themselves about my head was, to say the least, unusual. I was tempted to ask some of my old Sioux informants what such odd behavior might mean.

But the owl is a bird of ill omen, among Indians, and the number four is "strong medicine." If an ill interpretation were put upon the actions of the four owls, I might forfeit the confidence of my Indian friends. So I had to let it go.

Maybe I ought to paint myself white all over and wear weeds in my hair. But I shall never know.

For my part, I like the little owl, and do not mind saying so:

BURROWING OWL

Ghost of the prairie, perched on the open grave
Where he was hatched, and nests, and dies at last;
Droll puff of feathers without body born;
An empty target, shedding plumes, not blood,
And curtseying when a bullet passes near.

VARIOUS VARMINTS

Usually, in any region, the creature which has the most names and nicknames is the most bizarre and interesting. By this test, no fowl on the Plains is so popular as the Road-Runner, Chaparral Cock, Chaparral, Ground Cuckoo, Snake Eater, Desert Cock, Medicine Bird, "Bird of Paradise," Churella, or Paisano. He even has a cockeyed Latin name: *Geococcyx Californianus.* And no wonder.

New Mexico, which has the habit of trying to appropriate all the color of the Southwest to its own uses, has named the Road-Runner its State Bird. But the fowl is to be seen streaking it down the road ahead of cars and teams and footmen in every state in the region. From Kansas to Mexico, from Oklahoma to the Coast, the Road-Runner dashes along, as if going to a fire, only stopping, if he needs to stop, to kill the snakes along the way. Legend says he can swallow snakes laid end to end as fast as he can run. He is so ga-ga that everybody hangs a tale on him. He is cuckoo in character as well as by family tree.

J. Frank Dobie has published all the lore of the Paisano in the publications of the Texas Folk-Lore Society, Number XV, giving a most complete account of this long-legged, ingenious, serious-minded, crested clown among the birds, describing its curious antics and most intelligent methods of dealing with snakes and snails. Here we may be well content to quote Eve Ganson's lines for a perfect portrait of the fantastic creature; the lines are from *Desert Mavericks Caught and Branded by Eve Ganson or Who's Who on the Desert,* Santa Barbara, California, 1928, and are used by permission of the publisher, Wallace Hebberd.

THE ROAD-RUNNER

The Road-Runner runs in the road,
His coat is speckled, à la mode.
His wings are short, his tail is long,
He jerks it as he runs along.
His bill is sharp, his eyes are keen,
He has a brain tucked in his bean.
But in his gizzard—if you please—
Are lizards, rats, and bumble bees;
Also horned toads—on them he feeds—
And rattlesnakes! and centipedes!

Hydrophobia was a great curse on the Plains in early days. Mad wolves ranged the prairies biting men and animals. Even buffalo sometimes went mad, but the animal most feared when rabid was the skunk. The skunk is a quiet animal, small and nocturnal in its habits. A mad skunk could get at a man in camp before his presence was suspected. In the old days there was no remedy. Men therefore carried "madstones"—balls of hair retrieved from the bellies of ruminants—which, if properly manipulated about the wound, were believed to absorb the poison. These balls, composed of hair the animal had licked from its own back and swallowed, are still held to be talismans on the Short Grass, as elsewhere. In Oklahoma, the use of madstones is forbidden by law.

The skunk is a creature which treads softly and carries a big stink. It was common on the Plains, and so strikingly marked as to be readily seen. In the evening he and his mate might go for a stroll down the trail, and anyone who met him turned out or halted to let him pass. In the evening, families of skunks could be seen playing or hunting together, but they were seldom disturbed unless they were too near the chicken farm. The skunk's method of self-defense made him respected, and his deliberate manner and superb aplomb struck admiration in all those who emulated him in carrying deadly weapons. A skillful gunman was described as "cool as a skunk in the moonlight." Apt: one cannot appease a polecat!

It is claimed that the skunk is unable to launch his gas attack when picked up adeptly by the tail. As a precaution the picker-up should hold the skunk facing him. So long as he holds him so, it is said, no ill effects can follow. But nobody has yet volunteered precise information as to how best to set the animal down again. Hence the widespread expression for a man in trouble: "He's got a skunk by the tail."

Even coyotes generally left the skunk alone, and emulated him in attacking the farmer's chickens. The chicken farmer does not like either of these animals.

But, as one of their defenders has put it, "What of that? After all, a chicken farmer makes *his* living robbing bird's nests."

THE GHOST DANCE

The Ghost Dance religion was originated by a Paiute Indian in Nevada, a dreamer named Wovoka, who believed himself to be Christ come again to earth. Because the white men had rejected and crucified him at his first coming, he said he had come this time to the Indians, who were certainly in need of a Messiah now that their whole world had crumbled about them. Wovoka promised a new dispensation and taught that a new earth would come to cover the old, and with it vast herds of buffalo and all the dead Indians brought back to life. The white man was to be destroyed by supernatural power and the quick and the dead were to live happily ever after in the old Indian way. All that was necessary was that the Indians should believe in their Messiah and dance the Ghost Dance at regular intervals.

In the dance, the leader threw the dancers into trances in which they often saw and talked with their dead relatives. Naturally, this new faith, with its strange mixture of Christian and Indian elements, aroused tremendous enthusiasm and set many men to dreaming. Some of these men could scarcely distinguish reality from visions. In these visions they often hunted buffalo. On several occasions, the hunter, on waking from his vision, found himself in actual possession of a piece of buffalo meat, though the buffalo had been practically exterminated on the Short Grass more than a dozen years before.

The Plains Indians are objective thinkers. Facts to them are stubborn things, and many of them found it very difficult to accept the new doctrine or believe in the promised restoration of all they held dear. Since the faithful had been taught that those who did not believe would be destroyed along with the white man, they used every means to persuade their recalcitrant relatives to accept the new Messiah. Nothing proved more convincing than a piece of juicy buffalo meat between the teeth.

That winter of 1890-91, a devout dreamer roused from his trance after a dance held at Cantonment on the upper Canadian River. In his vision he had been butchering a buffado—and now, here in his very hands, he held a hunk of fresh buffalo meat! His vision was true—and the Messiah's teaching must therefore be true also. Quickly, the head men of that camp were called to council, no longer doubting. They decided to send a part of the meat to Darlington, the agency, by special messenger, in order to convince their relatives. A man named Good Bear was selected; they gave him his instructions and the meat.

There was snow on the ground, and it was cold. At that season, Indian ponies were thin and weak from lack of proper forage. Moreover, it would be cold riding. Good Bear thought he could make better time afoot. It was about sixty miles as the crow flies. Good Bear belted his blanket about him, packed up the meat, and set out.

It was a long march through the snow, but on the

second afternoon Good Bear knew he had only a few miles to go. He arrived at the agency camps after dark, very cold and hungry. The tipis were strung along the river, hugging the shelter of the timber which marked its course. Good Bear made for the nearest tent, eager to feel the warmth of the fire which lighted it up from within.

His moccasins made no sound in the soft snow. No one was stirring outside. On the drying rack behind the tent Good Bear saw some half-frozen slabs of muscle meat hanging like towels on a wash-line. These, hard as iron and stiff with cold, made no appeal. But among them, twining like a snake, hung a long beef gut, ruddy with the fresh blood confined within it. The sight of that blood sausage made the man's mouth water. Impulsively, he cut one end of it with his knife, and swallowed in haste as much of the tepid liquid as his stomach would hold. Then he went into the tipi.

The old woman made him welcome. Her husband was out, but on learning what was up, she quickly sent one of her sons to inform the chief.

The strange news spread like wildfire through the camps, and within a few minutes her small tent was jammed with visitors, who crowded in, filling every foot of space—except that occupied by the fire in the middle. They sat and stood and squatted, listening in amazed silence to the wonderful story Good Bear had to tell.

The messenger thoroughly enjoyed his importance, and made a good story of it, dwelling upon every detail at some length, speaking with deliberation and gravity. They listened patiently, eagerly, watchfully; they were Cheyennes, not easily fooled. Good Bear worked up to his grand climax, dramatically opened his pack and produced the meat. *"Nohetto!"* he said. "There you are. Buffalo!"

The nearest Indians looked at it respectfully. One or two women sobbed with joy. A man hummed a hunting song. Those of a more skeptical turn looked closely at the meat, smelled it, even dared to poke it with irreverent fingers. The younger Indians had never eaten buffalo meat, but the old-timers had devoured tons of it. They knew that buffalo is not like beef—it is dark red in color, and of coarser fiber, like mutton. Was this buffalo? Some believed. Others watched Good Bear; was he lying? No one, however, ventured to call him a liar to his face. The discussion went on.

But Good Bear had no fears; it was evident that his mission would prove a success. The excitement was almost more than that small tent could hold.

Now any tipi, however large, with even a small fire inside, is very snug and warm in the coldest weather. When filled with people, such a small tent as the old woman's soon became insufferably hot and stuffy. Good Bear had just come in after two days on the cold prairies. His stomach was full of blood from the sausage he had looted. The excitement and the heat began to make him feel sick. But before he could get up and start out of the lodge, it was too late. He vomited up all that he had swallowed. Physical discomfort was joined with the shame he felt at being found out.

None of those Indians had ever seen a man lose so much blood and live. But, to their amazement, Good Bear, instead of dying, or even seeming sick, appeared to be all the better for his hemorrhage. Before, they had regarded the meat with divided hopes and doubts. But that Good Bear could survive at all was a plain miracle. It was a portent.

Good Bear was immensely relieved to find that they mistook the matter. Having stolen the food, he could make no explanation. Everything seemed to be going his way. He smiled and said nothing.

Importantly, the chief rose and pushed through the crowd into the open air. There he began to shout the good news up and down the river with a voice like a soprano roaring, a crier's voice. The women crowded around Good Bear, sobbing and laughing, stroking his face in blessing. They regarded him as their savior. Now they would not be buried with the white men under the new earth; they would have their old life back, their buffalo, their dead relatives. All were happy, many overwhelmed. Even the former skeptics had nothing to say. The miracle had swept away all doubt. The Messiah's messenger was genuine.

But the old woman, in whose tent all this had happened, had to clean up the mess. She was a practical, hard-working old soul, whose life had been spent in packing wood and water, tanning hides, butchering beeves, pounding out pemmican, packing mules—all that hard, down-to-earth labor of the savage housewife. To her this miracle was just another dirty job to do.

As she bent to do it, her sharp eyes saw several hairs swimming in the blood. Red hairs, white hairs—hairs that were manifestly from the hide of an agency cow! She had butchered too many of them to make any mistake about that. Instantly suspicion jerked her erect. She exclaimed under her breath, got up, and ran out of the tent. There, on the rack, hung her limp, deflated sausage. There, in the snow, were the tracks of the thief. Following them to her tent door, she came charging in, scolding at her guest at the top of her rusty lungs. Dramatically, she pointed to the hairs in the blood, and called Good Bear thief and liar to his face!

The messenger of the Messiah hung his head.

The crowd stood slient, then began to laugh and jeer. The chief broke off his loud oration. Good Bear was discredited, his mission a failure. Quickly, Good Bear stooped through the tent door, and hiding his head in his blanket, turned back to the darkness and cold of the snowy plains. . . .

A typical leader of the Ghost Dance was Black Coyote (*Watan-gaa*) of the Arapaho Tribe. Born about 1850 while the Indians were still running buffalo on the Plains, he was a thorough Indian with all an old-time Indian's love of the wandering hunter's life, and deeply interested in tribal religion, "medicine," and cere-monies, always to be seen at the annual Sun Dance, and a great believer in dreams.

The Arapahos are imaginative people with a volumi-nous mythology and a friendly, accommodating charac-ter, and also gifted with rich artistic talent. This did not prevent them from being valiant warriors, and their Sun Dance was a rigorous ordeal.

Black Coyote had all an Indian's love of personal prestige and aspired to be a leader in everything that concerned his people. When they agreed to go on the reservation in 1869 he made an honest effort to adapt himself to new conditions and "managed to accumulate considerable property in wagons and livestock, including three wives." (In the Fourteenth Annual Report of the Bureau of Ethnology, there is a section called "The Ghost Dance Religion and the Sioux Outbreak of 1890" by James Mooney. The quotations which follow are from this.)

He set his feet in the white man's road and at forty years of age had earned his full share of honor, being a tribal delegate to Washington, Captain of the Indian Police, and deputy sheriff of his county. He was a "good natured fellow, vain of his possessions and titles, but at the same time thoroughly loyal and reliable in the discharge of his duties and always ready to execute his orders at whatever personal risk." But he had a natural predisposition to religious matters and it was the ambition of his life to be a great priest and medicine man. This ambition led him to make the long trip to Nevada to visit the Messiah and bring back the first songs of the Ghost Dance.

"Black Coyote in full uniform, with official badge, a Harrison medal and an immense police overcoat which he procured in Washington, riding with his three wives in his own double-seated coach, was a spectacle magnificent and impressive. Black Coyote in breech-cloth, paint, and feathers, leading the Ghost Dance or sitting flat on the ground and beating the earth with his hand in excess of religious fervor was equally impressive."

At one time several of his children had died in rapid succession, and following the custom of his people, he fasted for four days, hoping to avoid further disaster. During his fast he heard a voice like the cry of an owl or the low bark of a dog. The voice warned him that if he wished to save his remaining children he must cut seventy pieces of skin from his body and offer them to the Sun. He at once cut out seven pieces, held them up as an offering to the Sun, prayed, and then buried them.

But the Sun would not let him off so easily. A second warning followed that the full number of seventy pieces must be sacrificed to save his children. This time Black Coyote obeyed instructions, sitting very erect and bracing himself firmly while a friend pierced his arm or chest with an awl, lifted the skin from the flesh and sliced it away with a thin-bladed knife.

The pieces of skin were cut out in various patterns: crosses, circles, and stripes. Some of these were several inches long and nearly half an inch wide. The largest was a representation of the sacred pipe of the tribe. Black Coyote boasted that he never flinched once during the ordeal. The scars of these wounds are to be seen in his photograph in the Smithsonian Institution in Washington. It is comforting to know that the sacrifice was not in vain; he lost no more children.

Under the leadership of Black Coyote and another Arapaho chief, Sitting Bull (not the famous Sioux Chief), the Ghost Dance grew and flourished among the Arapahos, until in September, 1890, Plains Indians to the number of 3,000 assembled and danced every night.

By ill luck a commission arrived at this time to treat with the Cheyenne and Arapahos for the sale of their reservation. On the advice of the leaders of the dance, the chiefs signed the agreement, believing that they needed the money and that the Messiah would restore the country to them within a short time in any case.

White missionaries had told the gospel story to the tribesmen, and the Indians had been deeply shocked, if not surprised, to learn how white men had cruelly put to death the Son of God. They knew He had been rejected, having no place to lay His head.

Accordingly the Indians made a home for the 'Messiah, pending His arrival, on a small red butte—Coyote Butte—not far from the town of Geary, Oklahoma. They pitched a fine tent up there and eqipped it with an iron bedstead, mattress, fine blankets and new comforts, and all other necessary furnishings. When the Ghost Dancing failed to bring the Messiah, these pathetic offerings remained on the hilltop until they fell to pieces and disappeared.

This butte and the white men's town, Watonga, both named after Black Coyote, are memorials of his leadership and his vain hopes.

HAUNTS AND HORSES

Indians at first felt that the white man was a disgusting animal with hair on his body and face like a beast, with odor stronger than that of two porcupines, and a pale yellow skin like the corpse of an Indian who had bled to death. The white man thinks of a ghost as white, but Indian ghosts were yellow. They had a bad habit of inhabiting living creatures sometimes. I knew an old Indian whose later years were made miserable by the fear of his dead wife who haunted him in the form of a white dog. Wherever he went, this white dog would appear, sometimes in the distance, sometimes at the door of his tent. At night he would hear it howling and see it in the moonlight. He did everything possible to avoid the creature. He cut his hair, dressed differently, changed his name, and moved away to another agency, but the white dog kept after him, following his trail wherever he went. He lived to a ripe old age in spite of his terror, but never was free from his domestic haunt.

He was almost as badly off as another old Indian who believed he had a skunk in his belly.

It was considered unlucky to have to sell one's saddle. In fact, it was unlucky, since a man could get a horse or get the use of one readily enough, while a good saddle cost a cowboy several months' wages. It was part of his equipment which he had to provide for himself.

To be buried in Boot Hill, the community graveyard reserved for men who died with their boots on—in other words, in a fight—was regarded by some as a disgrace, since the men so buried were not buried by their friends, but (as it were) in the Potter's Field. However, many Westerners not only expected to "die in the smoke," but looked forward to it. Buffalo Bill is a notable exception. The fear of dying in the arena of his show was his bugbear.

Of course, far more frontiersmen died by reason of falls from a horse than ever died by bullets. Kit Carson and Major Frank North are notable examples. A large proportion of rodeo riders have had their lives shortened if not abruptly ended by accidents or injuries sustained while working with "outlaws."

The optimism of Plains folks was due in part to the fact that in the new country they had to make a fresh start and throw overboard most of the ideas and customs of the regions from which they had come. The slate was washed nearly clean of misgivings because all the old omens were lacking. People who look for omens see them, always with the same sad results of fear and hesitation.

10. High, Wide, and Handsome

IN THE good old days on the Buffalo Plains, when an Indian orator had reached the passionate climax of his speech, and wished to overwhelm his hearers with the force and validity of his remarks, he would suddenly step forward, let fall his blanket, jerk off his breech-cloth, and display the tokens of his manhood to the admiration of the world.

Since those days, that virile, magnificent gesture has been the inspiration of countless Westerners, who have imitated it (in essentials, if not in detail) to their own great profit, and the glory of their kind. In fact, the underlying idea has been raised into a cult, poems have been written, songs composed, paintings and monuments created, and a whole industry built upon this worthy theme. One may say, metaphorically, that the history of the American Frontier is strewn with discarded breech-cloths.

For the white frontiersman, being in fact an immigrant into Indian country, necessarily accepted the aims and technique of his Indian hosts. He had to fight, to adopt the warrior culture dominant there. And as there was next to nothing to fight for, Glory became his goal, as it was the Indian's. He came to practice the savage's whole-hearted pursuit of Personal Prestige. That ideal dominated the Old West; and it still holds, so far as conditions permit. From Captain John Smith to the latest movie cowboy, it is the staple theme, the key to everything. Many admirable men came out of the West, bringing valuable gifts. But whatever else they left behind, most of them contrived to bring samples of ballyhoo. It was the most valuable product of the Frontier.

In its manufacture, the white man had great advantages over the Indian. For Poor Lo remained at home, lived in a small community of jealous rivals, had to produce witnesses to his exploits, had to produce the hair of the men he claimed to have sent to the Happy Hunting Grounds. He had no chance to get away with anything.

The frontiersman, however, was not so hampered. He was a rover. Moreover, he did his broadcasting in the settlements, where few could check his statements (or statements made about him); he could profit enormously by the western habit of ballyhoo. He could get away with murder. There is no western type, and hardly any famous western individual, whose reputation did not profit somewhat from the universal habit of glorifying everything and everybody from the West.

Had there been no Indian, there could have been no Frontier, no wars, no pillage, no adventure, only a mob of lusterless clodhoppers moving into the empty wilds a little farther each season. But with the Indian present, there were all these things, and the noble art of self-advertisement was discovered and improved upon. Not to grasp this is to miss a great part of the meaning of western history, and the consequent march of present-day events. There is no understanding of the West possible without constant reference to vanishing gee-strings. It all boils down to What a Man!

And what a man it boils down to! Mounting steadily from the first explorers (most of them rather prosaic persons), those who followed trailed ever greater clouds of glory to the peaks of national and international renown. Scientists like the Prince Maximilian von Wied, artists like Catlin, fur barons like Kenneth "Red Coat" McKenzie wining and dining in lone majesty in his fort in the wilds, and the humble, if even more imaginative, trappers—all of them had accepted to some extent the Indian's lordly manners. On the Plains, however, John Charles Frémont was the first man to do the thing in a big way. He made a national hero of the unassuming Kit Carson; his propaganda spread far and wide, and soon brought over the sympathetic, if somewhat condescending, tribe of English sportsmen and writers, such as George Frederick Ruxton and Lord Dunraven. By the end of the Mexican War, the West had already a glamor that refused to fade.

By the end of the Civil War, the tradition was well established. And with the great trek westward which followed the opening of the goldfields, the frontiersman was glorified out of all recognition. Everyone on the Frontier—slackers, draft-dodgers, fugitives from justice, horse-thieves, and murderers—shared in the benefits of romance which clothed every man of the West. Even Jesuit missionaries caught the spirit, and did not fail to record with gusto their contacts with the Indian chiefs whom they were saving from Sin and Soldiers. Father Pierre-Jean de Smet had a wonderful time in the camp of Sitting Bull; it was adventure with a capital A.

Then came the military and the wars of the seventies, with Custer and Buffalo Bill leading the parade in buckskins and long hair. Before that time, Indians killed by white men on the Plains had not been many. Trappers had told tall tales, of course, but the actual carnage was slight. Even the soldiers were modest: Generals Sully and Sibley claimed so few enemy casualties in 1863 and '64 that a senator objected to the campaign on the ground that a million dollars a head was too much to pay for dead Indians. But on the advent of the veterans of the Civil War, publicity improved; every frontiersman had victims to his credit. Indeed, if all the red men alleged to have been slain during those decades were laid end to end, they would reach from the house of Ananias to the castle of Baron Munchausen. By actual count the Indians reported killed by whites in those campaigns total considerably more than the entire population (men, women, and children) of the tribes involved, even taking the figures of the Indian Bureau's annuity contracts as the basis for our census —no modest estimate. Yet those tribes were not exterminated.

It was General George Armstrong Custer who first demonstrated to the West the true beauties and profits of advertising; he was quite as successful in aping the Indians in ballyhoo as in his haircut and costume. His report on his reconnaissance of the Black Hills in '74 (the expedition which caused the wars in which he lost his life) is a classic deserving of study by every realtor in the country. "The valley presented the most wonderful as well as beautiful aspect. Its equal I have never seen—In no private or public park have I ever seen such a profuse display of flowers. Every step of our march that day was amid flowers of the most exquisite color and perfume. So luxuriant in growth were they that the men picked them without dismounting from the saddle. It was a strange sight to glance back at the advancing columns of cavalry and behold the men with beautiful bouquets in their hands, while the head-gear of the horses were decorated with wreaths of flowers fit to crown a Queen of May. Deeming it a most fitting appellation, I named this Floral Valley. . . . Through this beautiful valley meanders a stream of crystal water so cold as to render ice undesirable even at noonday." And when they got into the Hills, "Instead of being among barren peaks, we found ourselves wending our way through a little park, whose natural beauty may well bear comparison with the fairest portions of Central Park."

He goes on to rhapsodize about "rippling streams," "beautiful flowers, grazing whose only fault, if any, was the great luxuriance. . . . I know no portion of our country where Nature has done so much to prepare homes for husbandmen and left so little for the latter to do as here. . . . Nowhere in the States have I tasted cultivated berries of better flavor than those found growing wild here . . . hundreds of acres. . . . Wild strawberries, wild currants, gooseberries, blueberries, wild cherries, in great profusion. Cattle could winter in these valleys without other food or shelter than that to be obtained from running at large."

If anything more idyllic or appetizing than that has

been penned by a western booster, it ought to be written in letters of gold in pictures of silver. Just what all these berries and posies had to do with establishing a post in the Black Hills to overawe the Sioux is not very clear. But when we learn that Custer had ambitions extending to the White House and was about to add that he had found gold in the grassroots, the purpose of his amazing military report becomes manifest.

And so Custer rode magniloquently on his way in his fringed buckskins and his flowing hair, followed by the flower-decked troopers, heading—as he imagined—for the presidency. But evidently the gods considered his ballyhoo for the Black Hills too good to be wasted on a mere temporary fame like that. It led to the stampede of miners into those hills, brought on the Sioux Wars, caused Custer to die valiantly and mysteriously on the bluffs by the Little Big Horn, and so attain a renown which the realization of his ambitions could never have secured. Custer's fate added mystery to the romance and adventure of the glamorous West.

Custer, however, was not the only white hero who owed his fame to Indians, and to Indian methods of publicity. When Sitting Bull fled to Canada in '77, the Royal Northwest Mounted Police was a new organization, and virtually unknown. But, as an historian of the force, Longstreth, has well shown, Sitting Bull made it famous. His actions were front-page stuff around the world after Custer's fall, and whenever he was mentioned during his five years north of the line, the Red Coats were mentioned too. Having had greatness thrust upon them, thanks to the Sioux, the Red Coats valiantly maintained it, and may be relied upon to furnish thrills

for a long time to come. They always get their publicity.

With the surrender of Sitting Bull came the end of
Indian wars. No longer could men gain renown by
shooting redskins, real or imaginary. From that date
the Glory of the West began to fade. Not, at first, per-
ceptibly. Buffalo Bill took care of that. Seizing the tradition before it died, he proceeded to cash in on it by
glorifying the American frontiersman. For a while that
was a great success. He was the Ziegfeld of the Plains.

From Custer's fall in '76 to Buffalo Bill's command
performances at Queen Victoria's Jubilee in '87 was
the golden period of western glory. For Buffalo Bill,
though not comparable with Custer as an historical figure, being (as some malicious military critic has put it)
"just a beef contractor" (of buffalo beef), was nevertheless far more kingly, gracious, and impressive than the
undersized and somewhat arrogant general. And as
Buffalo Bill's ambitions were entirely commercial, he
was more willing to share his publicity with those who
could help him.

With the end of the Indian wars, the hero business
declined. Much as his press agent and publisher made
of his renown as an Indian fighter, Buffalo Bill had
small chance to retain his place as a romantic hero; he
was becoming a curiosity, he was heading for the museum. He saw that he must take the Indian into partner-
ship, or go out of the hero business. And so he hired
Sitting Bull to travel with the Wild West in 1885.

Sitting Bull was the sensation of the Show. Whenever he appeared in the arena, the crowds hailed him
with curses and cat-calls, spitballs and empty bottles.

Cries of "Hang him! Kill him!" resounded through the
stands, and often enough Cody had all he could do to
quell the riot. The people in the States hated the chief,
whom they thought the "murderer" of Custer; he
aroused more excitement than anybody on the program.
Buffalo Bill called this Sitting Bull's "unpopularity."

In Canada, Sitting Bull was quite as great a problem
in another way. The Canadians had no illusions about
the Toms, Dicks, and Harrys of the American border.
They had observed how quickly the Royal Mounted
had put a sudden stop to their antics north of the line.
They considered, as *Punch* says of the cavalry, that
Buffalo Bill called himself a frontiersman so as to "lend
tone" to what would otherwise have been a lot of vul-
gar brawlers. They were not taken in by his kingly
presence; they did not think him typical of the class he
did so much to make romantic and respectable. Sitting
Bull, however, was the real thing, and a superior article.
Mayors and Members of Parliament thronged to his
tipi to do him honor, greeted him with congratulatory
addresses. The Canadian press gave him three times the
space allotted to Buffalo Bill. One way or another, the
Indian was stealing Cody's Show.

For somehow everyone who thought twice about the
matter saw that the long-haired frontiersman was only
a sham Indian, and naturally preferred the real thing.
And this was a true hunch. All the most famous of the
Plainsmen took their place because they were less of
a sham than others, more like the Indians. Kit Carson
and Jim Bridger with their *coups* and their tipis and
their squaws; Buffalo Bill with his scalp of Yellow
Hand; Custer with his long hair and buckskin fringes.

Every one of these men owed a large share of his renown not merely to fighting Indians, but to aping them.
They were imitations, not realities, as much actors as
any movie cowboys of our day. It was the old breech-
cloth trick with modern trimmings.

What wonder that, when the novelty of the Wild
West Show palled, people began to suspect that the
Indian fighters were not all they had been cracked up
to be! By 1890 the Indian had been so thoroughly pacified that press agents were utterly unable to maintain
the public's enthusiasm at its old level.

But in 1890 came the Ghost Dance, and the Indian
was once more front-page stuff. The Sioux, especially,
were mentioned, and when the Sioux were mentioned
Sitting Bull was dragged in too. Buffalo Bill saw a daz-
zling opportunity to gather heaps of free publicity and
restore his waning glory; he persuaded General Nelson
A. Miles to give him authority to arrest Sitting Bull.
Had he been permitted to attempt it, he might have
added thousands to his gate receipts. But the Indian
Agent, Major James McLaughlin, wanted to make the
arrest himself; he managed to get Colonel Cody's order
rescinded. Thereupon followed a revival of the old feud
between the Indian Bureau and the War Department,
with the result that Sitting Bull's arrest was forced
through, and the old man killed. Buffalo Bill was thus
the indirect cause of the death of the one man whose
fame could have kept the Wild West Show going at its
former speed.

From that day, the Wild West showed a constantly de-
clining profit. After Buffalo Bill there were Pawnee
Bill and other Bills, until at last the business had to

combine with the circus, and the hero was lost among the clowns. War paint gave way to grease paint. Colonel Cody's magnificent effort failed. The good old racket was moribund.

Marshals and Bandits and Vigilantes did something to keep up the heroic tradition. But there was always a lurking suspicion that the "killings" of the newer West were unnecessary and often murderous. It was not magnificent, and it was not war. Gunmen and marshals proved a poor substitute for "Injuns," no matter how madly the old gee-string flagged the breeze.

Westerners began to be suspicious, resentful, touchy. They talked about "God's country," and obviously con-sidered it Man's duty to love and approve all their ways. Tenderfeet had to go through an initiation at the hands of these vicars of God, before they could be tol-erated. And if they ventured to express the least dis-satisfaction with the region, they were asked indig-nantly, "If you don't like this country, why in hell don't you leave it?" The natives had to inculcate a spirit which no longer flourished spontaneously. The tradi-tion was gone to seed.

And then, suddenly, by a queer turn of fate, a stran-ger came. An asthmatic youngster, a conscientious he-man, a Harvard graduate—if you please, an Eastern politician appeared. Theodore Roosevelt. He donned the gay fringed buckskins, gripped the trusty rifle, climbed into the old horned saddle, rode the Plains once more. He shot big game, made a terrible failure of his cattle ranch (never mind that), challenged the Marquis de Mores, a nobleman (even more "effete" than a Harvard man) to a duel, and went about dutifully exclaiming at all the stock sights and stunts of the now thoroughly codified legend. He made the West a good show once more, and how the Westerners loved him for it! We folks beyond the Missouri found Teddy a regular shot in the arm; he made it all seem possible once more. When you get a President into the cast, you can afford to raise the price of seats.

Moreover, Teddy *was* a fighting man. There was the Spanish war. The big felt hat, the guns and saddles and marksmanship were useful after all. Nobody cared to question the tradition in the West after that for a while; there were too many Rough Riders about.

But even the Rough Riders have suffered a decline. There may be no more great men owing their fame to deeds of valor (real or imaginary) on the Plains. The cowboys (now more numerous than ever before) are all very well as a class; but who is *the* great cowboy? Think of a Trapper, Kit Carson leaps to mind; think of an Indian fighter, and Custer is seen brandishing his carbine. But say Cowboy, and you think of Hollywood; nobody was ever a great cowboy of international renown. The greatest is only one of many.

When this was realized, the western vogue of strong, silent men came in. When there was so little to tell, why tell it? Stern-lipped silence was better than a feeble yarn. The garrulous Jim Bridger has been succeeded by the taciturn cowboy, who is not unaware that somebody, some low-down son-of-a-what-not, has called him "a hired man on horseback," and "chambermaid to a cow." And so the cowboy had to call on rank outsiders to bolster his shaken rating; he put chaps and sombrero on Calvin Coolidge, photographed the result, and took courage. To such a pass had come the fashion set by Roosevelt.

The professional he-man of the Plains has by now dwindled pretty completely into the dude on the dude-ranch. The dude upholds the dress-up and show-off tradition; he carries on. For, once you scan them carefully, you observe that nearly all the famous early frontiersmen were actually dudes, runaway boys playing Injun, who have now grown wiser and sadder, and sold their trappings to the tourists, who are their legitimate successors.

The Indian is the one figure on the Frontier who has not lost caste because of the civilizing of the region. He still stands for something; he is the genuine article. His prestige has not suffered appreciably; small boys are still afraid of his long hair. The trappers and the explorers, the fur barons and the scouts, the soldiers and the showmen, the bandits and the cowmen, all have taken their turn upon the Indian's stage and performed the old Indian trick to satiety. They are through. But the Red Man, master of ceremonies, remains.

He too will pass, is passing. Old-timers are few now. But the West will be a long time forgetting the good old game he taught it. Ballyhoo still has a surefire appeal for those who are hardly awake to modern life. The front-page heroes for some time to come will follow the Indian's method. Breech-cloths will still be waving. The West will be histrionic to the last.

On the Short Grass Plains, however, there is ample justification for this state of mind, which is not merely indigenous and traditional, but enforced by the land

and its climate. For the Short Grass is a region of superlatives, of extremes, of incredible excesses.

It grows the shortest grass—and the tallest; has the widest rivers—with the least water in them; the thickest dust and the deepest mud, the least rain and the heaviest downpours; the hottest days and the coolest nights; the brightest sunshine and the blackest clouds; the strongest winds, the most magnificent electrical storms, the longest summers, and the shortest winters, the biggest hail, the loudest thunder, and the brightest moonlight in the whole Mississippi Valley.

There the cattle had the longest horns and the shortest tempers. There the water makes you thirsty, the squirrels live underground, and the spiders have fur. There the riders have legs like a pulley-bone—they are so bowlegged they sit around a chair, not on it.

The native animals are all superlative in strength, toughness, stamina, or speed. The Plains buffalo is bigger than the woods buffalo, the antelope is swifter than anything that runs, with more curiosity than a goat— and hollow horns which it sheds like a deer. The jackrabbit is speedier than any other hare, the centipedes have more legs, the scorpions sharper tails. Rattlesnakes are bigger and more venomous. Wolves are fiercer, coyotes more cunning than in other regions. And in addition to greater power and size, these creatures were more numerous than elsewhere.

Even imported animals soon acquired superior toughness on the Short Grass. The mustang, running wild, became swifter, hardier, warier than his ancestors. He hardly ever gave in, and almost never gave out. As that great Texan, Charles Goodnight, said of the Staked

Plains, "It produces better cattle, why shouldn't it produce better men?" This opinion (quoted here from J. Evetts Haley's biography of Goodnight) is accepted as an obvious fact by all truebred Plainsmen, and supported by the statement of Henry Fairfield Osborn, the great paleontologist: "All recent ethnologic and physiographic evidence points in the same way, namely, that intelligent progressive and self-adaptive types of mankind arise in elevated upland or semi-arid environments where the struggle for food is intense and where reliance is made on the invention and development of implements as well as weapons." Osborn's evidence appears in an article entitled "The Plateau Habitat of the Pro-Dawn Man," *Science*, 1928.

In such a country and with such a tradition, we shall expect some outward and visible signs of the faith and experience of the natives, and this we find in the customary wearing of cowboy hats and boots. These are no longer restricted to cowmen, but are worn at times— if not all the time—by every man who fancies himself or his profession as something special. He adopts them as a mark of his superiority, independence, and loyalty to the local mores. Oilmen, businessmen, showmen, politicians, writers, artists, superintendents of schools, hotel men, college boys—and college deans for that matter—affect the boots and big hats.

The boot is comfortable as a slipper, free in the heel, with a firm sole supporting the arch, and is excellent protection against wet and cold—as well as cactus, stones, and snakebite.

It is ideal for driving a car in winter, keeping the foot warm and the ankles free from drafts. It does not bind the leg, and in the saddle the stiff sole takes all strain off the arch, no matter how the foot rests in the stirrup.

Moreover, the boot is a symbol of more than racial and heroic tradition, more than a comfortable footgear. Nobody can walk far in high-heeled boots without discomfort or burning blisters on his heels. To wear boots is therefore evidence that a man can afford to ride outdoors, and sit indoors—a mark of caste.

Men who prefer boots but have to work on their feet wear high-heeled "boot-style" shoes—high lace shoes that prevent the heel from slipping up and down and so causing discomfort.

Moreover, boots are decorative and expensive, as well as comfortable. Owners take pride in having them custom-made, rather than machine-made, and also in the name of the bootmaker, choosing him with quite as much care as any English gentleman uses in choosing a tailor in Bond Street.

A good pair of boots from Nocona, Amarillo, San Antonio, or Fort Worth may cost from $17.50 to $75.00. Poor men wear them plain, rich men have them made of two-toned alligator, while college boys, dudes, and rodeo riders buy boots with tricky inlays, wing tips, fancy stitching, and designs of diamonds, spades, or hearts, birds, flowers, and butterflies applied in bright-colored leathers, on a background of black, tan, or white. Some are high boots for dress, others low for comfort. But all have the high sloping heels, the pointed, square-ended toes, the characteristic tops.

And so with hats—worn with crowns flattened, crushed, or cleft, brims straight or rolled according to local custom or personal taste. A "John B. Stetson" of "genuwine beaver" may cost as high as sixty dollars. An old-time cowboy thought no expense too great when buying these prime parts of his equipment. That lavish tradition persists today.

Indeed it is thriving as never before—just as knighthood in Europe flourished most colorfully after gunpowder had put the armored knight (the tank of those days) out of business, and the tournament had supplanted war. And why not?

In all ages fighting men of spirit have gone in for colorful clothes and equipment—armor, uniforms, paint and feathers. It is reassuring to know that the rule still holds among ourselves, considering the kind of world we live in.

The cowboy who follows the rodeos must be a man of iron nerve, and takes quite as many chances as your soldier does.

And so one finds homesick boys from the Short Grass shedding their city shoes for cowboy boots when they come home to the boarding house at night. One reads of a Texas aviator flying planes to Britain in Texas boots "to bring him luck."

Maybe the lonely expanse of the Atlantic reminds him of the High Plains, where—as the Plainsman puts it, with inverted pride—"you can see farther and see less than anywhere else on earth."

This spirit of manhood unashamed is a greater asset to the nation than the oil and cattle of the High Plains. May it never die.

11. Black Blizzard

IN MOST countries the weather is unusual some of the time; on the High Plains it is unusual all of the time. It is generally agreeable. But if you do not like it, never mind; in half an hour's time it will be different.

One hot day a man was driving a team, when one horse died of sunstroke. Before he could get the harness off the dead horse, they say, a norther struck, and the live horse froze to death.

This country climbs steadily westward to the base of the Rockies, where it reaches an altitude of some 5,000 feet above sea level. It is nowhere below 1,000 feet. That, more than anything else, explains why the High Plains are so different from the Prairies east of the Missouri and the Mississippi. The first thing one must do, to understand the Plains, is to give up, once and for all, the notion that prairies and plains are all alike. Of course, people refer sometimes to "the prairie" on the Plains, meaning the open, grassy portions—but merely as a distinction from the buttes, breaks, canyons, mountains, and sinks which diversify the High Plains. Prairie and Plain, however, must never be confused. They are as different as a gentle lady and a tough old squaw.

Moreover, the region is not a unit in climate or

topography. Plainsmen, at any rate, feel this strongly. Once Charley Russell, who painted the Northern Plains with such mastery, was invited down to the Short Grass to paint the life of that region; his host, owner of a vast ranch, offered Charley every facility and all expenses for a prolonged stay. But Charley declined. He said, "A man can't paint a country unless he has lived in it for years."

All over the Plains, from Texas to Canada, the annual rainfall is about the same—even during the growing season, when most of it occurs. Of course, there are local variations, but throughout the region the annual rainfall probably averages between fifteen and twenty inches.

North of Kansas, where there is less sunshine and the northerly winds blow off the mountains, the humidity is generally sufficient for wheat farming. During the growing season sudden changes of temperature are rare, and the winds keep along the surface of the earth, so that the moisture they pick up from the soil is not lost. Rains there are commonly gentle and last for hours. The humidity remains.

But in the Short Grass region south of Nebraska conditions are very different. Down there the sun is hot and keeps on shining. The summers are longer, the altitude higher, and drastic changes in temperature more frequent. Under such conditions, air near the earth is swept upwards, to carry away with it the moisture it has taken from the grass. The evaporation is great.

But this is not the worst. For almost three thousand hours every year warm southerly winds blow across the grass at an average rate of more than ten miles an hour.

Sometimes these winds reach a speed of sixty miles an hour, and occasionally are so hot that even at night a windowpane is unpleasantly warm to touch.

These hot winds not only parch grass and soil, but cause vertical disturbances of the atmosphere and so bring the rain in violent downpours of brief duration and local extent. On the Short Grass it never rains but it pours!

These sudden storms are soon over, and after a morning drenching, the road will blow dust in the afternoon. In effect, the Short Grass has a *dry* climate.

The open winters, the early springs, the sunny, crisp autumns make the Short Grass generally pleasant eight months in the year. Even in summer, the nights are cool, and sleepers-out need blankets. But the hot summers are overlong, the sun strikes hard and heavy through the clear air. To this is added the everlasting wind, warm, dry, blowing hour after hour, day after day, month after month, scouring the hard-packed earth, winnowing the grass, blowing away everything that is loose.

For the *four months*—June, July, August, September —of a sample year at Dodge City, the following figures are eloquent:

WIND

Average mean velocity: 11 miles per hour.
Average maximum velocity: 45 miles per hour.
Duration of south wind: 1,420 hours.
Calm (no wind): 27 hours.

In such a windy country, a man gets tired just doing nothing. To stand and take it is wearing on the nerves;

to walk against it is like wading upstream in a torrent
or into a heavy surf; even to ride into it becomes fa-
tiguing in the long run. Strangers find it trying, become irritable and touchy, while women sometimes give
way entirely. In the old days when people were less shel-
tered and more alone than now, many a good woman
went crazy with the wind.

But people get used to the wind in time, "get to
where they never notice it," even get to *miss* it, when
a rare hour of calm supervenes. Such an interval of
calm is as startling to a Plainsman as a piece of level
ground is to a mountaineer.

But when the everlasting wind is at its hottest, dryest,
and swiftest, the tension grows severe for those who are
not acclimated. It parches the skin, burns the face, dries
up the nostrils, splits the lips. A weather-beaten skin is
turned to leather where it is not burned to a peel. Even
Indians find it hard to bear. Many a white man lost his
life because some sunburned naked savage coveted his
shirt.

Yet there are compensations for those who find the
hot winds hard to take. For the worst season—summer—
is also the time when the most people take their vacations, and can get away to the Rockies or the Ozarks,
to the lakes or the seashore for a cooling-off. In many
parts of America people have to spend the worst part of
the year at home and find summer vacations their only
respite from bad weather. On the Short Grass, folks are
more fortunate—the time they spend at home is the best
part of the year.

But the worst trial on the High Plains is a by-product
of the wind: dust. Sometimes this gets so bad as to be

frightening in certain places, with the result that the whole region has become popularly known as "the Dust Bowl."

The Dust Bowl is rather a recurrent condition than a definite locality. Drouths have been known on the semi-arid plains since the earliest records ever made. Old Kiowa Indian calendars painted on hides in a spiral of mnemonic pictographs record drouths as early as the 1850's. These have recurred as have the earthquakes in California, the floods in the Mississippi Valley, the hurricanes on the Atlantic coast, the blizzards of the North Central States, the forest fires in the woodlands, the landslides and cloudbursts in the mountains. Moreover, the loss in life, health, property caused by drouth on the Plains has been generally far less than that caused by regional disasters in other parts of the country.

Each drouth has had its migration. The last disaster was greater because it coincided with the Depression. In the past, when the drouth came, the Short Grass farmer, if unable to hold on, was always welcome in the factories and cities, but in the 1930's the Depression had already sent multitudes back to the land and the "busted" farmer had no place to go.

He found himself "burned out, blowed out, eat out, and tractored out." Free, white, unwilling paupers, all the men of the Dust Bowl asked was a chance. Their diet had become "little or nothing, boiled down," and they ate it up "faster than they could make it." The land had dried out five years handrunning. The wind which brought the rain in ordinary seasons now swept the soil itself away, buried the farmer's tools in dunes of sand, filled the very flowers on the fruit trees so that insects could not fertilize them. Where his plowed fields had been, sand dunes piled up forming a waterless beach. The wind erected its own monuments.

It was a hard life, but the farmer was true to his pioneer tradition. "He didn't aim to set there and let nobody feed him." He was as "nigh to nothin' as ever was seen." The farmer would have "toughed it through" rather than "turn the land loose," firm in his convictions that "it used to make good, maybeso it will again." Section after section dried up and blew away and it seemed that a man *must* sell out or "give out." Some just walked out and never stopped to shut the door. All they had to start with was a family of kids. It seemed to them that the old Biblical text expressed the situation perfectly:

"And thy heaven that is over thy head shall be brass, and the earth that is under thee shall be iron.

"The LORD shall make the rain of thy land powder and dust: from heaven shall it come down upon thee until thou be destroyed."

In the end, the soil became as fruitless as the barbed wire that enclosed it. The simple devices used in the past—a good well, a dirt tank to water the garden truck, fields of kafir corn, milo maize, feterita, Sudan grass, sorghum and beans, watermelons, cantaloupes, cows, hogs, plenty of chickens—all these vanished. The traveler saw only a parched, half-buried shack, a haggard windmill, a wagon or hayrake bogged forlornly in the dunes of drifting sand, a barbed-wire fence clogged with mounded tumbleweeds. Any living beasts were starving to death, and the man with a mortgage, the sharecropper, the tenant found himself unable to stick.

He didn't want relief, as a rule. But he could not sit still and watch his wife go mad from monotony and blasted hope. He wanted to grow what he ate, to go where she could live "decent." He had not lost all faith in the land. He knew that dust bowls form and heal like sores; but he hadn't the means to carry on while the land was convalescent.

Conditions were generally worst where Kansas, Colorado, Oklahoma, New Mexico, and Texas come together, centering about the Panhandles of Oklahoma and Texas. This Panhandle country had been depopulated more than once before. In 1855, there had been drouth; in 1868, grasshoppers devoured everything; in 1874, the summer was one of the hottest and driest ever known; and two years later the grasshoppers plagued the land again. In the late 1880's, western Kansas was almost swept clear of farm folk, who gladly abandoned their homes and rushed into the Cherokee Strip and old Oklahoma when these lands were thrown open to settlement. In 1893 and '95 again, the Panhandles were depopulated.

But the farmer always came back.

More and more were able to hang on through the drouths after 1900 and at the time of the first World War. When the rains fell no country could compare with the Short Grass in the eyes of the natives. Green prairies, spangled with flowers, were breathtaking in their beauty in the spring. Except for the drouth, all evil seasons were of short duration. Cloudbursts, blizzards, tornadoes, all were of short duration and passed quickly. In that high country, rising to more than 5,000 feet above sea level, the glorious skies and clear air soon made a man forget his troubles. He did not ask for much—not merely because he did not expect it, but because he did not think too much civilization was good for a man. The Plainsman had something of the old Indian spirit. In an Indian house, you will find an old warrior sleeping in his blanket on the hard floor in the same room with an unoccupied bed with springs and mattress, which he keeps for visitors. The luxuries of the Plainsman have seldom been of the sort that soften a man.

Few regions have a better all-round climate, though it is not of the enervating type which attracts tourists. Even in wet seasons, the weather is seldom muggy. High humidity and high temperature rarely occur together, and then only for a day or two. This year, as I write, the Panhandle country, refreshed by plentiful rains, is blooming like a garden.

But beginning in 1931, the Depression cut farm profits to the bone. Workers left, foreclosures multiplied, and the use of farm machinery was forced more and more upon the owners. Scarcity of labor caused machinery to take the place of horses, so that more and more pasture-land was plowed up. Merchants failed, schools dwindled and died, churches languished. In Texas, where the poll tax disfranchised poor men, the men who suffered most could get no help from Congress.

American pioneer farming was organized in the old days of the Frontier when it was taken for granted that a man could supply himself with wild meat, and raise his grain and vegetables on the land. With the destruction of the game and the hot winds which made the dried cornstalks rattle in the field, the old conception of the farm as a means of subsistence faded. Farms were becoming food-factories, and the factory-hand found himself out of a job. The very leaves on the trees dried up and dropped off before the frost.

But it is time to let the Short Grass folks speak for themselves. I have selected two letters from friends, narrating their adventures, and some impromptu verses to follow them.

In the Town

"February 27, 1935, we were visited by our first dust storm, I say 'visited' as we had dust of every color and type, entirely foreign to our soil.

"It so happened that a group of the Bridge Club were having a seven o'clock bridge luncheon at our home. In the late afternoon we had our tables set for twenty-eight guests. We noticed it was getting dark. Looking out we could see what looked to us like a cloud of smoke; it continued to grow darker and darker, and coming nearer and nearer, it was not long until the dust was sifting in at every crack. We started pulling window shades, then commenced grabbing anything and everything available to cover our tables and food.

"In the midst of this the electric current went off, leaving us in complete darkness. After lighting a few candles, we decided to try to locate some coal-oil lamps. I had two (relics of old days). We got these cleaned, filled and burning, then phoned other club members and borrowed what they chanced to have.

"By this time the phone commenced to ring and always it was the same question, 'Are you going to have the party?' Our answer was, 'Why, of course. Do you think you can make it?' 'Oh, I think so, we have a flashlight.'

"Next we got out the dust cloths and took turns dusting until the guests arrived. This wasn't supposed to be a mask party, but almost turned out to be one as the guests arrived wearing old shawls, coats, and even quilts to protect their clothing.

"Their faces were so covered with dust that you couldn't tell them from colored persons.

"One gentleman came with a black eye, it being so dark that he missed his car and struck the side of a building.

"We disposed of the wraps, directed the way to the bathroom so each might wash his face, and with many a joke and all having a good time went on with the party.

"Before the evening drew to a close the lights came on and by the time the guests departed the stars were shining and the dust had passed on to some other locality.

"It brought to our minds the old saying, 'Every cloud has a silver lining. . . .' "

ON THE FARM

"The dust storm that made the most vivid impression on me occurred one Saturday, about the middle of March, 1935.

"Our first storm came during the last week of February and storms continued until May 20th.

"Sometimes only one severe storm in a week and sometimes three or four.

"On this particular day my husband was to work on a lake project fifteen miles from our home. He always rode to his work with two neighbor boys and as he had to walk three-quarters of a mile across a pasture to meet them, he had to leave home by a little after six o'clock.

"That morning was clear and quiet when we wakened, and I set about my day's tasks with a feeling of cheerfulness.

"Our cattle were a constant worry. Daily they were growing weaker on their poor ration of Russian thistles, moistened with a little molasses-sweetened water.

"There had been no bad storms for several days now —maybe the worst was over.

"I got breakfast and packed my husband's lunch and as soon as he had eaten he started on his walk across the pasture.

"It was just coming daylight.

"He had been gone hardly more than two minutes when I heard a low sighing moan through the cottonwood trees—first warning of a rising wind—(I doubt that screaming sirens in air-raid-threatened cities of Europe have much more terror for the inhabitants than the sound of a rising wind came to have for the Dust Bowl dwellers that spring).

"My heart seemed to leap into my throat; I felt sick and weak. I went out of doors and with wetted finger felt for the direction of the wind. Almost west, just a little south of west, and my husband out there in the pasture would be facing right into it!

"Scarcely more than another minute had passed until the nauseating smell of greasy dust was brought by a stronger puff of wind, and then I could see the tumbling cloud of dust, rolling down the slope of the pasture toward the house, wiping out the familiar landscape, as completely as a spit-wet palm wipes the drawing from a slate.

"My husband had vanished into that shrieking, whirling, tossing bedlam. I went back into the house, hastily covered the table with newspapers and an old cloth, covered the water pail, covered all the unwashed cooking utensils, made my bed and spread an old denim comfort over it and peeked into our son's bedroom to see if he was awake yet. His head was covered and I did not speak to him.

"Next I put on an old stocking cap to protect my hair, an old jacket to comfort my shaking body, and sat down by the kitchen range with my feet on the oven door.

"The room soon filled with a dust haze through which the coal-oil lamp made a pale light, and for the first and only time during the dust storms I abandoned myself to an orgy of weeping. There was no danger of waking the boy with my noisy crying for by this time the din of the elements completely overwhelmed any noise a human might make.

"An hour passed. Long shuddering sobs still racked my body. Occasionally I put a stick of wood in the fire.

"Then—there was a fumbling at the door knob, the door opened and my husband staggered in. Except in general outline he hardly looked like a human. His eyes were bloodshot, the lashes caked with mud formed from dust and tears. His lips and the end of his nose were crusted with mud, but he was back in the shelter of home again, so nothing else mattered.

"He had tried to reach the road, thinking that the boys might have started a little early and be waiting for him. He thought by keeping the storm full in his face he could walk straight enough to reach the road. But when he finally stumbled into the head of a small ravine that he recognized, and which was not quite half way to the road, he gave up, followed the ravine to a hog-lot fence, and the fence back to the buildings. By this time the boy had gotten up and I fixed him a scanty breakfast while his Dad 'cleaned up.' 'Cleaning up' included washing the eyes with boric acid water, gargling the throat with an antiseptic and swabbing out the nostrils with vaseline.

"This dust was very irritating to all delicate tissues, and we had already heard of deaths from dust-pneumonia farther west.

"Then we started a fire in the living room, lighted the gas lamp, and sat down to pass the time as best we could until the storm passed.

"Between nine and ten o'clock we heard a noise on the porch, and looking out we saw a hideous face pressed against the window of the door. The boys my husband had started out to meet had reached our place.

"They had left home a few minutes before the storm struck and thought it easier to come on three miles with the storm than to try to turn around and go back three-quarters of a mile into it.

"They had taken turns walking a few steps in front of the car. The headlights would show the walker, but would not light the sides of the road—and much of the road was on a fairly high grade. They were hustled to the kitchen for the cleansing process.

"When noon came it was still too bad to prepare a meal. The men had their lunches so I fixed sandwiches, fruit and milk for Sonny and me. The sandwiches and freshly wiped apples I put in paper sacks. The milk in pint jars with screw tops.

"Between two and three o'clock in the afternoon the wind eased, so that there was visibility for several rods.

"The boys left with the first easing of the storm as they knew their mother, a widow, would be frantic with worry.

"Husband and son got out and watered and fed the chickens, and turned the stock out to water.

"I went to the kitchen to the dreary task of cleaning, almost as weary as though my body had actually been beaten by the storm.

"So much dust collected in the hair on the backs of the cattle that when they shed in the spring, hair and dirt came off together, leaving patches of hide as bare as if they had been shaved.

"Some of the girls who taught in rural school had a time. One of them tied three children together one night, with her own stockings, and took them to a barbed wire fence they could follow home. Their Daddy was away, the mother had smaller children to care for and the nearest road to their home was blocked with dust drifts."

KANSAS DUST

Oh! I am so tired this morning,
  So tired of the dirt and grime.
The wind blew all day yesterday
  And my house with dirt is lined.

I wearily got the breakfast
  And then I sat down with a sigh,
And then I thought, "This will get me nowhere,
  There's no time to sit and cry."

So I roll up my sleeves and get busy,
  I scrub every corner and nook,
For I think when I am finished
  How nice it is going to look.

There is a real satisfaction in cleaning,
  But I well know if it doesn't rain,
The wind will blow tomorrow
  And I shall have to do it all over again.

"OKLAHOMA RAIN"

Feeding the family was a hard job, and at first it seemed as if everybody would starve to death. Food was no sooner placed on the table than it was covered with what seemed a layer of fine black salt. Every morsel was grit between the teeth at the first bite, and then mud on the tongue. Hungry children, tired men, could not down such food, and quickly gave up trying. Milk and coffee were liquid mud, and added to disgust was the fear of infection.

But as storm after storm followed, smart housewives

found ingenious ways of preparing food with a minimum of dust. Liquids they put into Mason jars with screw tops and rubber collars. They learned to mix dough in a bureau drawer—almost closed—thrusting their arms through two holes cut in a cloth covering the opening. They baked nearly everything in the oven of the range, and fried meat on a hot stove, so that the warm air, rising from the pan, carried the dust upward. All food was kept in covered containers, and those women who had ice-boxes and electric refrigerators sealed tight against the outer air counted themselves lucky, and thanked God for American ingenuity. As soon as food was cooked, it was served from the stove piping hot, and every plate was immediately covered by a cloth. Milk and coffee were drunk through straws from bottles.

The moment the first sign of a coming dust cloud appeared, everyone hurried to fill every available container with drinking water to last through the ordeal. At that, the only person who got his ration clean was the baby at his mother's breast.

People learned not to leave the house during a storm, and if caught driving, would stop and park the car to wait until the storm was over, though it lasted half a day. Men on foot clung to some shrub, or tree, or followed a wire fence hand over hand until they reached shelter. It was a perfect blackout.

As for sleeping—how could anyone sleep with his bedding and clothing thick with dust? To leave the window open or the door ajar was intolerable. Yet to keep them closed on a warm night was suffocating. Everyone was coughing and wheezing, and a man who could spit at all, spat mud. The only way one could sleep was with a wet cloth masking the face, and young children were in danger of their lives because they threw off their masks. No one could watch them, for no one could see to watch. Houses in the Southern country are not so tightly built as they are in the North, and the dry winds had a way of warping wood, or finding crevices around windows and doors, even of stone or brick buildings. Nothing, it seemed, would keep out the dust. You could not see a person across the room. At school, with the lights on, the teacher could not see the pupils in the second row. The dust seemed able to pass through the very walls and windowpanes.

Sometimes the dust storm was followed by thunder, lightning, hail, and rain. People rushed out when the rain began—only to find, as the drops fell through the dusty air, that these had turned to pellets. Their clothing was ruined. It was raining mud.

Travel was dangerous, for no driver could see the ditch, or make out his radiator cap in such a fog. Headlights helped hardly at all, and cars bumped into each other fore and aft, went into the ditch, or swung crossways of the road. The road itself was so blocked with drifted sand that it was often impassable. Worst of all, dust got into the motors and stalled—or ruined—them in a few minutes' time.

Those who drove horses or mules were "just as bad off." The eyes of the animals soon filled with dust, mud would form from the tears, and the lids stuck together and remained sealed as the mud dried and locked the eyelashes together. For, if the people suffered, the livestock suffered more. Dust clogged the noses of the helpless creatures, soon turning to mud and hardening there, so that all were choked and suffocated. When the farmer swilled his hogs, or poured milk in the trough for his calves, the stuff turned to mud before it could be swallowed. Forage was blown away while the bawling, blinded cattle drifted with the wind and cut themselves up on barbed-wire fences. Horses went frantic with the dust, coughing and snorting. And chickens smothered—even in the snuggest henhouses.

No sooner had the dust stopped blowing than people began to laugh and joke about their troubles.

It was reported that dust had been found in the vault at the bank, that a banana crate used as a waste-paper basket by the local editor was full and running over with dust. One man claimed that gravel had come through his windowpane and wakened him during the night. Another, finding his car stalled by the grit in the engine, opened the door and shot ground squirrels overhead which were tunneling upward for air! A local paper reported finding gold nuggets in the street which had been blown from the mines in New Mexico. The county farmer advised his clients that it would be unnecessary to rotate crops in the future, since the wind was rotating soils. One of the natives proposed a test for wind velocity: "Fasten one end of a logchain to the top of a fence-post. If the wind does not blow the chain straight out from the post, the breeze is moderate. You have a calm day."

Allergy in its various forms became so common that, it was said, even the snakes had learned to sneeze; in the night you could tell when a duster was coming by the sneezing of the rattlesnakes on the prairie. Everyone jestingly referred to a dust storm as an "Oklahoma rain." A man caught some huge bullfrogs, so he said, and put them in his watertank to multiply; but, he said, the poor things all drowned immediately. It hadn't rained for so long that they had never had a chance to learn to swim.

A housewife claimed that she scoured her pans by holding them up to a keyhole. The sand coming through in a stream polished them better than she could by the usual method. One old lady, on hearing a man compare the climate to that of hell, put her chin up and declared that if the good Lord sent *her* to hell, he'd have to give her a constitution to stand it.

They laughed about the Black Snow which covered their fields. One farmer said he was going to leave Texas and move to Kansas to pay taxes—"There's where my farm is now."

Another said he could not keep up with his farm, which had taken a trip north. "But next week she'll be back," he said. "I can plow then."

One leather-faced dry farmer said, "I hope it'll rain before the kids grow up. They ain't never seen none."

Those dust storms were magnificent and terrifying, huge walls of tawny cloud, or black, sweeping in ominously to black out the world, sky-high, swift, horrible. But the Short Grass folks laughed them off.

People talk about the horrors of bombed London— and no doubt they are bad enough. But vital statistics show that the death rate on the Plains was as high as that in bombed London at its worst. Nobody lauded the Dust Bowl heroes, for nobody wanted to fight their war. What's more, none of them asked anybody to fight it.

The Men of the Short Grass are a hardy breed. And their humor, their gameness, is every whit as admirable as any shown anywhere. A hero is without honor in his own country.

Most of the people who live on the High Plains live there from choice, for most of them could find homes elsewhere where it would be easier to make a living. When the drouth was at its height in the 1930's, a farmer proposed to give his wife a holiday and take her back to Georgia where her parents lived.

"Molly," he said, "we have been out here forty years. You have worked hard and deserve a vacation. We can afford it now. Let's go back where your folks live for a visit. It will do you good."

His wife, brown as a berry, looked at him, startled into alarm.

"Why, Jim," she protested, "do you think I'd go back there where they have all that water and rain all the time? Not me. It ain't healthy."

In the days of this dry cycle it is often forgotten that not so long ago, before the grass had been grazed off and while the water table was only a few yards below the surface of the earth, the great plague on the Plains was malaria. Nowadays malaria is almost unknown there.

The man who knows he may not make a crop for five, or even seven, years is not going to be cast down by any temporary difficulty or minor disaster. He plants and cultivates, and loses his crop. The next year he repeats, with the same result. Again he tries and fails. This discipline forces him to take the long view, to hope and work and wait—and then do it all over again. Like the Indian hunter, who might have plenty of fat buffalo one moon and be starving the next, the farmer on the Short Grass was neither discouraged nor ashamed when the drouth or the grasshoppers destroyed his crops. He knew that it would rain again sometime; when it did, he would pay off the debt, make a fresh start. He stuck.

For seven lean years there was no crop. He stuck. He had faith, he had hope, and he had charity for the fellow less well off than himself. He was what Short Grass folks call "friendly." His labor was his prayer, and in the long run it got results. Such prayers are strong.

When, finally, the dust storms robbed him of the very soil under his feet, he still stuck—if it was humanly possible. The tune of the migrants to the Coast is always the same: "I'd rather be back in Oklahoma, if I could make it go." Those who left the Plains generally did so unwillingly, and, in the midst of their disaster, with a joke on their lips: "Well, the wind blew the dirt away. But we haven't lost everything. We still got the mortgage!"

12. The Biter Bit

A NY account of humor on the High Plains might well consist of two words. One might simply write the name Will Rogers, and let it go at that. His humor was characteristic, and the proof of that is the reception it got on the Short Grass. Everyone there recognized it, enjoyed it, loved it.

People argue about the difference between British and American humor; they say that British humor often consists of understatement, American of exaggeration. But on the Short Grass—that land of extremes and excesses—humor, like the weather, embraced both. There were yarns and jests that consisted of delicate innuendoes, and others that dealt flatfooted with gross exaggerations. At the core of all good jokes on the Plains, however, there was a core of *truth*. Wit—in the sense of exact expression—was found in the same package with humor. There was social criticism, but little moralizing. Sometimes the jest was an escape from hard conditions, often it was a form of self-assertion by a man lost in the vastness of the open country, or his reaction to the haphazard dangers he faced. Laughter is Man's cure for nervous strain. Also, it was what made *good will* in a region where men carried arms and grew crusty from long solitude.

On the Plains, everyone joked—or learned how to take jokes. Practical men, living outdoors, like practical jokes. Their humor was seldom malicious or sneering. However elaborate, it was generally sympathetic, recognizing human frailty, but calling attention to the necessity for controlling that. It was hearty.

All men on the Plains were humorists. They felt that he laughs best who laughs often.

What jests the Spaniards made in their first explorations have not been recorded. Perhaps they did not jest; they were too intent on gold, on serving the King, for that, maybe. Or they felt such matters were unfit for their official reports to His Majesty.

But there are abundant records of Indian humor. For, except when the occasion called for dignity or stoicism, nobody was so carefree and laughter-loving as the redskin of the Plains. He was a free individual, hardly subject to discipline from his parents even. Unlike the Pueblo, the Plains Indian was not priest-ridden, or trained to labor at the command of a chief. Most of his activities were to him opportunities rather than duties. And he was always ready to relax, always ready to laugh. Particularly, he liked to match yarns against his companions.

In the long nights of winter, when natural forces were "dead," he freely talked about the mythological beings of legend, and many of the stories—even those which preached a moral, were humorous. Then he liked to tell tales of Old Man, or Coyote, creatures curiously compounded of god and man and animal, and of their foolish antics. These tales were innumerable, and in the evening by the tipi fire, old men told them, and at the end of each yarn the teller would invite competition, saying, "Tie one to that!"

Coyote and Hollow Tooth

One day Coyote was trotting across the prairie when he heard something rattle in the grass. Coyote stopped and scouted around, and pretty soon he saw a small snake. Coyote laughed. He said, "How little you are. Too bad you are not like me. I am big."

The snake did not say anything.

Coyote said, "Show me your teeth." So the snake opened his mouth wide and showed his fangs. Coyote laughed. The snake only had two. "Only two teeth— and they are hollow!"

Then Coyote opened his mouth and showed the little snake. "See my teeth? They are sharp. Suppose we bite each other? You could not hurt me much. But I could just about bite you in two."

The snake did not say anything. But when Coyote bit him, the snake bit Coyote back again. It was just like a tap. The wound did not even bleed.

Coyote hardly noticed the snake's teeth. "Well," he said, "I'm going over yonder in the tall grass. You stay here. Every little while we can call to each other, and see how we feel."

Coyote lay down, grinning, in the tall grass, and every little while he would call to the snake. Then the snake would answer. The snake's voice was so weak that Coyote laughed. "I guess he is dying," he said. So he kept calling to the snake—very loud.

But pretty soon Coyote began to feel bad, and did not call quite so loud. The place where the snake had bitten him began to swell up and hurt. And after a while Coyote began to swell up all over. And the more his body swelled the weaker his voice became. The snake called louder and louder, but Coyote did not answer.

Then the snake crawled over to the tall grass, and there was Coyote. He was dead—because he had acted so smart and bragged so loud.

The snake was small and said very little.

He had only two hollow teeth.

But *he* was still alive.

STEAMBOAT'S LECTURE

There was once a camp-crier, or herald, who was walking through the camp announcing the news and the plans of the chiefs for the day to come. Heralds were privileged persons, and often broadcast moral precepts along with their official statements. One day this herald, named Steamboat, admonished the camp as follows:

"I do not wish to urge you to be stingy. But be on the lookout for loafers and beggars, who make a nuisance of themselves by continually asking for the loan of a horse, or a saddle, a gun, or a knife. The man who does not own a knife is a worthless fellow; he does not deserve pity. Do not lend your knife to such a man; then he will see his mistakes and amend his ways."

No sooner had Steamboat given this excellent advice than he saw one of his ponies, which he had just staked out, wallowing on the ground. Its feet were caught in the lariat, and in another minute, the animal would probably have a bad rope burn. He ran to cut the rope, but found he had lost his knife.

Some boys were playing close by. Steamboat called to them, "Grandchildren, lend me your knife. My pony is in danger."

One of the boys made a quick answer: "No, we cannot. Steamboat has just warned us not to lend our knives to anybody."

THE EMBARRASSED GROOM

A party of white folks were gathered at the camp of a tribe of blanket Indians on the occasion of the wedding of two young Carlisle graduates. Among those present was a young lady from the East, whose curiosity far exceeded her knowledge of Indian terminology. She went about peering into all the tipis, and annoying the shy natives by her impertinent and irrelevant questions. One after another, the women whom she found making moccasins, got up and took their work into the privacy of their tents.

She was at a loss to understand the reason for this.

Finally she appealed to the young Indian groom.

"Oh, Mr. Wolf," she exclaimed, "why are your people so secretive? Wherever I go, they get up and leave without saying a word. Now, over in that tent they were making papooses. Why wouldn't they let me see?"

INDIAN PIG CULTURE

The Indian Agent on the Cheyenne Reservation did everything to get the Indians to adopt the new ways of the White People.

Kias was fast becoming one of the best Indian farmers in one of the districts. One day he came to the agency in his wagon followed by his pack of dogs. The agent was always glad to see him, for he had always tried to carry out the orders from the agency office.

The agent said, "Kias, you have tried nearly everything in the way of farming, but there is one you have not tried. Why don't you start raising hogs?"

Kias replied, "I would, Major, but I cannot. The hogs won't follow my wagon."

SATANTA'S BATTLE DRESS

Satanta, second chief of the Kiowa tribe, had a somewhat grim sense of humor. During the winter of 1866-67, he sent word to the commander at Fort Dodge that he hoped the government animals at the fort were fat and in good shape, since his own were getting poor, and he intended to come over shortly and run off the Army horses.

The next spring, a council was held at the fort, and Satanta was presented with a general's uniform. He went back to camp, put it on, and led his promised attack on the fort!

PERENNIAL JOKES

The Indian surely loved a joke, and being a pragmatic person liked a practical joke best of all. This trait also belonged to the cowboys who inherited his country, and many of their practical jokes were very similar to those in vogue among the redskins.

Thus in an Indian camp young bucks full of deviltry would ride through the camp, throw the loops of their lariats about the top of a tipi, and gallop away, pulling it over—to the discomfiture of the people seated about the fire. Pioneer riders used the same technique in wrecking privies on Hallowe'en.

Another trick of salty young bucks was to shove a colt into a tipi at night and listen with delight as the frightened animal barged about, trampling the people on their pallets. Cowboys used the same trick sometimes in the bunkhouse.

Indians would slip up on some young man wrapped in his blanket and courting his sweetheart and suddenly jerk off the blanket, leaving him naked. In like manner, cowboys shot off the hats of their butts. All over the Plains, badger fights and snipe hunts were organized for the dismay of tenderfeet and the delight of the natives. In those times there were few amusements, and people provided their own.

But among cowboys and nesters, as among sophisticates and savants, the best talk was often struck out spontaneously. Anecdotes that illustrated the mores of the people were always popular.

But best of all, Plainsmen liked a tall tale.

Such tales are innumerable, but they differ from the tall tales of the lumberjacks and other industrial workers in that, on the Plains, the narrator himself was always the hero of the yarn. From the great grand-daddy of all Plains tall tales (Hatcher's yarn of how he visited hell and made the acquaintance of the Old Black B'ar himself, recorded in Lewis H. Garrard's *Wah-To-Yah and the Taos Trail,* Philadelphia, 1850) down to the latest invention of a Panhandle cowboy, this holds good. Paul Bunyan is no native to the Plains; he came in with the oil industry. No regular Plainsman could squelch his ego to the point of making a hero of some other fellow; he wanted to swell himself up to the size of the country, and to make his listeners feel the exquisite absurdity of that magnificent gesture.

13. Hit the Trail

A N EASTERN artist once exhibited a picture showing an Indian walking. It was entitled "Out for
a Stroll," and aroused considerable mirth among those
who saw it. Indians did not walk unless they were going
somewhere; the notion of the "stroll" had never touched
their practical, objective minds. And, for that matter,
it has never "caught on" among the men who have inherited (a polite term) the Indians' country.

Indian and cowman alike were horsemen. They could
not make a living or long survive without a horse under
them. Horses were, too, almost the only personal property worth anything in early days. It followed that a
man was ashamed to be seen afoot, since it branded
him as a pauper. To this day, Indians and cattlemen
share this feeling.

Of course, neither moccasins nor high-heeled boots
are suited to hiking. Both were devised for the saddle.
And whenever an Indian or a cowboy got so "low"
that he had no shame in walking, his footgear were not
slow in reminding him that riding was more comfortable.

Moreover, in a country where distances are so great,
and landmarks so far apart; where the nearest town
might be eighty miles away, and the nearest neighbor

forty; walking was not only shameful, not only painful
—it was positively ridiculous! Imagine "taking a stroll"
on the Staked Plains! For that matter, imagine "going
somewhere" on foot! Like a mud turtle on a world
cruise.

WHERE PLOWMEN NEVER PLOD

People do not walk even to plow on the Short Grass.
Most of them drive tractors; some use riding plows;
others ride a horse and drive the team from the saddle.
Wheat is harvested by combines—huge machines that
do everything but butter the toast.

It is by no means uncommon for a man to go fly-
fishing on horseback, and shooting quail from the saddle is an old practice for anyone with a horse that is
not gun-shy.

Some of the ranches in Texas are so large that the
cowboys haul their horses out in trailers to work the
cattle, and rustlers operate in trucks. It is getting so
even the cattle are ashamed to walk.

But maybe that is a good thing; in some parts of the
Plains the cowboys are so busy imitating Will Rogers
that the dogies have to "git along" the best they can.

For all that, the people of the Short Grass love to
ramble. As the saying goes, "Some travel for their
health; others find it healthier to travel." No use having a horse under you if you don't get around. On the
Plains there is "a general absence of locality." And
where one place is like another, all alert men are nomadic. They are forever ready to pull up stakes and
move on.

The Plains Indian solved the problem of leading a

wandering life and at the same time having a comfortable home and a genuine family life. He loved his relatives, loved to visit them. Old Indians thought of their reservations—though half as large as Dakota—as simply prisons. When one tries to explain that their confinement to the reservation was not intended as a punishment, they retort passionately, "What else *could* it be?"

The Plains Indian travels now all over the West, but he is in this no different from his white brother. Everywhere one hears it said of the people of the High Plains, "They are the damnedest folks to travel!"

As a matter of fact, there is hardly any human trouble —barring incurable disease or bereavement—which cannot be cured by taking a trip. Even these may sometimes be alleviated by a change of scene. For life is short, and the world is wide; there is much to see before the final blackout.

On the Plains, when "a change of scene" is wanted, it generally means a jaunt of several hundred miles!

One reason Westerners travel so much is that a man never feels that where *he* lives is really West. The old song puts it best: "Out where the West *begins*." A fellow is always on the edge of it. It is just around the corner, over the hill. One might say, mutilating poetry: Man never is, but always to be—West!

It has been said that the rapture on the lonely shore is most agreeable when one may at any moment go home. And Dr. Samuel Johnson once declared that the finest prospect in the world was improved by a good inn in the foreground. But the reverse is also true, for a crowd is tolerable only to the man who knows where to find privacy. An inn may be more barren than the desert.

Knowing this, one may imagine how flabbergasted a Plainsman is to hear some tourist on his first trip across the buffalo grass, say, "Of course, I've never been in the *Desert* before!"

For the Plains are not like the Desert, but rather like the sea. Early explorers felt this strongly, and spoke of "making port," "navigation," and "the coasts of Colorado." At night on the prairie one might take the ranch-houses for convoys, and the towering grain elevators for lighthouses.

Of course, in these days of air travel, we are gaining a new conception of the shape of the earth. Our ancestors could see that the earth was flat; we have been taught that it is round; but when we go up in a plane, it is obvious that the earth is shaped like a saucer or a dish—for the brim is always on a level with our eyes.

The Plains are worth seeing from any angle. But they may best be seen from the air. Then one grasps the real scope of them, and the landmarks as well: endless straight roads running "to hell and gone"; lakes and pools and rivers of every color from rusty red to pale yellow; snaky streams marked by dark green foliage; cattle trails leading to the bare spots centering on a tank and windmill; curious patterns made by contour plowing; the branching gullies of eroded fields, showing like some anatomical chart of blood-vessels or nerves; flat-topped buttes, and flat-bottomed clouds; little towns huddled on the wind-bitten grass; and farmsteads at the corner of the sections, with their green roofs and red barns, so tiny and homelike in the midst of the flat prairies. If a man has not loved that country before, he must now; it makes him feel like Santa Claus.

Life on the Plains was transformed once—when the Indian acquired horses; again, when the white men bought motor cars; and now a new dispensation is at hand. The plane has come, and folks on the Short Grass welcome it. Surely there was never a land so well adapted to the flyer. The man in a plane can grasp this country at last. The Short Grass country becomes his own pasture or, rather, his private ocean. General Custer's description in his book, *My Life on the Plains*, is worth remembering:

"Starting from almost any point near the central portion of the Plains, and moving in any direction, one seems to encounter a series of undulations at a more or less remote distance from each other, but constantly in view. Comparing the surface of the country to that of the ocean, a comparison often indulged in by those who have seen both, it does not require a very great stretch of the imagination, when viewing this boundless ocean of beautiful living verdure, to picture these successive undulations as gigantic waves, not wildly chasing each other to or from the shore, but standing silent and immovable, and by their silent immobility adding to the impressive grandeur of the scene. These undulations, varying in height from fifty to five hundred feet, are sometimes formed of a light sandy soil, but often of different varieties of rock, producing at a distance the most picturesque effect. The constant recurrence of these waves, if they may be so termed, is quite puzzling to the inexperienced plainsman. He imagines, and very naturally too, judging from appearances, that when he ascends to the crest he can overlook all the surrounding country. After a weary walk of perhaps several miles, which appeared at starting not more than one or two, he finds himself at the desired point, but discovers that directly beyond, in the direction he desires to go, rises a second wave, but slightly higher than the first, and from the crest of which he must certainly be able to scan the country as far as the eye can reach. Thither he pursues his course, and after a ride of from five to ten miles, although the distance did not seem half so great before starting, he finds himself on the crest, or, as it is invariably termed, the 'divide,' but again only to discover that another and apparently a higher divide rises in his front, and at about the same distance. Hundreds, yes, thousands of miles may be journeyed over, and this same effect witnessed every few hours."

Men who move about a great deal have a habit of mind which differs widely from that of the earthbound. To them it would seem horrible to live in the same house in which they were born, much more horrible to die there. Their home is wherever they spread their bedroll, and they develop a certain inarticulate affection and intimacy towards the spot where they are camping. When they make camp they choose it for its convenience, for the proximity of wood and water, and the shelter, if any, of a cottonwood or cut bank. But after a man has slept in such a spot a night or two, the tree or the bank, the water hole, the very grass and weeds around his bed, take on a homelike quality which he feels quite as much as the fellow who feels lost without his familiar table or bookcase at home.

But travel on the Plains has undergone great changes. In the earliest times everything on the Plains moved north and south. The wind blew north and south; the buffalo migrated north and south; the Indian trails ran north and south, following the trend of the Rockies. This was the natural direction to follow, since the streams ran mostly from west to east, providing water and fuel at regular intervals, all the way from Mexico to Canada. Early explorers constantly report meeting Sioux and Crow Indians in Texas and New Mexico, fully fifteen hundred miles from home, but with the coming of the white man from the East all this was changed.

The white man followed the streams instead of marching athwart them. The Santa Fe Trail and Oregon Trail and the other trails moved in a general westerly direction. Only the cattle trails from Texas kept up the old line of march, and when the railroads cut across the Plains, even these were discontinued. Today, with paved highways running everywhere, most travelers head east or west with the streams and railroads. A car with a Montana license is a rarity in Texas and Oklahoma.

The Black Hills are more remote and unreal than the mountains on the moon to Texans. For all the Sooners know or care there may be mountains in Nebraska, though they are thoroughly familiar with Arkansas, Missouri, Colorado, Arizona, or California. Long journeys are to east or west. Trips north or south are briefer, more private, and local, though culturally of great importance.

The Plainsman has a complete disregard for distance.

He will drive five or six hundred miles a day for several days running when he is on the road; and energetic young men sometimes double that distance in a day's run, driving from southwest Texas to Denver and beyond in order to fish through the weekend. On those broad straight level roads in the Panhandle, where a man can see ten miles ahead, eighty miles an hour is the usual speed.

In some parts of America a man lived *at* a certain address, or at least *in* a certain town, but on the Plains a man lived somewhere *in the vicinity* of his county. He had room to turn around in—and he turned around.

There are plenty of ranches on the Short Grass with upwards of 100,000 acres. But nobody there would be guilty of mentioning so small a parcel of land as an acre. Short Grass folks think of land in terms of sections. A section is a square mile—640 acres. A quarter-section is 160, and there are people with such limited imaginations that they even speak of 40's!

When the Plains were opened to settlement, congressmen of Eastern states, who thought 40 acres a good-sized farm, made their silly homestead laws—which made a government claim only 160 acres.

Some of that land, fit only for grazing, had such scanty grass that one cow required 20 acres or more to subsist her. A claim of 160 acres would graze only eight head of cattle at that rate—and so far no man has ever been able to keep himself—let alone a family—on a "herd" of eight cattle.

The result was that settlers either sold out, leased their land to cattlemen, starved to death, or plowed the land for crops. Plowing that land eventually meant seeing it blown away entirely, when the next drouth came. Hence came the saying that free land meant only a chance to starve a good woman to death.

When the congressmen, the plow, and the drouth were through with it, the grazing homestead had often become a "gazing" homestead—all a man could do with it was to gaze at it.

The land in some parts became so worthless that a man who bought a section had to read his title deed carefully, or the seller would slip in an extra section on him.

In dry years, when there was no grass for stock, you might see a corral full of horses and a sign alongside. The sign read: "Take some, and SHUT THE GATE. Some more horses might get in."

A lot of criticism has been heaped on Plains Indians for not earning their living "with all that land." The Indian's allotment was 160 acres of grassland. You try it.

One might easily get the impression, while reading about pioneer days, that the pioneer was a person who had left the old civilization behind him, and had gone out to create a new one from scratch.

No doubt there were some who took to the wilderness as an escape, and who were later disconcerted to find the States catching up with them.

But for the most part the pioneers on the Short Grass had no such idea, and never thought of themselves in any such terms. They brought their culture with them, and regarded themselves as pioneers of the old American way. Nothing made them more resentful than having outsiders admire them in a patronizing way and express surprise at their progress and achievements, thus implying that their fathers had never enjoyed anything of the kind.

They did not—and do not—feel that they lack what older regions have; they feel that they have all that, and something more peculiar to the Plains, something the others lack.

In fact, many of the pioneers were people of education and refinement and in the early years, as since, were apt to make some display of their sophistication. Thus we find that Buffalo Bill and his compeers regularly served champagne instead of whisky at their parties, and Army officers at miserable frontier posts dressed for twelve-course dinners and led cotillions, keeping up the customs of the Service as followed in the East. Officers stationed at Fort Reno, when ordered to Fort Sill, carried with them in the baggage train a dance floor built in sections. Every evening this was put together on the buffalo grass, and the officers danced with their ladies to the music of the regimental band. Territorial capitals were centers of fashion and good living, and kept up with the vogue in the States with their horses and carriages, their elaborate parties, to the very best of their ability.

After the Plains were first opened to tourists a century ago, European noblemen and gentlemen were frequent visitors, traveling with every possible luxury, and living a truly baronial existence. Buffalo Bill and Wild Bill Hickok hobnobbed with a Grand Duke from Russia. Jim Bridger was guide and companion to Sir

George Gore. Lord Dunraven, Frederick Ruxton, and many another English sportsman made himself and the natives at home on the Short Grass.

When the cattle industry promised millions in the 1880's, a torrent of British capital flowed to the Plains, and with it came many young gentlemen, Scottish and English. These, nominally cattlemen, passed the time pleasantly, racing horses, shooting, and chasing coyotes with hounds. Quite a number of them remained in the West after the heyday of the range cattle industry had passed. Indeed, some of the largest ranches in Texas are still owned by Britishers.

In the early days, the country, as Mrs. Katherine Fullerton Gerould has insisted in one of her books, *The Aristocratic West,* was aristocratic, and nowhere more so than on the High Plains. This was nothing new there, of course. The Plains Indians, as one of the Jesuit missionaries put it, were "all gentlemen," with such a strong sense of personal dignity that to lay hands on one was to invite a fight to the death.

At one of the frontier posts a number of warriors were held captive in a corral. The commanding officer ordered them transferred to a nearby building. The Sergeant of the Guard and his men, fully armed, went into the corral to effect the transfer. Ignorant of the Indian language, the sergeant could not make himself understood. Signs also failed. As a last resort, the soldiers attempted to push the Indians in the desired direction. The warriors immediately produced knives which they had concealed on their persons, and within a few minutes all the Indians and most of the guard lay dead.

One could not take liberties with those wild knights of the prairie.

This haughty spirit was continued in a manner among the cattlemen; they were accustomed to have their own way about things, or to prevail, if necessary, by violence. The cowboy was not, and even now seldom is, a family man. He stood on his own feet, covered the ground he stood on. He had nothing to consider except his loyalty to his outfit. Being on his own and bearing arms, he, too, had his share of the aristocratic spirit. It is a matter of record that English gentlemen and cattlemen got on famously together.

The rude conditions of the frontier made luxuries seem all the more desirable, and the aristocratic spirit —the feeling that the best is good enough—still persists. Critics of the boosters and boomers have seldom traced this feeling to its source, and have generally attributed it to less worthy motives.

Americans have always been nomadic, and none more so than the farming population. The grass always looked greener over the hill, and generation after generation of farmers have moved on, living up to the tradition of "moving west" to settle on new land. Such seeking of opportunity was the great American privilege, and the best men sought it first.

Of course, it was inconvenient for the Californians when the Dust Bowl migrants moved in on them—so was the migration of '49 inconvenient for the Indians! If it is a crime to be poor, then a lot of people have broken jail lately. And if a man is not to be allowed to travel because he is poor, then most of the people can never hope to better their condition.

The government's investigators discovered pertinent facts about these travelers, as follows:

Most of them had a definite destination in mind. Half of those who registered for relief never applied a second time; most of them were going only a short way; most of them settled when they arrived at their destination. Only ten per cent asked repeatedly for aid, and their reasons were hard luck, illness, or unfitness for employment.

The vast majority of migrants were native-born white Americans, younger than the average of the population. The average family consisted of three persons, including both parents. The educational average of the migrants was higher than the average for the whole country. Most of the heads of these families were employables in skilled trades. Except for the farmers from the Dust Bowl, most of the migrants were city workers.

The farmers had stuck it out through hard times until they had no money, no crop, and no soil in which to grow one. They stayed until the very earth was gone. Such people cannot be called shiftless.

At first the young men went, men of few responsibilities, daring, restless young men—like young bulls leaving the herd. Most of the migrants were not neurotics or criminals, but ordinary Americans with a hope and a purpose. The governor of a certain state, when refusing to establish a "bum blockade" at the state line said, "Some of our worst crooks have come here in Pullmans and limousines; and some of our best citizens got here without a dime." It was the irony of fate that led these poor men to seek California as a "warm" climate.

No lover of the sun should leave the Short Grass for "sunny" California.

The Okies are not contemptible, as they were represented. These are the men who got away with 13,000,-000 acres of Indian land in Oklahoma in less than thirty years. Do the native sons of California think they are tougher than the Comanches? Perhaps they were right to be alarmed when the migrants showed up—men with the courage and vitality to go and get it, men who practiced the courage and initiative other people preached.

The San Francisco *Chronicle* said of the Dust Bowl refugees: "These people are of good pioneer stock. Their grandparents followed such men as Daniel Boone through the Cumberland Gap and settled Kentucky, Tennessee, and later farther west. Theirs is a history of generations of the soil, of decades of heart-breaking toil in the improvement and cultivation of their impoverished land."

Yes, the Okies are made of the same resourceful and heroic stuff as their fathers who peopled the Plains. Those earlier pioneers halted on the prairie, set down a covered wagon-box, pitched a tent, carved a dugout from the clay hillside, ripped slabs of sod from the earth for their building stone, or slapped up a shack of rough planks and tar-paper. The Indians did not want them, the cattlemen tried to run them out. But they came, they saw, they conquered. And there they stayed.

Just so their sons and daughters headed west in cars as dilapidated and overloaded as the old-time covered wagons. Once more they meet opposition, once more the landowners threaten and protest. Once more Uncle Sam backs them up.

If the one migration was heroic—a national glory— why not the second? They do not forget, perhaps, that Abraham Lincoln was a migrant as poor and as heroic as they.

14. Boot Hill

IN THE records of life on the Short Grass a century
and more ago, you will encounter a phrase "on the
prairie." Understand that, and you have the clue to
law and lawlessness on the High Plains.

Thus, when a man made a gift to a friend out of
sheer affection, expecting no return, the gift was said
to be "on the prairie." When an Indian woman, taken
in adultery, was driven from camp and left to the mercy
of any man who found her, she was "on the prairie."
When a man found himself unexpectedly near a hostile
camp, he hastened boldly into the nearest tipi, knowing
that, as guest and suppliant, he would be safe there;
but the moment he left the camp, his late host might
kill him without compunction, with impunity—he was
"on the prairie." Again, if a man found a stray horse,
and threw his rope on the animal, it became his own,
since it had been roped "on the prairie."

These examples will suffice to show the meaning of
the phrase—freedom from responsibility to the community, freedom to act as one saw fit, freedom to disregard the customs and sanctions of the camp or town.
This freedom—the Indian's Bill of Rights—was known
as "Prairie Law."

Prairie Law, however, was not statutory, not even

common law. It was simply the rule of necessity: a man on the prairie was not only legally, but actually, on his own. There was no authority, other than *force majeure*, which could control him. Indeed, the word "control" is inaccurate: "on the prairie" he could not be controlled, he could only be destroyed. On the prairie, might made right.

Thus, when an Indian war party invaded the hunting grounds of their enemies, they did not feel that they were trespassing; they merely felt that they were on dangerous ground. Trespassers could not be sued, much less prosecuted; they could only be killed or frightened away. On the prairie—any prairie—a man was a free agent. Not by law, not by custom—but actually.

Among the Plains tribes, moreover, the tribal government only functioned when some ceremony, tribal war-party, or tribal hunt was in progress. At such times, the chiefs appointed one of the Warrior Societies to patrol and police the camp; as soon as the emergency was over, the camp dissolved, the authority ended, and the government—for all practical purposes—ceased to exist. Moreover, this intermittent control was always extremely local, never extending far beyond the boundaries of the camp. As we have seen, nobody approached a lone Indian away from the camp; it was taken for granted that he wanted to be let alone. He was "on the prairie."

An example of this limited local government is that, not infrequently, when troops were known to be coming to attack the Indian camp, and some of the tribesmen wished to clear out, the Indian police—members of the Warrior Society appointed to that temporary duty—had to threaten them with violence to make them remain. For, once outside the camp, they were free men, "on the prairie."

We who live under laws which blanket the whole accessible world must use our imaginations to visualize a society in which the law ended within a few rods of a man's front door. But to understand the so-called "lawlessness" of the Short Grass, we must make the effort.

For these same conditions which created Indian "prairie law" had to be faced by the white settlers also. For centuries after the first white man set foot on the High Plains, there was *no* law whatever outside the camp, the village, or the town. That was not a theory, but a fact—which had to be faced.

Where there is no law, there can be no crime, in the strict sense of the word. A right, by the law and customs of our ancestors, is something a man can get away with (in the face of the community) for twenty years. Where there is no community, a man can get away with murder, and legally commit no crime. Therefore, when a man killed another "on the prairie," he had no sense of guilt; he merely feared vengeance. This fact was recognized by everyone: such an act was commonly known, in early days, as a "killing"; nobody called it "murder" until a verdict had been brought in.

There has been a vast misunderstanding on this score. For example, General Custer has been much criticized for ordering deserters shot on sight. But "on the prairie" it was not feasible to capture such men. They had decamped with horse and rifle belonging to Uncle Sam, they were not going to be taken alive, and if they had been taken, there was no adequate punishment prescribed in those days by the regulations. Nobody wanted to bring them back alive, for they would only run away again.

In any region, obviously, those men are most successful who best adapt themselves to actual conditions. Custer was such a successful man; he followed the custom and faced the conditions of the country. It is true that he failed at last; but he failed, not because of his methods, but simply because he bit off more than he could chew.

Just so it was with arrests of dangerous men everywhere: the phrase "dead or alive" commonly meant "dead." The verbal instructions were usually "Don't let him get away"—a sentence that was often interpreted (correctly, as a rule) as a sentence of death. Thus, when the Indian Police and the troops were sent to arrest Sitting Bull, most people seem to have understood that he was to be killed. Read the account of that affair in the New York *Herald*. It was so with many another "wanted" man: the man was not wanted; what was wanted was his death.

And so with everything else "on the prairie." The imported laws of the woodlands and hills to the eastward did not make sense on the Short Grass.

BILL OF SALE

Little Chief was camped on the Canadian River in the Cheyenne Reservation in Oklahoma. One day a white man came riding to his tipi, leading a fine chestnut running horse. Little Chief had visions of winning all the races at the next beef issue, and before long had persuaded the cowboy to part with the animal. Little Chief got it at an excellent bargain and spent the rest of that moon training the animal. The white man rode on.

When Little Chief went to the agency to draw his rations, he took the running horse along, but before he could arrange any matches with other race horses, the United States Marshal rode up and took the horse away from him.

Little Chief complained to the agent. The agent explained that the horse had been stolen and that Little Chief had no claim to him. The Indian looked so hurt and puzzled that the agent volunteered information, "On the White Man's Road, whenever a man sells a horse, he is expected to give a bill of sale, a writing. The next time a white man tries to sell a horse to you, ask him for a bill of sale."

Little Chief went back to his camp, more determined then ever to get a race horse and recover his loss. Before many days another white man turned up herding four or five good horses across the reservation. One of them was a fast bay, which made Little Chief's legs ache to ride it. He dickered with the white man and soon had possession of the animal, but this time he demanded a bill of sale in order to protect himself.

Once more he trained the horse for running races and turned up at the agency, confident that he could win against any horse in the tribe. Unfortunately, the marshal was on hand again and took possession of the animal, over Little Chief's vehement protests. Little Chief thereupon produced his bill of sale.

It read, "This certifies that I have this day sold to Little Chief one stolen horse. (Signed) John Doe."

HELL ON THE BORDER

Many a bad man did not set out to be bad. He killed somebody in self-defense, woke up, and found himself infamous.

It is also to be remembered that border lands are always lawless—witness the Scottish Border, where cattle-stealing was prevalent for centuries. Differences of race and culture breed border crime also, and the lawlessness which follows wars is always most pronounced on the border, where exiles and fugitives wreak their spite on all and sundry.

On the Short Grass, this cut several ways. There was, to begin with, the inevitable clash between Indian and white; between Indian and Mexican; between white man and Mexican; between Texans, lately Confederates, and Kansans, lately Union men, Yankees. Some of these wars had gone on for centuries. When the American Army tried to get the Navajos to stop fighting Mexicans at the end of the Mexican War, the aggrieved Navajos, allies of the States, protested: "This is *our* war."

Also, the Texans and New Mexicans had been at odds ever since the Texan-Santa Fe Expedition. Even today there is small love lost between Texans and New Mexicans, between Texans and Kansans. Oklahoma is still a house divided—part Southern, part Northern. And to top all this, there was the hostility between the Five Civilized tribes of eastern Oklahoma and the Plains tribes of the Short Grass. Besides, eastern Oklahoma, also, was chock-full of guerillas, who had taken refuge there after the Civil War, men who wanted to go on fighting law and order simply because it was Yankee law and order. These men often extended their operations to the High Plains.

The Comanches had been kidnapping and robbing everybody on their borders since the memory of man. They stole from the Indians and sold to the whites; stole from the Mexicans and sold to the Indians; stole from the whites and sold to the Mexicans. They had a regular yearly program for their raids, striking Mexico at one season, the Santa Fe Trail at another, and the Texans on any night when the moon was full. They had a lilting song: "Oh, how bright is the moonlight tonight! Tonight as I ride—"

The New Mexicans trafficked in stolen cattle, making their headquarters at Las Vegas, and meeting the Comanche looters in the neighborhood of Tucumcari. It is claimed that these *Comancheros* acted as fences for the Comanches to the tune of 100,000 Texas cattle. Big business—and it was all "on the prairie."

When the white men came to live on the Short Grass, they too found that, in the nature of things, such government as was possible was necessarily *local* government. Each town was a unit, armed, belligerent, acutely conscious of its rivals. From this intensely local government arose the County-seat Wars.

Even today, in the less modern parts of the West, there is intense rivalry between competing towns— towns which, any stranger can see, would progress faster if they could work together. But the old feeling persists; neither can trust the other to co-operate in anything. Each town might be properly organized, but between them lay the prairie—on which anything might happen.

When, after the Run into Old Oklahoma, towns and cities sprang up overnight, local governments were organized at once, each by the land company which had most at stake. But it was the better part of a year afterward before anything like a territorial government was set up. People in the West thought that government began at home. It had to.

Now, the failure and corruption of local government in the United States is notorious. Lord Bryce, in *The American Commonwealth,* has stressed this as the worst feature of our political organization. If lawlessness was, for a time, rampant "on the prairie," it was not helped much by the establishment of local governments scattered hither and yon over the Short Grass. The conditions of life under the Indian regime were at first only aggravated by the organization of local governments in the white man's towns and counties.

The boosters of the early boom towns carried blazing guns. Sedentary people—all legend to the contrary—are more bloodthirsty and vindictive than nomads. The impromptu wars of the Indians were not one-tenth so deadly as civilized battles.

For the earthbound man with title to a home or a stake in the country is like a bear at a bear-baiting. He must fight. He is tied by the leg to his real estate. He cannot ride away to fight again some other day. To the Indian it would have seemed as silly to die in defense of Hill 101 as to die for a given cubic yard of prairie air. The Indian was not defending any hill; he expected the hill to shelter him. If it did not, he looked for a better hill.

It was the same to a great degree with the cowboys. They fought for their boss, or to protect their cattle, their grass, or their water holes—or out of sheer high spirits. And so the cowboy has followed the Indian. He was not mean enough to inherit the earth.

In the late eighties men all over the Short Grass—but especially in Kansas—fought bloody wars for many a paper town which never materialized into the metropolis imagined by its defenders. These conflicts are known as the County-seat Wars.

Kansas was plagued first by the bushwhackers of the pro-slavery faction of the 1850's, by the struggles of the Civil War, by the Indian wars that followed, by the gun-fighting of cowboys and road-agents, and finally by the County-seat Wars. It seemed that Bleeding Kansas would never stop bleeding!

The men of those wars were smart, loyal to their friends and towns, and often formidable. Many early Kansans had come to the State on purpose to take a hand in the trouble there. They came with guns in their hands, resentment in their hearts, and a fierce determination to make their ideals prevail. They fought stubbornly in those guerilla campaigns. They were feudists with no mere personal grudges. And these men were not hirelings—they were leading citizens, holding high office in town, county, and State. Some were directors of railways, prominent lawyers, or journalists. Probably, but for the journalists, there would have been no wars. The most combative of them all was Colonel Sam Wood—a Quaker!

The cowboys and gamblers had killed personal enemies. But the plowmen who swarmed in to file on free land fought for their towns and their homesteads—grimly, ferociously, relentlessly.

With the farmers, all sorts of crooks and criminals went west—speculators, grafters, and demagogues. It was an era of opportunity. The county-seat boosters and land-hungry boomers too often had no conscience and no remorse. Many of the towns they fought for are ghost towns now—or ghosts of ghosts, since, never having lived, they never died. Some of the railroads existed only on paper. Elections were often settled by frauds, until voting had to be supervised by armed militiamen.

In the days of the Old West, before the Indians had been pacified, all men carried arms. By the time the Indians were put down, the superiority of the Colt's revolver had been thoroughly demonstrated. And so, although Winchesters, derringers, and shotguns continued to play their part in private war and self-defense, the six-gun was the arm most generally worn.

After the Indian wars, a wave of banditry swept the West. White men, no longer able to hunt buffalo or fight redskins, turned to stealing horses—first from the Indian reservations, afterward from anybody who owned stock. The ubiquity of horse-thieves, rustlers, road-agents, and gunmen made packing or "toting" a weapon obligatory upon anyone who traveled, anyone who wished to be let alone. This, on the Plains, meant almost the whole male population.

Public opinion on the matter is well illustrated by

the story about Judge Roy Bean, "the Law west of the Pecos." A man was brought before him, charged with carrying concealed weapons, and the evidence was conclusive. But the Judge ruled that a man had a right to carry a gun when traveling, and "if he wasn't traveling, how in hell could he be carrying it? Acquitted."

After towns and homesteads made the land more peaceful, men still kept guns in their homes and places of business, carried them on trips—as many still do. But the coming of oil and motor cars enormously encouraged crime on the Short Grass. Bank robbers and stick-up men abounded, and the habit of carrying arms revived with the revival of banditry. Every man who traveled at night carried a revolver or an automatic pistol in the glove-box of his car, in his clothes, or in his boot. On the train the weapon might go into his bag.

I remember that when I was an undergraduate I always traveled with a pistol among my things. I had no use for it, and it was a nuisance to get past customs officers in England when I returned to Oxford from my vacations on the continent. Another American, also from the Short Grass, was ingenious enough to discover a use for his weapon. Finding that his servant was drinking up his cognac on the sly, my friend left the gun alongside the brandy bottle, in his sideboard, thereby frightening the college "scout" into unwonted sobriety.

Neither my friend nor I was more bloodthirsty than other young men. We had simply never questioned the custom of taking a gun along.

Now, if Western boys carried six-guns to Oxford, you may be sure that some of their friends on the Plains went armed. At my college in western Oklahoma, sev-

eral of my classmates from the Texas Panhandle had
pistols which they carried to college lectures where they
took notes on Chaucer and Ben Jonson—who would
have understood perfectly. Nobody who knew of it was
either excited or offended. In no case was the young
man an uninstructed, gun-crazy boy. Men who habitu-
ally carry arms understand that their possession induces
deliberation and a sense of responsibility.

Such instances were rare, of course, but can seem
strange only in states where the incompetence of the
police has forced legislators to strip the citizens of their
constitutional right to own and bear arms. It is the old
American way. If all our citizens were handy with firearms, there would be less unrest at home, and less danger from abroad.

Later on, I became a college teacher myself.

There was a laugh hidden with the weapon, then. I
used to wonder whether some of my colleagues, arrogant young instructors from the east, would have been
quite so caustic in their comments, if they had known
that, quite possibly, some man in the class went armed.
There is nothing so conducive to good manners as the
society of armed men.

Nowadays one hears that "Americans learn their
manners at the filling station and the telephone booth."
As a teacher in this field, Samuel Colt's "Peacemaker"
was outstanding.

Was it Will Rogers who said that the voters sometimes elected a man to office so that they might have
someone to laugh at? Certainly in early days, in many
communities, the newest settler was regularly elected

town marshal. Sometimes he got shot; if so, that was one on him.

For, on the Short Grass, as in many adjacent regions of the West, nobody sought out the police except to challenge them to a fight. Problems were usually settled without benefit of law and order. The leading citizens were ready to ride and shoot whenever the community welfare demanded it.

I recall an instance from my own boyhood. A ne'er-do-well in the town ran a little hotel—or rather, his wife ran it, while he loafed around, making a general nuisance of himself. One day, in his cups, he killed his wife. Sobered by what he had done, and knowing the code of the country, he loaded his rifle and lit out of town. Before he had gone a mile, everybody knew what had happened. Almost every able-bodied man joined in the pursuit. The killer was chased into a cornfield.

When the self-appointed posse appeared at the edge of the field, the murderer stuck up his head and fired. Immediately everybody fired at him. He fell dead. They brought him back into town, loaded into a spring wagon, his head lolling over the end-gate. There was no inquest. Nobody knew who had killed him, nobody cared. The town was rid of him, gladly buried him, and forgot the matter. Justice had been served. I confess I never knew whether the town marshal was in the posse; it never occurred to me to ask. That detail was unimportant.

Even today, on the Short Grass, a man is somewhat ashamed to call in the police in any personal affair in which the offender is known. In any sudden emergency, those present are apt to take matters into their own hands. Self-help and community spirit prove adequate in most cases, and often settle affairs where delay and red tape might prove costly or even defeat justice. It is generally assumed that the average citizen is as smart and as honest as hirelings are likely to be.

Of course, lawyers must eat, like other men. If the law seemed likely to deal effectively with the criminal, it was allowed to run its course—as in the case of Abraham Lincoln and his first client. But not every criminal lawyer on the Frontier enjoyed the respect accorded to Lincoln.

Such spontaneous action on the part of a community is not practicable where people are too numerous to know each other well. In a city such informal vengeance would be simply a lynching by a mob. But in a small town where every man knows his neighbor, the common sense of *all* is often fairer and truer than the decisions of a court of law, especially where everyone is of the same tradition and the same race. The impromptu posse was simply the town meeting bearing arms.

These things are far in the past. But the tradition conditions the thinking of Short Grass folks. There, now as always, good will and freedom go together.

During a recent wave of burglary in an Oklahoma town, the police begged the citizens in the public press not to shoot at prowlers, since they might accidentally kill a neighbor. Old-timers regarded this as a slur on their coolness and accuracy with firearms. But it may have been justified; young men these days show a deplorable lack of familiarity with firearms, even on the Short Grass.

The American Republic was born of revolution and

its birth certificate was the Declaration of Independence. Every foot of the Frontier was gained by conflict with Indians or Mexicans, and the fighting was often in defiance of the laws and treaties made by the nation. Yet along with this spirit of rebellion went a strong admiration for the Founding Fathers, for their Constitution and the statutes growing out of it. This made everyone eager to "make a law." The multiplicity of these laws, seldom rigidly enforced, meant a multiplicity of crimes. Walter Prescott Webb sums the situation up in his book, *The Great Plains:* "Therefore the West was a lawless place. It was turbulent in the early days because there was no law. It was lawless in the later period because the laws were unsuited to the needs and conditions. Men could not abide by them and survive. Not only were absurd laws imposed upon them, but their customs, which might well have received the sanction of law, were too seldom recognized. The blame for a great deal of Western lawlessness rests more with the lawmaker than with the lawbreaker."

Strife was engendered by the fact that laws imported (often enacted *en bloc*) from other sections—woodlands and mountains—did not fit conditions, and therefore made survival difficult on the Short Grass. This is the reason why so many radical movements—like Populism —have originated there. The development of transportation and communication in our time have obscured this obvious fact.

It is significant that the best people—as well as the worst—often looked with much misgiving upon the establishment of federal control and the organization of state government on the Short Grass. They had got along very well, thank you, with their own local set-up. The fact is, that in a sparsely settled region, phrases like "the dignity of the law" and "impartial justice" have less meaning than in a densely populated country. The Short Grass folks had seen how laws are made, initiated, and forced through by minorities. They had no great respect for the laws; they knew the men who had made them.

In fact; in the Panhandle of Oklahoma, then known as No Man's Land, they wanted none. In that district, owing to a mistake in the treaties, no federal control existed.

When the government sent a Judge and a Deputy Marshal to No Man's Land to set up law and order, the whole population regarded it as an indignity and an infringement of their natural rights. There was talk of revolution.

The Judge used to tell the story: His Deputy, Chris Madsen, one of Oklahoma's triumvirate of peace officers known as the Three Guardsmen, was sent out to investigate the state of affairs. He went to the saloon in the little cowtown, and found three belligerent hombres lined up at the bar. They were lean, and brown, and carried their guns slung low-down, ready for action. They all regarded him sourly.

The Deputy saw that they were itching for trouble. A few words passed, and the nearest man went for his gun. The Deputy fired once, and downed him. He stopped the second gunman by breaking his wrist with a bullet. The third man lost heart, and ran for the swinging doors. The Deputy fired a shot into the door jamb beside the fugitive's ear, and the fellow threw up his hands.

The Deputy disarmed his prisoners, and made the two carry the man who was down. The little procession marched up to the hotel where the Judge was staying. There the Deputy made his report, as brief as his fight had been: "Judge, here's your revolution!"

In the old days Indian lands were regarded as belonging to Uncle Sam. Pioneers had no compunction, as a rule, in helping themselves to timber from Indian lands. In a certain Western town the foundation of the principal church was made of cedar logs taken from an Indian reservation. When reproached for helping themselves to Indian timber, the answer was generally, "Shucks, it all belongs to Uncle Sam, and we are Uncle Sam's boys." On the frontier, as in most other parts of America, public opinion was king.

Kansas and Oklahoma have been consistently dry states almost from the beginning. In Kansas this is due in part to the moralistic New England tradition. In Oklahoma it grew out of the treaties with the Indians which forbade the importation of liquor into Indian country. Of course anyone who wants a drink can get it, if he will take the trouble, but the voters are still overwhelmingly in favor of prohibition. They argue that the way to minimize the nuisance is to make it inconvenient for a man to get liquor, and that state prohibition is the handiest way to make this inconvenience prevalent. If dry laws do not cut down the sale of liquor, they ask, why are the men who make and sell it all against them? They claim that, if national prohibition was disastrous, that is no reason why state prohibition should be. They argue that a dry state surrounded by wet ones has all the advantages and avoids most of the disadvantages of the traffic.

In Western Oklahoma, as in other parts of the Short Grass, there were chapters of the Anti-Horse Thief Association. The members were usually the leading men in their communities, and where the law proved ineffective, they sometimes took matters into their own hands and dealt with their enemies by stringing them up to the nearest tree or telegraph pole. They represented public opinion, and few honest men objected to their proceedings.

On one occasion it happened that at such a necktie party, three men took part, among others. One of the three committed suicide afterwards, another skipped the country, and the third went crazy. They had discovered that they had hanged an innocent man.

Necktie parties, killings, and state prison probably did something to discourage rustling cattle, if only by decimating the cattle thieves, but year after year, week after week, since cattle were first brought into the High Plains, the stealing of livestock has continued. Today the loss has become a huge tax upon the industry.

In old days rustlers altered brands or branded calves and mavericks, sometimes building up considerable herds in this way. Many a cowboy set up in business as a cattleman by stealing the iron rod from the endgate of a wagon, bending one end of it into a hook, and branding everything that came his way.

This sort of thing is out of date now, for cattle rustling has been streamlined and modernized.

Nowadays the thieves are organized into rings or

gangs whose operations are interstate. The first step in stealing cattle is selecting or spotting the animals to be stolen. The spotter drives around the country in a car and picks the choice animals which have been fattened for market. Of course he prefers those in a pasture close by the highway and one easy to get into and get out of with a pick-up truck.

When the spotter has reported, the truck visits the pasture after dark. The men kill the steers, load the meat on the truck, and before sunup are a day's ride away, generally across a state line.

One large gang used a furniture van bearing the name of a furniture company. Within the van was all the equipment of a butcher shop. The cattle were skinned and butchered on the road while the van was moving, receiving the meat from the pick-up truck and delivering it at a distance to a third truck belonging to a butcher shop. The thieves disposed of the hides in one state and the meat in another, operating through confederates owning meat markets.

This ring was inordinately successful until the cattlemen hired detectives, who worked for nearly a year before the racket was broken up.

Cattlemen have agitated for strict brand laws and have encouraged even small farmers to brand their cattle, thus co-operating with the big ranches to put down the racket. They urge that a bill of sale describing the stock be required for every sale, even of a single animal, so that successive owners may be identified. Too often rustlers have been encouraged by slack prosecution, easy verdicts, paroles, or pardons. As the Indian still occasionally steals horses, so the white man has carried on the tradition of the cattle thief. Old customs die hard on the prairie.

There are plenty of people who admire a brave man, no matter how "bad" he may be; and some of the old-time bandits were certainly men of courage. However, the sentimental glorification of the real criminal has not "caught on" among the old-timers. They have long memories, and their recollection of those men is not one of admiration or even of tolerance.

Elmer T. Peterson had his say about them recently in *The Daily Oklahoman:*

"Pioneers in Oklahoma know that these outlaws were lousy loafers—poor sports who refused to do their share of the back-breaking labor of pioneering, scum of the civilization that came to the far outposts to tame the wilderness. They lived by stealing from those who did the real work, murdering them if they resisted. . . .

"The real building of the Old West was done by obscure, leather-faced, toil-bent men and women who never dreamed of notoriety or whisky-crazy gun-fights, except to uphold the marshals and sheriffs who stood off these criminal camp followers."

Of course, there were some pathetic cases, like that of a girl dubbed Cattle Annie. Life on the lonely farm was tough on a young woman, and sometimes the reckless valor of a bandit appealed to her more strongly than the stodgy men on the land. Cattle Annie was one of these waifs, who "threw in" with a young rascal, and became involved in his clash with the law.

In those days, one never spoke of a gunman's "moll." A woman who went wrong was commonly called a "soiled dove." Cattle Annie probably deserved no such name. But she resisted arrest, was taken, and sent to a reform school. Her pathetic portrait, forlornly holding a Winchester (evidently put into her hands—unloaded —by the photographer) is a striking witness that association with criminals does not pay.

Cattle Annie afterward married and was a thoroughly respectable person. But her plight has been recorded in ballad meter. Here are some of the verses:

CATTLE ANNIE

There was a fair girl, her father was poor,
An honest and God-fearing man;
But his daughter was lonesome and followed the lure
Of a boy in a bad outlaw band.

   Poor Cattle Annie, they took her away,
   They put her in prison, nobody knows where;
   Poor Cattle Annie, they cut off her hair,
   She was a good girl till he led her astray.

Cattle Annie jumped out of the window, they say,
And shot at the men on her trail;
Little Britches was caught as she hurried away,
Cattle Annie's brave fighting did fail.

   Poor Cattle Annie, they took her away,
   They put her in prison, nobody knows where;
   Poor Cattle Annie, they cut off her hair,
   She was a good girl till he led her astray.

But the "lawlessness" of the Plains had other causes, deep-rooted in American folkways. In the first place, Americans are idealists, and they have also, following the example of the Founding Fathers of the Republic, the feeling that their ideals should be legalized by enacting them into law. At the same time, they are practical people, and by no means given to letting law stand in the way of getting things done. The history of America is the story of how the Americans, faced with new conditions, learned to meet these, often by ignoring the laws they had brought with them from the Mother Country.

Those English laws have been cherished, much as we cherish an heirloom. But they have been held with "in principle" rather than "in fact." This, of course, is an old English folkway; it is a sorry Englishman who cannot approve an idea, and at the same time neglect it in the interests of expediency.

These heirlooms, these "keepsake" laws, were sometimes not necessities, and often not even conveniences. And it may be taken for granted that a man will do his best to survive—law or no law. In these states, laws and customs have never exactly coincided.

Ever since Benjamin Franklin made it a rule to practice one virtue—a different one—each day of the week, Americans have followed his plan, which has become a widespread—indeed almost universal—folkway. The code of laws in any given community is never enforced in its entirety at any one time. Traffic laws provide an obvious example: when things are going along all right, officers get lax; but let a bad accident occur, and they begin to crack down on violators. Just so it is with bank robbery or any other crime.

The fact is that our laws are not always, perhaps not even often, an expression of public opinion; some of them are merely propaganda. They are like the shotgun kept loaded in the home: a weapon to be called into sudden use whenever an emergency demands it. Even the Constitution is interpreted anew whenever public opinion demands it.

It is true, of course, that no politician, no man even, ever has a choice between pure good and pure evil; he has only a choice between two evils. But he must make no mistake in his choice, however slight the difference. He is forever torn between the law and the facts. In the long run, the facts will win.

After all, who would care to live in a society where all the laws were constantly and rigidly enforced? Certainly not the Plainsman.

15. He'll Do to Take Along

IN SOME parts of the States the attitude of natives toward a stranger might be expressed in such questions as: "Who was your grandpappy?" or "What school did you attend?" or "How's your accent?" or "How much money have you?"

On the Short Grass, the test question is simply, "What can you *do?*"

Few begrudge a man what he can do or get for himself on the High Plains. Fewer pay homage to wealth, breeding, or education which are merely passive or ornamental. In a new country—that is, one recently developed—wealth is a proof of prowess, not the hallmark of old authority. Manners are better than in most regions—if only because men so lately carried arms—but they must earn their way. The test of a man's education is his self-sufficiency and *good will.*

There is little bootlicking of wealth or power—a fact which is reflected in a lack of philanthropy—so called. Rich men on the Short Grass are public-spirited, but not many devote their wealth to endowments and benefactions. They are never able to feel themselves a class apart. Subservience comes high on the Plains—it is beyond the means of a millionaire.

On visiting some parts of the country a Plainsman

is likely to be shocked to find even college presidents thinking of culture in terms of dollars and cents—as if moral qualities and clear thinking could be produced in students at so many dollars a head. How simple life would be if that were true! One is reminded of the inept remark of Napoleon I on being told that France under his regime had no good writers: "This is the fault of the Minister of Education!"

In the early days in Oklahoma Territory it was bad form, as well as bad judgment, to ask a stranger his name or show any curiosity about his past. A popular song of the period expressed the people's secret thoughts when a stranger appeared.

> *What was your name in the States?*
> *Was it Thompson, or Johnson, or Bates?*
> *Did you murder your wife and fly for your life?*
> *Say, what was your name in the States?*

Of course, plenty of fine people, persons of education and breeding, came to the West. That fact provided the humor expressed in the song. It also expressed the hospitality with which strangers were welcomed.

This feeling about questions is nothing new on the Plains. Though today you may hear a Westerner rebuke a stranger, saying, "You ought to get a job as a detective; then you could get *paid* for asking questions," the same displeasure will be found expressed in the books of the earliest travelers on the Short Grass.

When Francis Parkman was encamped near Bent's Old Fort on the Arkansas River in Colorado, the Volunteers were passing along the Santa Fe Trail to the War with Mexico, and visited his camp. He well ex-

presses the disgust of the Plainsmen, his companions,
at the inquisitive behavior of the men from the woodlands. The passage occurs in *The Oregon Trail:*

"One morning, as we were descending upon a wide
meadow, where we meant to rest for an hour or two, we
saw a body of horsemen approaching at a distance. In
order to find water, we were obliged to turn aside to
the river bank, a full half mile from the trail. Here we
put up a kind of awning, spread buffalo-robes on the
ground, and Shaw and I sat down to smoke beneath it.

" 'We are going to catch it now,' said Shaw; 'look at
those fellows; there'll be no peace for us here.'

"And in truth about half the volunteers had strag-
gled away from the line of march, and were riding over
the meadow towards us.

" 'How are you?' said the first who came up, alighting
from his horse and throwing himself upon the ground.
The rest followed close, and a score of them soon gathered about us, some lying at full length and some sitting
on horse-back. They all belonged to a company raised
in St. Louis. There were some ruffian faces among them,
and some haggard with debauchery; but on the whole
they were extremely good-looking men, superior beyond measure to the ordinary rank and file of an army.
Except that they were booted to the knees, they wore
their belts and military trappings over the ordinary
dress of citizens. Besides their swords and holster pistols,
they carried slung from their saddles the excellent
Springfield carbines, loaded at the breech. They inquired the character of our party, and were anxious to
know the prospect of killing buffalo, and the chance
that their horses would stand the journey to Santa Fe.

All this was well enough, but a moment after a worse visitation came upon us.

" 'How are you, strangers? Whar are you going and whar are you from?' said a fellow, who came trotting up with an old straw hat on his head. He was dressed in the coarsest brown homespun cloth. His face was rather sallow from fever-and-ague, and his tall figure, though strong and sinewy, had a lean angular look, which, together with his boorish seat on horse-back gave him an appearance anything but graceful. More of the same stamp were close behind him. Their company was raised in one of the frontier counties, and we soon had abundant evidence of their rustic breeding; they came crowding round by scores, pushing between our first visitors, and staring at us with unabashed faces.

" 'Are you the captain?' asked one fellow.

" 'What's your business out here?' asked another.

" 'Whar do you live when you're to home?' said a third.

" 'I reckon you're traders,' surmised a fourth; and to crown the whole, one of them came confidentially to my side and inquired in a low voice, 'What's your partner's name?'

"As each newcomer repeated the same questions, the nuisance became intolerable. Our military visitors were soon disgusted at the concise nature of our replies, and we could overhear them muttering curses against us. While we sat smoking, not in the best imaginable humor, Tete Rouge's tongue was not idle. He never forgot his military character, and during the whole interview he was incessantly busy among his fellow-soldiers. At length we placed him on the ground before us, and told him that he might play the part of spokesman for the whole. Tete Rouge was delighted, and we soon had the satisfaction of seeing him gabble at such a rate that the torrent of questions was in a great measure diverted from us. A little while after, to our amazement, a cannon with four horses came lumbering up behind the crowd; and the driver, who was perched on one of the animals, stretching his neck so as to look over the rest of the men, called out,—

" 'Whar are you from, and what's your business? . . .' "

On the Santa Fe Trail the traders welcomed all comers who wished to join the wagon train. Moreover, the wagon master would feed the strangers free for nothing all the way from Kansas to New Mexico. All that he asked in return was that every man would take his turn at guard duty. This custom well expresses the feeling which still persists on the prairies, that freedom carries responsibilities with it.

An anecdote illustrates this: I have taken it from Lona Shawver's *Chuckwagon Windies and Range Poems* (1934), with the permission of her publishers, The Naylor Company of San Antonio:

"In the early days there were certain rules concerning the etiquette of the cowboy during work on the range. For the breaking of these rules a fellow was tried by Kangaroo court. Some of the rules that might cause a cowboy misery if he so forgot himself as to break one, were:

"Not to jump into chuck until the cook called, 'Chuck, come and get it.'

"If one went near the waterbucket and found it empty he must fill it immediately.

"No scuffling or kicking up the dirt around the chuckwagon, during a meal or when food and cooking utensils were exposed.

"Scraps from the plates must be raked into the fire to prevent flies.

"Never saddle a horse near a wagon.

"Never run a horse into camp.

"One must be called only once to get up mornings.

"Keep mouth shut about the other fellow's business or past.

"For violating these rules a man might receive a booting, a ducking in the creek, or other punishments. Practical jokes were often played on the tenderfoot. After everyone was asleep at night some fellow would drag a lot of trace chains across the tenderfoot's bed and yell 'Whoa'; of course the greener would come off of his roll scared out of his senses, much to the amusement of the cowboys."

Competence was not enough, on the Short Grass; the stranger must prove himself a man of good will. The community was too small to tolerate any voluntary deadheads. Whatever was not social was not virtuous.

Democracy was inevitable on the Plains, first because no one could be sure of making a go of it without the help of his neighbors, and secondly, because nobody could be compelled to help. It was too easy to pull out, skip, vamoose.

Beryl Williams-Palmer tells of this early help-thy-neighbor spirit in *Echoes of Eighty-Nine*:

"We had dust storms in those days. All the roads were dirt, and horses, cattle, mules, oxen and wagons traveled

them. We didn't call it a dust bowl. The government
didn't have to step in and give us a lift. We were not
mentioned even for politics' sake. We had cheap wheat,
but when we did, we had a banner crop to make up for
it. Our taxes were low and living accordingly. The farmers planned ahead. Nature was our great stabilizer and
took care of us. But it was dead certain a poor worker
had poor pickings. Money wasn't the big thing then.
We always had about everything we needed, and sometimes all we wanted. But I don't remember crying
around for pennies or nickels as kids do now. We
bought in quantities of bushels and pecks, not in paper
sacks. It was a wholesome life, with a moral fiber sadly
needed right now, happy in the simplicity of things, an-
ticipation, realization, contentment. We had no union
alliance of reliefers telling the taxpayers where to
head off.

"Radio, electric lights, automobiles, gas, paved roads,
telephones were not for farmers then and mortgages
were a disgrace—something to be rid of as soon as possible.

"Let us catch that help-thy-neighbor spirit again, but
not as the guys in Washington would have us do."

On the Short Grass, drouth, recurrent, meant that a
man might make no crop for years on end. Success in
making a living therefore meant spreading the risk over
a period of several years, either by individual thrift, or
by some form of community planning. The Plains Indians followed the latter method, organizing their
hunts on a tribal scale, and taking up the slack by a custom of personal generosity. The cattlemen, with their
large capital and large profits in good years, their al-

most feudal system, could carry on through lean years and fat. The nesters had a more difficult time, unless they were members of an organized community. Such organized communities (generally religious bodies) are still to be found scattered over all the Plains: Mennonites, Amish, Dunkards, Mormons.

But the old-time American farmer cared for none of these things. He wanted to go it alone. He was no joiner. He liked local government, and damn little of that. He had a hearty distrust of regimentation, and felt that the price of liberty was hanging on to all the liberty he had. The whole tradition of his kind taught that nobody was likely to help him half as much as he could help himself. He expected to take the world by the horns and crack its neck. He was a good neighbor, helpful and generous, but he resented favors. On the windbitten Short Grass he found he had a tough assignment.

The Indian went at it differently. No Plains Indian ever went hungry while another man of his tribe had meat in his tipi. The Indian required no invitation to the feast; it was his *right* to share with all men of his own blood, and he walked right in, sat down, and expected to be served. Moreover, he *was* served; the Indian was nothing if not hospitable. I have seen a stranger enter a tipi where the family had been served with everything the kettle afforded. Immediately, the woman of the family gave him a clean plate, took a little food from the plate of every member of her family, and so made the uninvited guest welcome.

Only once have I seen that custom violated—under provocation. I once invited myself to dinner in a strange camp of Indians, when I was miles from home.

The old warrior—who had evidently been so used by some stingy white man—led me out, handed me the ax, and pointed to the woodpile. I knew Indians well enough to realize what caused him to act so, and I began to make the chips fly. Before I could split a second stick, he took the ax from me, led me in, and told his wife to serve me.

Some weeks later, when passing that way, I made it a point to repay his hospitality by carrying a big watermelon into his tent and placing it before him. The old man sat there speechless, hanging his head in shame. I had had no intention of embarrassing him, and hurried out, as ill-at-ease as he was. This is the sole instance in years of experience. I never knew an Indian to demand payment for a meal.

By his code, good hunters and successful horse-thieves not only expected to contribute constantly to the poor and unfortunate, but positively looked forward to doing so. A man might have only wildcat or "dead horse" on the day's menu, but he never hid what he had from the passing stranger.

Today, if you ask an old Indian to recount his honors, he will not be content merely to recite his war honors; he will also relate with honest satisfaction every generous contribution he made to the welfare of his people, every occasion on which he was able to care for the helpless or give away all he possessed for the benefit of others.

Thus, if a quarrel broke out in the tribe, the true-bred Cheyenne would risk his life, stepping between the feudists with the peace-pipe in his hands. If he had a child, he would take the little one with him, pleading with his people to think of their children and set aside their differences for the common good. If they listened to his plea and smoked the pipe in communion, he would then make presents all round, satisfy everyone, and restore peace to the camp.

Again, if a man had lost his wife or his brother through sickness or war, the chief would call upon him, give him a new suit of buckskins, dress him in it with his own hands, give him ponies, a new tent, weapons, and a buffalo robe, or even organize a war party to go and avenge the deaths of his relatives.

Such generosity was expected of leading men, and they gloried in it. The wish to perform such generous deeds was, in fact, the principal motive among Plains Indians for the acquisition of property. As a result, the chief was often the shabbiest man in the camp, and lived in the sorriest tent of all. He expected no return for such gifts.

One summer day in the eighties Chief Little Robe was heading toward the government agency on the Cheyenne reservation. The next day was ration day and all Indians were required to be present at the beef issue. As he drove his wagon along he passed the homes of members of his band strung along the river. Some of these tents were unoccupied, with two crossed sticks across the doorway as a sign that the inmates were away.

Before he came in sight of the agency he saw a young woman in her blanket trudging along on foot, packing a baby boy on her back. When he came even with her he saw that she was crying. Little Robe pulled up his team and saw that she was the wife of White Bear. He called to her and she stood to listen. "My niece, what

are you crying for? What are you doing walking all
alone like this? What is the matter? Tell me. I may be
able to help you."

She stopped and wiped away her tears. "Uncle, it is
my husband. At the last dance he gave away our only
tent just to show off, and now we have no tent to camp
in at the agency tomorrow. You think I want to go
there and hang around some other woman's tent? I told
him to go alone or ask one of his relatives to get our
rations for us, but he has no ears. He would not listen.
He insisted on coming, saying we could share his cousin's tipi. When I refused he lost his temper, said he was
through with me, and told me to leave his camp. So
here I am. He is all alone at home."

Little Robe felt sorry for her. "Did he strike you or
abuse you?" he demanded.

Mrs. White Bear shook her head. "No," she replied.

"Then," said Little Robe, "get into our wagon. We
will go back and see your husband."

She climbed in and they drove back to the place
where White Bear's tent had stood. There they found
the husband very busy repairing his harness. He was
evidently still upset, for he at first ignored them, and his
jerky movements showed his agitation.

Little Robe called him over as if nothing had happened. When White Bear stood before the Chief, Little
Robe told him what his wife had said. White Bear
quickly admitted everything.

"Well now," said Little Robe, "my nephew, you just
allowed your temper to get the best of you. But since
no blows were exchanged between you, I ask that you
both make it up and live together peaceably. Look at

this baby boy of yours; take pity on him. Remember, if the Indian Agent hears of this you are likely to be punished. See, here in the wagon I have an extra tent. Take it, keep it, and do not be so foolish as to give it away another time."

Little Robe got down and pulled a wall tent, nearly new, out of his wagon, and gave it to them. White Bear's ill temper gave way to smiles of satisfaction. He shook hands with the Chief, hugged his wife, and said: "My Chief, my heart was on the ground, but now it is strong again because you have brought my wife back to me and given me this tent."

Little Robe got back into the wagon and headed for the agency again. The reunited couple hooked up their team, put their new tent into the wagon, and rumbled happily along the trail behind.

The Indian thought thrift a kind of cowardice. If a man were unwilling to give away whatever he had, it must be because he was afraid he could not get the like for himself again. This made the Indian a generous giver, since he preferred prestige and good will to wealth. Somewhat the same spirit animated the cowmen who followed him.

Owing to the independent habit of Indians of making individual wars, owing to the lack of authority of Indian chiefs, owing to the conflict of authority among the War Department, Indian Bureau, and civilian local government, owing to the fact that most men went armed, and owing to the size of the country, there arose a confusion in the minds of some men as to where war left off and crime began.

Thus, in war on the Plains, horses were prime booty; taking them was dangerous, but thoroughly honorable. So, to this day, Indians on the Plains get sent to prison for stealing some miserable rack of bones not worth the attorney's postage bill. The Indian has not learned up-to-date methods. He gets caught.

Again, when cattle ran wild and uncared for, every man carried an iron and branded them wherever found. In the beginning there was no pretense of breeding the stock. The cowman, like the Indian stealing ponies, was entitled to any he could get his rope on. It was only later that branding mavericks was looked on as a crime. And so, to this day, rustling goes on all over the Plains.

Yet, with all this stealing of cattle and horses, which has never stopped, and which has at times run into thousands and thousands of head, petty thievery on the Plains was unknown. The cattle thief would scorn to take a saddle or a rope; the Indian horse-thief never touched the small possessions of his fellows left in camp. Two sticks crossed before a tipi door made it safer than the vault of the United States Treasury. I myself have left all my possessions lying under a tarp on the grass in the middle of a camp of 5,000 redskins for two weeks at a time, and never lost so much as a tent-peg. Indian traders, who sold to redskins on credit to the tune of thousands of dollars, have told me that they never lost a dime. At a treaty council, an old chief once stated the simple fact: "Indians do not steal."

The traveler was welcome, however, to help himself to forage or fuel wherever he made camp or stopped to boil coffee. He fed his animals with corn from the nearest field.

In like manner, anyone passing by was free to enter and bed down in anybody's house, free to cook up a meal, burn wood, and help himself to groceries. In return, he was expected to cut wood to replace what he had used, to leave supplies or money for what he had eaten, and to clean up the mess he had made. He expected the get the same fair treatment from any stranger who visited his own home in his absence. Until within ten years past, hardly anyone on the Short Grass ever bothered to lock his door; many householders had no keys whatever.

Even the stores were left unlocked in country districts, so that any neighbor passing by could help himself by day or night, leaving his money on the counter, or a note signed with his initials. Such storekeepers never lost a dime; petty thievery was virtually unknown.

But times changed with paved roads and motor cars. One after another, these harassed storekeepers called their patrons together, and red in the face, explained the case: "There must be some stranger in the county. I'm losing a lot of stuff. I reckon I'm going to have to put a lock on the door. I didn't want you to mistake me." Then, like as not, the storekeeper gave a key to each of his regular patrons.

Again there is the Indian angle on this unpleasant novelty in Western life—petty thievery. The tale goes that an Eastern tourist stopped his car and hailed the blue-coated Indian policeman at the agency rodeo. "Will it be safe to leave my car here?" he demanded.

The Indian looked gravely up and down the road, then turned to the tourist. "I guess so. I don't see no white men around."

The Indian extended his fair play even to the animals on which he was dependent. He felt himself a brother to all living things and—far from despising the wild creatures—envied them their specialization and powers quite beyond anything he himself possessed. The Indians loved the ground beans, and squaws passing over the prairie with their digging sticks were delighted to find the little cache of seeds buried in the ground by the "bean mouse." But the Indian woman did not rob the little creature. She was as tender toward the mouse as Robert Burns. When she took the beans she replaced them with an equal quantity of Indian corn.

But the friendliness of people on the Plains seldom extends to subservience. Personal service is not easily commanded, and on the Short Grass, fortunately, one seldom encounters strangers who attempt to treat their employees as servants or inferiors. There is no peasantry on the High Plains. The burden of courtesy rests upon the employer, who walks carefully to avoid offending the self-respect of those who serve him.

Thus, if you organize a pack train to go into the mountains, and need a cook, you will do well not to ask any old cowman outright to be your cook. However poor he may be, he expects better treatment than that. The proper technique is to hire enough men to wrangle your horses and pack your mules—with no mention of a cook. One of these men, of course, will have been hired to perform that duty, and everyone knows which man will have it to do. After the train has been organized, the boss will then say, carelessly, "Well, somebody has got to cook for the outfit. Who's it to be?" Then the man employed for the purpose will volunteer and no feelings are hurt.

On one occasion, a refugee of noble blood came to the Short Grass and put up at a boarding house in a small town. He was not arrogant and meant no harm when he demanded breakfast in bed. But his landlady, red in the face with indignation, informed him that he was able-bodied and could get down to breakfast like other people. The nobleman had the good grace to comply; or maybe he was just hungry.

Cowboy Democracy

On the Short Grass there were social differences, but they were not the kind that have to be enforced by artificial barriers, servants, clothes, press-agents, and ostentation. Goodnight, Kit Carson, Satanta, men like these did not have to attend exclusive schools or belong to the right clubs to maintain their superiority. Everybody who met them acknowledged it. It was manifest. They did what others did, and did it better. It was so with Odysseus, who was the best sailor on his ship.

G. W. Christian tells a story in *Echoes of Eighty-Nine:* "Lots of funny things happened in the early days. In the fall of 1890, about October, a neighbor of mine built a new log house. When they got the house enclosed, a dance was given for the young folk of the community. After the dance got under way, some cowboys from the Strip cow-country came in with their spurs on

and their six-shooters buckled to them. The girls refused to dance with them. The cowboys said that if they
couldn't dance nobody could, so they proceeded to
loosen their guns and let cool air in the place by shooting out the windows. The occupants lost no time in
vacating the room. The girls, in a group, were found
the next morning about three miles north on the
prairie. They had become lost when they ran out into
the night. I hadn't taken any girl to the dance that
evening."

GREAT OPEN SPACES

A Plainsman must be able to "see out"—at least in
one direction. He does not love crowds. One of these
men, a young fellow from a small town on the Short
Grass, recently returned from a trip to Miami. "Yes,"
he reported, "we had a good time. But we had to drive
for miles out of town to find a beach where we could
have our party. Around Miami all the beaches were
covered with people, thick as fleas; nobody could have
a good time in a mob like that."

For it is the man who has solitude enough to make
him independent who makes a good neighbor. He still
has something of his own to give. In crowded places, a
man might feel that he has to be on his guard—even be
haughty, surly, or rude to maintain his privacy. This
sometimes mars his capacity for friendship. But where
there is plenty of room, a man can afford to be friendly,
and still be his own man. That is the feeling of the
Plainsman.

The most living tradition of any people is often unconscious—some pattern of life which everyone takes for granted. And so in the Short Grass.

In that treeless country there is a strong feeling that to enclose one's yard—and particularly to shut it in with a hedge or wall—is little short of anti-social. Strangers who do that find themselves the object of unfriendly criticism. And some towns have even enacted ordinances which compel the citizen to leave his front yard unfenced. Where barriers are permitted, public opinion favors low hedges, wire, or fences over which, or through which, any passer-by can easily see. In many towns nearly all the yards remain entirely open—front and back. The houses stand, like so many tipis or frontier shacks, on the prairie. It is the old tradition of the High Plains—of man standing alone on the grass.

Some have attempted to justify the custom on esthetic grounds. They say that good architecture should bear relation to the surrounding landscape, and so, where the country is open, a house shut in by walls stands in a false relation to it.

This feeling against shutting out the public is illustrated by the old story of the cowboy in the frontier hotel, who broke down the bathroom door of a terrified dude, saying he "just wanted to know what in hell was so damn private in there."

But there is a feeling which runs counter to that one —a love, amounting almost to reverence, for a tree or a stone. These, being so rare on the plains, are treasured. The man who needlessly cuts down a living tree is regarded generally as a skunk, unfit for human society.

Individuals and city fathers go to great trouble and expense planting trees, shrubs, and flowers. Even the poorest shacks will boast a burning bush or morning-glory vine carefully tended. Cottonwoods and red cedars stand guard wherever soil and water permit. And this passion, organized in the garden clubs, has encouraged people to enclose their *back* yards with woven-wire fences on which vines may climb, with tall hedges, or—more rarely—with solid walls.

For there are many who find great spaces and high winds exhausting, even frightening. These seek some shelter from "all outdoors." They want a nest, a hole to crawl into. The country is too big for their taste. They are kin to the lady tourist driving through, who stopped to ask about the road. "And," she declared, "it's the *road* I'm interested in; I've had enough *scenery!*"

The absence of shelter even affects health. There is the story of the woman from the woodlands who carried a bush on her car, behind which she could hide when Nature compelled a halt.

But your true-bred Plainsman cannot thrive shut in on all sides. He loves trees, but the forest smothers him. He loves rocks, but cannot endure living in a valley ringed round by mountains. He must be able to see out on *one* side—or go crazy. He must have "room to breathe," and space "to turn around in." On vacations in the Rockies he hurries through the pines and makes camp in one of the natural "parks" or open valleys; if he goes above timberline, where only grass grows and the horizon is far away, he draws a sigh of relief.

He loves privacy, too—none better. But he knows there is no privacy like that in the middle of a plain. There he can converse in complete confidence on any subject. There he is at home. There are those, of course, who cannot love any land unless they can tamper with it—plant and dig in it. But these are the earthbounds, chained to the thing they keep. It is a curious fact that such people are far more ready to pull up stakes and move on than are the hunter and the cattleman.

History shows that it is always the so-called "nomad" who fights most bitterly to avoid removal. Our cities are full of farm boys, but you will find mighty few cowboys or Indians there. They will endure anything rather than abandon the country they love.

Like the rest of the world, the people of the Short Grass know that the United States is the greatest nation on earth, that its greatness is due to a combination of factors, any one of which would make a lesser nation great and powerful: a vast area of good land; a huge population of diverse talents and origins, intelligent and resourceful; an industry and trade of immense scope and potentialities; an enormous arsenal of resources; and a form of government more flexible and so more stable, under which all these components continue to progress and develop.

To share in the glory and power and safety of all this, the man of the Short Grass welcomes everybody—but insists that these newcomers share also the ideals and responsibilities which are its foundation. Anyone who belongs may buck any aspect of the set-up—but woe to the stranger who attacks it from the outside. To criticize us with impunity, a man must speak our language.

The Short Grass believes that it should be obvious to anyone that democracy is the best system for Americans. It would be so, even if it were less well administered than other systems—or, for that matter, even if our people had not the highest standard of living on earth. It would be so because it best expresses the old, deep-rooted tradition of America.

A long-established form of government becomes a set of folkways, and can never be essentially altered; does history afford a single example of a nation—retaining its autonomy—which altered its essential form of government through revolution?

Before the Revolution, the German people trusted experts, bowed to a kaiser, thirsted for domination, relied upon military power, and blundered diplomatically. Their legislature existed merely to give the Kaiser what he wanted.

What is changed now? Only the men who rule the Germans.

Before the Revolution, Russia was, in effect, a nation of serfs, ruled by an ignorant despot surrounded by greedy, incompetent yes-men, terrorized by secret police, swept by pogroms.

What is changed now? Only the men who rule the Russians.

And so with every nation. Nothing changes except the personnel. Nothing *can* change.

Is anyone so dumb as not to see that Americans will maintain the essential functions of their way of life in spite of all attempts to change them?

When a man advocates revolution in this country he is therefore not, as he claims, advocating any essential change in our government—since he must know that he is powerless to produce any such change. He is simply advocating a change of personnel; he wants political power. And, if he advocates change by violence, it must be because he despairs of achieving power by legal means. In other words, he is not the politician of our choice.

Of course, in any country, power is forever passing from one man or group to another. No party is strong or wise enough to hold it long; if they were so, they cannot live forever. Now, since we believe in the consent of the governed, we prefer to have this power go to people who will not shed our blood in the process of getting it. That is what elections are for. We prefer elections to purges.

We are not averse to violence in dealing with underhanded minorities—summon up the ghosts of the horse-thieves and bandits on Boot Hill! But violence that involves us *all* is a different matter. The fellows who start that had better be plenty strong. And if they are so strong, why resort to violence?

The people of the Short Grass have demonstrated that they can take it—and dish it out.

Where are the Indians who annoyed the Texans and the Kansans in early days? Not in Texas. Not in Kansas. Some of them left their bones—to be sold for fertilizer. The rest of them had to get out. There is an obvious moral here.

Moreover, it must be clear that whoever wishes to gain power by violence must be either a blind fanatic or a plain fool. Otherwise he would not crave political power where assassination is in use as a political weapon. Dictators retire in wooden overcoats. Ask the ghosts of those who were purged in Russia and Germany if revolution was worth it. For that matter, ask the refugees.

Free speech is the right of every American. It entails the responsibility that the speech be not only free but *honest, well-informed,* and *in the interest of all.* Only such honest, informed, and broadly benevolent speech can stand the strain put upon it by facts.

These, I take it, are the convictions of the people of the High Plains.

On the Short Grass you may sometimes call a man a son-of-a-bitch—if you smile when you say it. But no smile will save you, if you call him a coward or a liar.

The first epithet may be a term of endearment—it may mean that the speaker recognizes a kindred spirit. But to call him a coward or a liar means that he is an outcast, that he is anti-social, *that he does not belong.*

No one should expect more of human nature than human nature can give. But we should expect good will, some public spirit, and a decent respect to the opinions of mankind. For without these no society can long exist.

When the Dust Bowl migrants from the Short Grass went west to the Coast, they sent home word, "The people out here are not friendly."

California is, I suppose, as friendly as most other states infested with tourists. But the friendliness of the Short Grass is hard to match. Probably its best expression is the saying so often attributed to Will Rogers: "I never met a man I didn't like."

That bewildered complaint of the Okies lights up the outstanding virtue of the High Plains people. They do not care where you come from or who you are. You are welcome.

This attitude puts the maintenance of cordial relations squarely up to the stranger. Short Grass folks give him the benefit of the doubt; it is up to him to deserve their trust. If the stranger can deserve it, he will receive the highest praise the Plainsman can give: "He'll do to take along."

16. The Gold Dust Bowl

THE MEN on the Short Grass have been lucky fellows, and their good luck is reflected in their perennial hopefulness.

There are many reasons for this. The Plains has always been a young man's country, whether the young man was a cowboy, a nester, a townsman, or an oilman. Men were not earthbound, but moved freely to greener pastures when the old ones went sour. There were always friends and neighbors to take up the slack, always a chance to start over. Food was more or less free for the asking or the getting, equipment was simple, and nearly everyone possessed the needed skills from boyhood. Women were few, sought after, and therefore well content. Great resources lay untapped. Moreover, the present was not conditioned by the past—for the past no man regarded. Wealth came and went, and there was little in the way of caste.

On those High Plains there is more good will than there is grass even. In Amarillo, Texas, they hold an annual Mother-in-Law's Day, and give prizes to the oldest, the youngest, and the "most" mother-in-law.

THE LONG VIEW

Much of the land sold originally for such a nominal price that one good crop would return the investment in full. A man with a little capital, therefore, found it possible to carry on for years without a crop, since his first crop had fully reimbursed him for his original investment. Year after year he would plant wheat which never came up, or came up so scantily that in five years' time he never put a combine in the field. Then, when it rained, all the seed previously planted might germinate and grow. Thus it was sometimes possible to have a crop in a year when no seed had been planted.

They say that the use of colchicine will enable scientists to develop perennial wheat. If they do, the wheat farmer in the Dust Bowl will be ready to plant it. He already has the notion.

In the shallow well district of the Panhandle the water table lies a little more than a hundred feet below the surface. Wells driven beyond that depth provide a bountiful supply of water if the drouth is not too severe. Farmers rig up centrifugal pumps driven by the motor from an old Ford truck and are sometimes able to pump out a steady stream of water nine inches in diameter to irrigate their land. They claim this is more economical than buying water from a large irrigation company, since such a company expects annual payments whether the water is needed or not. Whether this method will prove successful during severe drouths, when the water table falls sharply and may decline to 200 feet below the surface, is not yet known. Pumping water from a depth of 200 feet is too expensive for irrigating land in the Dust Bowl, as a rule.

Out there, they say, water is a matter of life and depth.

Where the climate makes a good crop impossible for years on end, men must learn to take the long view, to carry on and hope for the future—which always arrives, eventually—to gamble on their guts and brains, to prefer a grand adventure to a petty daily security.

The Indian always knew how to endure hardship, adapt himself to the course of nature, and make the most of his opportunities. The cowman learned the lesson quickly, since his herds could be quickly increased or reduced. But the plowman from the small-farm rainy regions to the eastward was long a-learning.

Often he had not the means to plan far ahead—he was geared to a shorter cycle. He could not always stick it out in a country that made a crop only once in four years.

Time has relentlessly sifted the chaff from the wheat on the Short Grass. The men who stayed and "took" it are the salt of the earth, men with courage, faith, hope, and vision. They are not hand-to-mouth people. They believe that there is surely a way out, if *only* they can find it. And the odd thing is that those who do not understand their approach to life accuse them of being mere opportunists and improvisers, satisfied with makeshifts. Nothing could be more absurd.

These men prefer to work for themselves; they expect life to be better for their children than it was for them. They believe that the future of these States will be greater than their glorious past.

The Boosters

In early days, every citizen had high hopes that his town would turn out to be a metropolis of the prairies, rivaling Kansas City or Wichita. To insure this, he wanted railroads and improvements there, and therefore was determined to make his town the county seat. Most of the settlers were men of modest means, and the readiest way to raise money was through the sale of bonds. The population was sparse and shifting and each town in the county, and particularly those near the geographical center of the county, became bitter rivals in the struggle. Sometimes there would be as many as four or five contestants for the prize. One election after another was held, always with conflicting results and mutual charges of fraud. Then there would be a quarrel over the possession of the county records—which were sometimes stolen, commandeered by force of arms.

Thus in Howard County, 1870, Boston and Elk Falls contended. Each claimed to have won the election, but Elk Falls had the records. The armed citizens of Boston, 150 strong, marched in a body to Elk Falls, loaded the records into a spring wagon and carried them away. When the sheriff attempted to recover these, Boston posted sentries all around the town and concealed the records. Other residents of the county sought to end the controversy by having the county divided, which was done in spite of the combined efforts of the two warring villages, which now found themselves away off in one corner of the new county. Neither was successful in becoming the county seat. Boston vanished completely, Elk Falls dwindled to a hamlet.

In Grant County in the late 1880's, Appomattox and Ulysses were rivals in a similar struggle. The leaders of the two communities met and signed a written agreement not to engage in any fraud in the forthcoming election. It was also agreed that the winning town should underwrite the expense of the election. When this became known, the citizens of Appomattox, feeling themselves wronged by their leaders, formed a mob and threatened to hang them. The men saved their lives by making up the money which had been spent. Appomattox now had everything its own way and the drouth of 1889 and the movement of settlers into the Cherokee Strip in the early 1890's left Ulysses apparently at the mercy of the bond-holders. In 1909, however, the citizens got out from under by putting their shacks on the running gears of wagons and moving the whole town overnight to an unmortgaged site a few miles away.

Syracuse, one of the most delightful towns in western Kansas because of the trees in its streets, had a long fight with Kendall, while one election followed another and charges flew back and forth. At one time Kendall threw up breastworks of barrels and bales of hay around the court house to protect their county records, but in time Syracuse was successful and Kendall ceased to exist.

Many of these county-seat wars were fomented by the local journalists, who delighted to bombard each other with picturesque vituperation. Samples of their editorials may be found in "The Battles of Phantom Cities" by Elmer T. Peterson, in the *Saturday Evening Post,* 1927, a detailed account of the county-seat wars of Kansas.

Goodland was a rival with several other towns for the

county seat and at each election sent an armed delega-
tion to count the votes. The county books, however,
were at Eustis and Eustis had the law on her side. The
citizens of Goodland decided to use guile, and sent their
sheriff to arrest every voter in the rival town. Every
charge in the law books was made against one man or
another, from wife-beating to arson. Each of the victims,
arrested separately, and knowing that he could clear
himself in court, submitted without resistance. The
judge connived and kept the trials going while a posse
in Goodland carried off the records. In time, the Supreme Court confirmed the designation of Goodland
and the other towns were left with no recourse. No one
was killed.

In Wichita County a war broke out between Leoti
and Coronado in 1886. Both towns imported gunmen
from Dodge City and Wallace. The ringleader at Leoti
was a man named Coulter. He and his roughs drove to
Coronado and challenged it to a pitched battle. The
Coronado men were not daunted, shot Coulter and another man dead and mortally wounded a third. About a
dozen of the Coronado men were tried, but none was
convicted. At the next election Leoti was declared the
county seat.

A prolonged conflict was maintained between Cimarron and Ingalls. A wealthy financier named Soule
financed the election completely and dug a canal ninety
miles long, built a town and a railroad, and put the
journalists and the gunmen of Cimarron on their metal.
But Cimarron had the records which it refused to give
up, even under a court ruling. The men of Ingalls
marched upon Cimarron, where a battle followed. Only

the traditional innocent bystander was killed, but the Ingalls men remained in possession of the field. Mr. Soule lost interest after the battle and left his ditch to dry up. Within ten years Cimarron was made the county seat.

The most malignant conflict of the kind was between Hugoton and Woodsdale. Woodsdale was founded by Colonel Wood, the fighting Quaker, a journalist, promoter, and a leader in the Free State Party. He was a bold man who drove alone into the rival town after his life had been threatened there, but Hugoton won the election. Charges of fraud were hurled back and forth and the militia came down to quiet the disturbance. The Hugoton marshal, a man named Robinson, had pistol-whipped one of the Woodsdale men. A warrant was issued and given to the Woodsdale marshal to serve. The two marshals shot at each other in Hugoton until the Woodsdale marshal lost heart and retired.

South of the Kansas line in what is now the Panhandle was a strip of land that was known as No Man's Land. As I have pointed out, this land was not included in any governmental unit, through a mistake in the wording of the treaty, and, therefore, had no law-enforcement agency. Any killings taking place there were outside the jurisdiction of the existing courts. Robinson, perhaps to avoid further trouble, went on a hunting trip into this neutral strip.

The Woodsdale marshal, Short, organized a posse— if you can call it that—and tried to trap Robinson there, but Robinson made his get-away on a fast horse.

Short sent for reinforcements and the sheriff from Woodsdale led a second posse into the strip. One summer night in '88, the sheriff, three deputies, and a boy named Tonney camped near a hay stack on the banks of Wild Horse Lake. The Hugoton men took them by surprise. The sheriff and his three deputies were immediately shot down. The boy played dead and afterwards managed to get back to tell the story of the massacre. The militia was ordered out, but no arrests could be made under existing organizations.

Colonel Wood, persistent as ever, finally brought twelve Hugoton men to trial in Texas and convicted five of them of first-degree murder. The Supreme Court of the United States ordered a new trial, but this was never held. In 1891, when leaving the court held in the Methodist Church, one of the witnesses for the defense shot Wood in the back in the presence of his wife. Woodsdale was finally abandoned.

The high hopes of the early settlers is well expressed in the following advertisement, found in the back of a book by Charles L. Youngblood entitled, *A Mighty Hunter: The Adventures of Charles L. Youngblood on the Plains and Mountains,* published by Rand McNally and Company, New York, 1890:

COOLIDGE, KANSAS

"Coolidge is now a full-fledged city, the metropolis of Hamilton County and of Western Kansas. Although only a few years ago it was but a 'trading-post' called Sargent, made up of an old sod fort and a flag station when the Santa Fe first went through, it now has about 1,500 bees, with the drones and moss-backs nearly all driven out, fine stone blocks, schools and churches. The

Peck Water Works Company furnishes the City and the Railroad with the finest quality of water in the State, and a fire protection second to none. Its location, on the western line of Kansas, is almost identical with that of Kansas City on the eastern, and twenty years from now may find it as large a city; for its intermediately high altitude and one of the finest climates in the world (there having been only about forty stormy days in 1889, it being just near enough to the mountains to escape the storms of Eastern and Middle Kansas, and far enough away to avoid the cold from the snow in them), and its Artesian Waters, possessing highly curative properties, are fast bringing Coolidge into prominence as a legitimate health resort. Everyone recommended to go to the mountains for pulmonary and throat troubles will find it wise to stop here and get acclimated. The change from a low altitude to that of Manitou, Colorado Springs, and Denver, is so great that many well people cannot stand it, while invalids are often seriously injured, whereas if they had acclimated themselves at Coolidge, they would in most cases recover. The Artesian Water has effected some remarkable cures of chronic kidney and liver troubles. The address of those cured will be promptly furnished on application.

"Coolidge is situated on the Main Line of the Santa Fe Railroad, which has here its Division Round-house, Work shops, and Eating-house, and pays out monthly about $8,ooo. It is also situated in the Valley of the Arkansas River, surrounded by the most fertile lands in the West, and as a stock-growing locality it is incomparable.

"Youngblood, after having traversed the plains for twenty years, here decided to pitch his tent, finding here the best natural resources, climate, and water, and knowing that a prosperous City must eventually raise its walls in this favored spot.

"All inquiries will be promptly and courteously answered by the City Clerk, or the Coolidge State Bank."

I have just consulted the *State Guide to Kansas,* 1939 edition. The index contains no reference to the town of Coolidge.

DOODLEBUGS

In the West you can always tell a phoney from a man. The phoney loses his courage with his money. The man gains courage as he needs it more. Security— if by that one means money—is an illusion. But—if one means by security a moral quality—it is as indestructible as Pike's Peak. From time to time people everywhere have to learn this lesson. The folks on the Short Grass have always known it. They are like the Indian who could not find his camp, and was accused of being lost. "No," he said, "Indian not lost; Indian here. Tipi lost."

The odd thing is that even men with money share this folkway. There never were men more persistent and hopeful in making money, or men who cared less for it, than the cattlemen and oilmen of the High Plains.

Of all born optimists, oilmen and cattlemen take the cake. Both are accustomed to large profits in good times and to scratching the bottom of the barrel in bad. It is an even bet which of them is the more incorrigibly hopeful.

There is a world of amazing legend about the oil

game, much of which has never been printed, and a whole lingo peculiar to the industry in all its many ramifications. Many of these tales have to do with finding oil with doodlebugs. The term "doodlebug" is commonly applied to any gadget, from a hazel switch to elaborate machinery mounted on trucks—any device in which men have faith.

I once asked a practicing oil geologist why he did not publish some account of the doodlebugs he had seen at work. He was horrified at the suggestion. "Not me," he said emphatically. "It would ruin my profession. More oil has been found with doodlebugs than by regular geologists."

In some cases the doodlebug was simply a divining rod like that used by water-witches—a forked stick held in a certain way so that the free end turns downward at the spot where the well, as is believed, should be drilled.

There are also men known as "creekologists," who locate oil fields by studying the lay of the land and the direction of the creeks and water courses. This may have some logic, since creeks sometimes run along faults in the structure. At any rate, creekologists have sometimes been lucky.

Then there are machines which consist of a pendulum or steel cone hung on a cord, a device much like the "sex indicators" used on eggs. If the pendulum swings from side to side it is believed that the egg contains a cock. If it swings round and round, the egg beneath it is believed to contain a hen. Similar indications have been used in locating oil wells.

Then there are elaborate machines of the Rube Goldberg order—machines big enough to fill a truck with coils and radio and rods connected to wires to be thrust into the ground. This enormous gadget has been used to estimate the production of a producing well, and its champions swear by its accuracy. Skeptics, however, maintain that there is a man inside who controls the indicators.

There are those who attempt to locate oil by soil analysis. These men say that gas seeping upward over long periods of time leaves chemical traces near the surface which may be an indication of oil far below.

The seismograph is perhaps too scientific to be called a doodlebug in the strict sense of the word. These operators set off charges of dynamite and record the reflections from structures far below. These have often found oil, but sometimes have accomplished nothing more than a breaking of all the eggs and windows in the adjacent country. Wherever large stakes are involved, men tend to become superstitious and make horses of their wishes, believing in any method which seems to promise results.

Those early oil towns, such as Borger, Pampa, Burkburnett, and Amarillo were often hectic places, quite as tough as any of the cowtowns of an earlier period. Some were already built before oil was discovered; others, like Borger, were built where the oil was found. In one of these towns where there was no jailhouse, prisoners were kept on a "trotline," like a picket line used in the Army. A drill cable was strung between big timbers planted in the earth and the prisoners chained to the cable.

Sometimes greenhorns would strike matches to see if

the oil of a new gusher would burn. They found that it would.

In all these oil towns the same crowd was found, men who followed the oil booms wherever they occurred, as a race-track crowd follows the races.

In each town one found the same newspapermen running the local sheets—papers which were distributed in incredible numbers all over the country to advertise the field. The same merchants carried their fixtures from town to town, and one would see the identical signs hung out over their new establishments which had graced those in earlier boom towns. In one case a physician had his hospital prefabricated in sections so that he could carry it with him and set it up wherever business was good. It was like a carnival.

In the old days, before men learned to wash the free acids out of the "soup" or nitroglycerine used in shooting the wells, transportation of the explosive was accompanied by many accidents. These old shooters' wagons or trucks had a safety box on the back and a boot below that to catch any leakage from the cans held rigidly above, for if only a drop or two reached the running gears the friction would immediately cause an explosion. When this happened the driver, the team, and the wagon might disappear completely. In one case the only trace of the outfit was one horseshoe and the driver's false teeth found at the distance of a mile.

One day a farm boy was hauling nitro tins packed in straw. He made the journey of fifteen miles without difficulty and arrived safe, ignorant of the fact that one of the cans had sprung a leak. Turning home, he drove along for ten miles, when the wagon struck a hard bump. At that the loose nitro in the rear of the wagon blew up. The driver was not hurt, but the rear wheels and most of the wagon bed were utterly destroyed.

The driver left his team and hurried to the nearest telephone. He called the company and said, "I'm quittin'. I ain't hauling nothing that blows you up ten miles from where you leave it."

There's More in the Man Than There Is in the Land

Scots rule and largely own the British Isles, they dominate the dominions, they and their Scotch-Irish brothers are everywhere in America—and one striking fact about their culture is their faith in education. A bright Scottish lad is seldom doomed to ignorance and oblivion. The career is open to the talents. In every Scottish village the best building of all is the schoolhouse.

So it is on the Short Grass. There every wind-bitten tank-town, with its wooden churches and false-front stores, has at least one brick building, modern and trim —the schoolhouse.

All the states which include parts of the Short Grass partake of this faith In Kansas the New England influence is patent. The number of state institutions of learning in Oklahoma is a constant problem for would-be budget-balancers. And what other state in the Union is so overrun with colleges as Texas?

Anybody can—indeed, everybody must—enter school. Those who stay come through to the top. In a certain one-horse town I used to know (pop. 500) practically every able-bodied boy and girl went through high school. The year I was there, every high-school graduate went to college. Their records since have all been creditable.

Shortly after, I taught in one of the oldest and largest high schools in another part of the country. The curriculum was entirely college-preparatory. Yet during my two years of service there, out of hundreds of boys, only one entered college—and he was promptly sent home. I report this with no desire to belittle another region; I believe that particular community has better schools than many others. It just happens that I taught there, and saw what I saw.

In Oklahoma Territory, when the college I attended was opened, "the" building was not ready when the college assembled for the first time. Classes were held in empty store buildings and gambling halls wedged between false-front saloons. Out in front, at the hitch-racks, cow ponies dozed in the sun and blanket Indians squatted on the boardwalks. The town marshal pushed his handlebar mustaches against the breeze, packing an ivory-handled Colt's. During the pauses in the professor's lecture, the sound of clinking glasses and the voice of the faro dealer came through thin partitions from the saloons next door.

But in those flimsy halls there burned a passion for learning which I have never seen so bright elsewhere —no, not at Oxford or the Sorbonne. The student whose course required him to read *The Odes* of Horace read *all* of Horace—secretly. If assigned one play of Plautus, the student read them all, and never let on. Some of those boys rode horseback to classes through all

weathers, or herded a team of broncs towing a dilapidated buckboard to school. One cripple walked to
school—eighty miles—and arrived with a dime in his
pocket. It seemed the opportunity of a lifetime. Some
of the teachers were equally keen. One read himself
into brain fever. Another became a scholar of international reputation. To them, as to the students, life at
that college was a series of exciting adventures among
masterpieces.

The union of Oklahoma Territory with Indian Territory to form the new State of Oklahoma brought politics into the state schools, and somewhat blurred that
bright enthusiasm, though producing an amusing—if
unprintable—classic entitled *The Sculptor from Tennessee.* Later, the coming of oil brought in many who
put their faith in money. But the old belief, the old enthusiasm, is something the people there will not let die.

One of the greatest and most representative Plainsmen was Charles Goodnight, pioneer and cattleman.
He founded a college. Valiant, able, and wise, he expressed the faith of the region in no uncertain terms.
J. Evetts Haley, in his biography of Charles Goodnight,
quotes the pioneer's words: "We should bear in mind
that we must meet by brains in the West the problem
that is being presented by numbers in the East. . . ."

This respect for intelligence found expression in a
calm, even humorous acceptance of the consequences
of one's decisions. When a man had invested all his
money in a new town which did not "grow up" and so
lost it, he would grin and say, "I guessed wrong. My
town got so low, they sold the church bell for old
brass!"

Finally, the memories of a small farmer, George Washington Sturgeon, as set down in *Echoes of Eighty-Nine,* are eloquent of the same belief:

"In the fall of 1889, we organized a Sunday School and built a log room on the northwest corner of my father's place. The room was full to overflowing every Sunday and everybody was happy.

"In the fall of 1889, we built our first schoolhouse of logs with a dirt roof. There were 50 or more pupils.

"We got seed wheat from the railroad company and planted our first wheat in 1891, each family being allotted 10 bushels of wheat. We also raised corn. Some folk had cattle; some hogs. We had free range for a few years.

"On May 10, 1891, we organized the first church, the Cimarron Valley Baptist Church, in the schoolhouse. Later we built a church house on the present location, four of us giving the land, each one acre for the cemetery and church sites.

"My brother was the first to pass away from our group. There was no cemetery at the time, so he was buried in my father's dooryard. Later, after the church and cemetery were located, his body was moved to the cemetery. He and a small boy were the first to be laid in the new city of the dead.

"There were many Indians, but they were harmless to our people. We all were kind to them. Only once they tried to give trouble, but were talked out of it by our friend, a Mr. Todd, who had married an Indian girl years before. The cowboys to the north also were good to us.

"There was plenty of wild game, such as prairie

chickens, wild turkey, quail, ducks and geese, some bear and hundreds of deer.

"The settlers soon learned when to put out their crops and gardens and what to plant. Times were hard for several years. We could get only 3 cents for chickens, 5 cents for butter and eggs, and had to go all the way to Kingfisher to market, which took us two days. Agricultural enterprise has favored us in this settlement ever since. God has been good to us and left most of us here."

It is the faith of the Short Grass that America has never been licked, and never can be. This year, once more, the hopefulness and confidence of the people of the High Plains is justified. The drouth is over, the rains are falling, turning the Dust Bowl gold and green again. A thousand pulpits resound with the words of the prophet Joel:

Fear not, O land; be glad and rejoice: for the Lord will do great things.

Be not afraid, ye beasts of the field: for the pastures of the wilderness do spring, for the tree beareth her fruit, the fig tree and the vine do yield their strength.

Be glad then, ye children of Zion, and rejoice in the Lord your God: for he hath given you the former rain moderately, and he will cause to come down for you the rain, the former rain, and the latter rain in the first month.

And the floors shall be full of wheat, and the fats shall overflow with wine and oil.

And I will restore to you the years that the locust hath eaten, the cankerworm, and the caterpiller, and

*the palmerworm, my great army which I sent among
you.*

*And ye shall eat in plenty, and be satisfied, and praise
the name of the Lord your God, that hath dealt won-
drously with you: and my people shall never be
ashamed.*

Index

299

082799